Reinforcement Learning for Developers

Earnest Wish

ABOUT THE AUTHORS

Earnest Wish

With 25 years of experience as a programmer and hacker, Earnest Wish has consistently demonstrated a profound passion for exploring the ever-evolving landscape of technology. Early in his career, he immersed himself in the world of hacking, actively participating in bug bounty programs and authoring a book on advanced hacking techniques. This insatiable curiosity for mastering intricate systems seamlessly transitioned into a focus on artificial intelligence, where he has recently concentrated his efforts on reinforcement learning. Today, he is committed to sharing the valuable insights and knowledge acquired through his deep dive into this dynamic field with fellow developers and technology enthusiasts.

Table of Contents

FOREWORD

As a programmer, I have always been captivated by the immense potential of artificial intelligence to address complex challenges and create more intelligent systems. Among the various subfields of AI, reinforcement learning (RL) particularly intrigued me, especially after witnessing its groundbreaking success in applications like AlphaGo. However, my initial foray into learning RL made it clear that the path ahead would not be easy. The concepts were intricate, the algorithms were complex, and at times, it felt as though I was navigating uncharted territory.

Like many others, I faced significant challenges in the beginning. From grappling with the theoretical foundations to attempting to implement the algorithms in real-world scenarios, there were moments of frustration and confusion. Yet, with each obstacle I overcame, my understanding deepened and my confidence grew. Through countless hours of coding, extensive research, and learning from both successes and setbacks, I steadily gained a firmer grasp on reinforcement learning.

It was during this journey that I realized an important truth: my experience was not unique. Many developers, like myself, are drawn to AI but find the steep learning curve of reinforcement learning particularly daunting. It became evident that by sharing the lessons I had learned, I could help others navigate this challenging, yet rewarding, field more effectively.

This realization is what ultimately led me to write this book.

This book is written with the programmer in mind—someone who, like me, is fascinated by the potential of AI but may be uncertain about how to begin their exploration of reinforcement learning. It is not intended to be a purely theoretical textbook. Instead, it serves as a practical guide, informed by my own experiences. I have made it a priority to explain complex concepts in simple terms, provide hands-on examples, and offer clear guidance on implementing algorithms. The goal is to make reinforcement learning accessible, even to those who are just starting to explore this exciting field.

My hope is that the insights and knowledge I have gained through my own struggles will help others avoid some of the obstacles I encountered, shorten their learning curve, and inspire them to explore the world of reinforcement learning with greater confidence. AI is evolving at an unprecedented pace, and with the right tools and understanding, developers like us have the opportunity to play a pivotal role in shaping its future.

Let's embark on this journey together, and may this book serve as a valuable resource on the path to mastering reinforcement learning.

The example code can be downloaded from the following site. https://github.com/multicore-it/rl-kdp

Chapter 1
Getting Started

1. Getting Started

This book is written for many Developers who were interested in reinforcement learning but gave up because it was too difficult. Although reinforcement learning was first introduced to the world through AlphaGo, it is now being widely used to solve various real-world problems. In the field of stock trading, trading bots using reinforcement learning algorithms are under development, and Google DeepMind has developed software to assist in diagnosing eye diseases like glaucoma and macular degeneration based on eye scan data using reinforcement learning.

Why Study Reinforcement Learning?

Artificial intelligence can be broadly categorized into machine learning, deep learning, and reinforcement learning. Generally, machine learning is used to analyze structured data, while deep learning is used to handle unstructured data like images or natural language. A key feature of these data-driven learning methods is that they require large amounts of labeled data. To train on such large datasets, very large artificial neural networks are needed, and this in turn demands high-performance computing power.

As such, data-driven artificial intelligence requires not only technical skills but also significant financial resources. Data labeling requires manual labor, and to label large datasets, many workers need to be employed. Computing power is also a matter of capital; the more money you have, the better performance you can achieve, with access to high-performance GPUs and large clusters of parallel computers.

However, reinforcement learning can overcome many of these challenges through technology. Unlike traditional machine learning, reinforcement learning does not rely on pre-labeled data. Instead, it generates its own data as the agent operates, reducing the burden of data preparation. Additionally, while having more computing power is beneficial, high computational speed does not necessarily guarantee better results. Much of the success in reinforcement learning depends on a deep understanding of the algorithms and strong programming skills for solving specific problems.

Reinforcement learning is particularly suitable for environments like South Korea, where financial resources may be limited. Many business problems can be solved through programming skills and reinforcement learning algorithms, enabling the development of better services and products based on these features.

Features of This Book

To study reinforcement learning, one must understand a range of mathematical and statistical theories, as well as optimization algorithms like Markov Decision Processes. It is no easy task for a programmer to grasp all of this while learning reinforcement learning algorithms.

This book is structured in a way to help Developers easily understand reinforcement learning:

1.   **Foundational Statistics and Math**: All the essential statistical and mathematical theories required for understanding reinforcement learning are explained from the basics. Key concepts are explained in detail, while less crucial concepts are introduced briefly, with guidance on how they are used in reinforcement learning, allowing readers to grasp their practical application without needing to look up additional resources.

2.   **Visual Explanations**: Concepts that are difficult to convey through text alone are illustrated with diagrams. Complex theories are often difficult to grasp and require multiple readings, but the use of diagrams helps resolve these difficulties, making the material easier to understand.

3.   **Consistent Example Throughout**: A single example is used to explain both concepts and theories. For foundational reinforcement learning theory, we use an example of a ship

navigating an island, progressively developing the concepts. All algorithms are explained using the Cartpole game, eliminating the need for readers to set up or understand multiple environments.

4. **From Theory to Practical Application**: The book explains everything from basic theory to tuning, all the way to applying reinforcement learning in real-world scenarios. It not only introduces the latest reinforcement learning algorithms but also provides detailed knowledge and methodologies for tuning, ensuring the book is comprehensive enough for practical use despite being an introductory guide.

Who Should Read This Book

This book is written for anyone interested in reinforcement learning. However, basic programming knowledge is required.

The most important prerequisite is programming knowledge. Most Developers are likely familiar with Java or C. It is recommended that these readers first study basic Python syntax. Instead of reading a beginner's Python book, a basic understanding of Python for data analysis, which can easily be found online, will suffice. Although Python offers many features, only a small portion is used in the field of data analysis.

This book is suitable for readers who already possess basic programming skills and fall into one of the following categories:

1. **Those Who Want to Improve Their Work with AI**: Reinforcement learning, introduced through AlphaGo, has been widely applied in gaming but can also solve various problems in business environments. While traditional programming can automate tasks using loops and conditional statements, reinforcement learning allows you to automate and intelligently handle tasks by designing appropriate reward systems.

2. **Those Who Want to Create Intelligent Software Bots**: Software bots that handle repetitive and rule-based tasks can easily be created by anyone. However, implementing software bots that can autonomously handle tasks based on data is not easy. With a basic knowledge of reinforcement learning, you can upgrade simple software bots to include intelligence.

3. **Those Who Want to Develop Innovative AI-Based Products**: Many software startups are emerging, and while many claim to use AI technology in their products, achieving product-level accuracy in tasks like image recognition or natural language processing is extremely difficult. However, reinforcement learning can deliver impressive performance if you design an appropriate environment and reward system.

Structure of the Book

This book consists of five main parts: basic reinforcement learning concepts, AI concepts, value-based reinforcement learning, policy-based reinforcement learning, and tuning problems.

• **Basic Concepts**: The book first covers the statistical and mathematical theories needed for reinforcement learning, followed by an explanation of the process from probability theory to DQN algorithms.

• **Artificial Neural Networks**: Introduced next are artificial neural networks, which have greatly contributed to the development of reinforcement learning. Rather than directly explaining what neural networks are, the book takes a step-by-step approach starting from linear regression.

• **Value-Based Reinforcement Learning**: This section focuses on the DQN algorithm, explaining it primarily through code since value-based reinforcement learning is relatively easier to understand.

• **Policy-Based Reinforcement Learning**: The core reinforcement learning algorithms are introduced here, including REINFORCE, A2C, and PPO algorithms, with explanations and code examples to run them. This part is longer because, although policy-based algorithms are harder to understand than value-based ones, they offer more stable performance.

• **Tuning**: The final section explains tuning problems, covering essential neural network theories and efficient parameter tuning methods like Bayesian optimization.

Reinforcement learning is theoretically one of the most challenging AI techniques, but it is also the most practical in terms of achieving visible results if understood well. If you are an individual or part of a small-to-medium-sized business wanting to create something using AI, I highly recommend studying reinforcement learning right away.

Chapter 2

Basic Concepts of Reinforcement Learning

2. Basic Concepts of Reinforcement Learning

In this chapter, we will briefly explore what reinforcement learning is and cover the necessary knowledge before delving into reinforcement learning algorithms. Since reinforcement learning algorithms are among the most challenging technologies in the field of artificial intelligence, it is beneficial to first strengthen your foundational knowledge before jumping directly into the algorithms.

2.1 What is Reinforcement Learning?

Reinforcement learning is an optimization method that finds a policy to control an agent's behavior by utilizing a well-designed reward system, encouraging the agent to take positive actions. In reinforcement learning, an **agent** takes specific **actions** in an **environment** according to a **policy**. The **state** of the environment changes depending on the action, and the agent receives a **reward** based on whether this change in state is positive or negative.

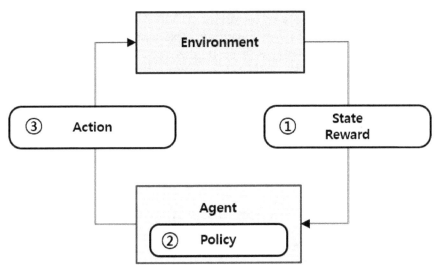

Components of Reinforcement Learning

If the policy determining the agent's actions is excellent, the environment will continue to improve, and the rewards will grow accordingly. The goal of reinforcement learning is to accumulate all the rewards received from actions and find a policy that maximizes this cumulative reward. In simple terms, reinforcement learning aims to find the best policy, and the best policy maximizes the total accumulated reward.

Basic Concepts of Reinforcement Learning
(https://pixabay.com/)

Think of a child crossing a flower bed without being able to see the ground but only looking straight ahead. If the child successfully avoids stepping on any flowers, none will be crushed, but if the child missteps, many flowers will be trampled.

Imagine that each time the child takes a step without crushing a flower, they are praised, but if they crush a flower, they are scolded. After countless attempts, the child will eventually be able to cross the flower bed without stepping on any flowers. This is because the child accumulates memories of being praised for certain steps and can use this experience to know where to step to avoid the flowers. In this example:

- The flower bed is the **environment**,

- The flowers are the **state**,

- The praise and scolding are the **rewards**,

- The child is the **agent**, and the steps taken by the child are the **actions**.

As we grow, we learn many things through reinforcement learning without even realizing it. Whether it's learning to walk, speak, or ride a bike, these skills are naturally ingrained through a reward system of successes and failures, praise and scolding, pain, and a sense of achievement.

When the number of actions and states is small, it is possible to calculate the optimal policy. However, as the number of actions and states increases, finding the optimal policy through calculations becomes difficult. In such cases, artificial neural networks are used. While the concept of reinforcement learning introduced so far may seem abstract or unfamiliar, as we delve deeper into the necessary concepts, you will be able to make it your own knowledge without much difficulty.

2.2 Probability and Stochastic Processes

2.2.1 Probability

To understand reinforcement learning, the first concept you need to grasp is **probability**. According to its dictionary definition (Wikipedia), probability is a method of expressing knowledge or belief about whether an event will occur or has occurred. Probability also refers to the rate at which specific outcomes occur given the same cause. When you think of probability, the concept of a **dice game** might come to mind. A die has six faces numbered from 1 to 6. The probability of rolling a 1 is 1/6, something we understand intuitively. However, if you actually buy a die from a store and roll it six times, will a 1 definitely come up once? Not necessarily. A probability of 1/6 means that if you roll the die an infinite number of times, on average, a 1 will come up once every six rolls. Therefore, the concept of probability is intertwined with randomness. When we say something is probabilistic, we can think of it as random. However, like in the dice game, probability can be calculated based on the number of possible outcomes.

2.2.2 Conditional Probability

Conditional probability refers to a special case of probability that describes the likelihood of an event occurring under a specific condition. For example, the probability of event B occurring given that event A has occurred is denoted as P(B|A), and this is called the conditional probability of event B given event A. Let's assume we have a classroom with 5 male students and 5 female students.

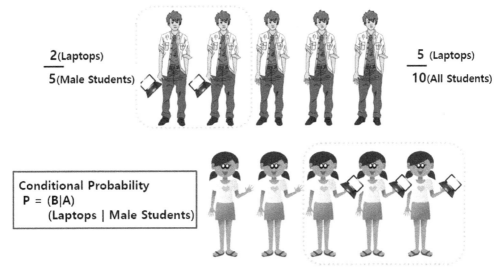

Conditional Probability (https://pixabay.com/)

Now, let's say that 2 male students have laptops, and 3 female students have laptops. The probability of selecting a student with a laptop from the entire class would be 5/10, which is 1/2. However, the probability that a male student has a laptop is 2/5. In this case, event A is selecting a male student, and event B is selecting a student with a laptop. In other words, we are referring to the probability of selecting a student with a laptop under the condition that the student is male. So, what is the probability that a female student has a laptop? It is easy to see that the probability is 3/5.

2.2.3 Stochastic Process

A **stochastic process** is a combination of the concept of **stochastic** (probability) and **process** (a sequence of steps). As mentioned earlier, stochastic refers to something that may appear random in the short term but follows certain rules over a longer period. A **process** is something that is related to the passage of time. Processes like growth, development, and evolution are determined by the flow of time. Therefore, a stochastic process refers to a state that moves randomly (probabilistically) over time.

$$\{ X_t \}$$

- X : Random Variable
- t : Time
- { } : Set

Stochastic Process

There are various ways to mathematically express a stochastic process, but a common representation is {Xt}. Here, **X** represents a random variable, and **t** represents time. The curly braces **{}** denote a set, meaning that a stochastic process can be represented as a set of random variables occurring over time.

The concept of a stochastic process was created to solve specific problems. To solve a scientific concept, the first step is to represent the phenomenon mathematically. If a phenomenon can be mathematically represented, it can be programmed, making problem-solving easier. Therefore, a stochastic process can be defined as a mathematical representation of a state or environment that changes randomly over time.

A prominent example of a stochastic process is **Brownian motion**. Brownian motion is a phenomenon discovered in 1827 by the Scottish botanist Robert Brown, who theoretically explained the irregular movement of pollen particles on the surface of water. Previously, it was believed that only living organisms could move by themselves, but Robert Brown demonstrated that the same irregular motion occurred even when using inanimate materials like dust or glass.

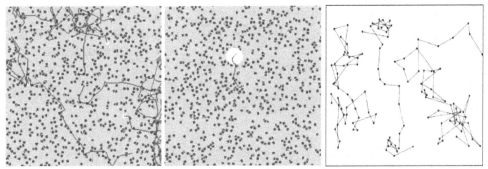

Examples of Brownian Motion
(https://en.wikipedia.org/wiki/Brownian_motion)

If pollen starts at a specific point and moves randomly at regular time intervals, after **n** movements, the distance from the starting point can be measured. If **n** is large enough, the probability of where the pollen will be located can be calculated.

This phenomenon, discovered by Robert Brown, was further elaborated by Einstein. Einstein showed that the cause of Brownian motion is the collision of liquid molecules and formalized this phenomenon in mathematical terms.

The concept of Brownian motion is widely used in fields like statistical mechanics and economics. In economics, Brownian motion is often used to explain the rules that govern market movements.

2.3. Markov Chain

2.3.1 Markov Property

The Markov Property is named after the Russian mathematician Andrey Markov. It is a special form of a stochastic process, characterized by a lack of memory. This "memory" refers to the temporal record of past events. In other words, it disregards everything that happened in the past and predicts the future based solely on the current state. If a variable has the Markov property, it means it is only influenced by the immediate prior state.

Why, then, do we ignore past events and consider only the present? The answer is simplification. Imagine trying to predict the future by accounting for every past and present condition. The amount of data to consider would be overwhelming. By focusing on the current state, which most strongly influences the future, it becomes much easier to solve the problem.

This property can be represented by conditional probability as follows:

$$P[\ S_{t+1}\ |\ S_t\ ] = P[\ S_{t+1}\ |\ S_1,\ \ldots,\ S_t\ ]$$

Figure 2-6 Markov Property Expressed by Conditional Probability

It represents the probability of the state being S_{t+1} at time $t+1$, given that the state is S_t at time t. In other words, S_{t+1} is determined solely by S_t; knowing S_t is sufficient to determine S_{t+1}.

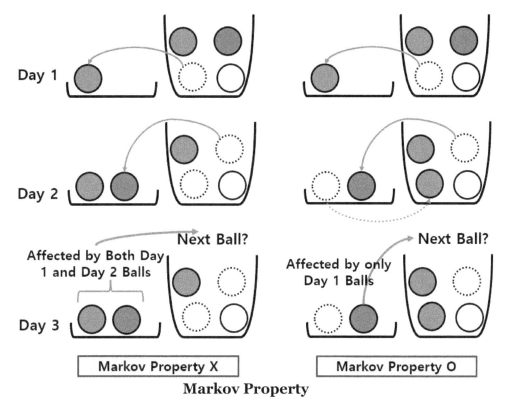

Day 1

Day 2

Next Ball?

Affected by Both Day 1 and Day 2 Balls

Day 3

Markov Property X

Next Ball?

Affected by only Day 1 Balls

Markov Property O

Markov Property

Consider a situation where you are drawing balls from a bag containing two red balls, one blue ball, and one yellow ball—four balls in total. If today you draw one ball and set it aside, and tomorrow you draw another ball and also set it aside, the ball drawn on the third day will be influenced by the balls drawn on both the first and second days. This situation does not satisfy the Markov property. However, imagine that after drawing a ball today, you set it aside and then return it to the bag after the draw. In this case, the ball drawn on the third day is only influenced by the ball drawn the previous day because each ball drawn is returned to the bag. This scenario satisfies the Markov property.

2.3.2 Markov Chain

A Markov Chain describes the changes in the state of a system over time, which adheres to the Markov property. In other words, when the future state is conditioned only on the current state, independent of the past, this is known as the Markov Chain. If the state space is discrete, it's called a Markov Chain, while a continuous state space is called a Markov Process.

A Quick Note
• Discrete and Continuous
The term "discrete" means separated or distinct. In contrast, "continuous" implies being connected or uninterrupted. Thinking in terms of numbers makes this easier to understand. For example, integers like 1, 2, and 3 are distinct and separate, so they are considered discrete. On the other hand, real numbers like 1.000000001 and 1.00000000002 are difficult to distinguish precisely and are connected, so they are considered continuous.

A Markov Chain consists of two elements: a set of states (S) and a state transition matrix (P). The state transition matrix is a matrix that organizes the probabilities of each state transition.

$$\cdot\ S : \textbf{Set of States}$$

$$\cdot\ P : \textbf{State Transition Matrix}$$

$$P_{ss'} = P[S_{t+1} = s' \mid S_t = s]$$

Components of a Markov Chain

Let's use a weather prediction system as an example. Although simplified, suppose statistical analysis of past data has determined the probability of the next day's weather based on today's weather.

Weather Prediction	Tomorrow's	
	Clear	Rainy
Todays Clear	0.6	0.4
Todays Rainy	0.7	0.3

$$P = \begin{bmatrix} 0.6 & 0.4 \\ 0.7 & 0.3 \end{bmatrix}$$

State Transition Matrix

State Transition Matrix

Assuming two weather states, clear and rainy, there are four conditional probabilities: (1) Clear → Clear, (2) Clear → Rainy, (3) Rainy → Clear, and (4) Rainy → Rainy. For example, if today is clear, the probability of another clear day tomorrow is 0.6 (based on historical analysis). The probabilities for the other transitions are 0.4, 0.7, and 0.3, respectively. This can be represented in a matrix, known as a state transition matrix.

Using this state transition matrix, we can predict the weather three days from now, assuming it is clear today. Since the Markov state ignores historical data, we only consider the conditional probabilities for future events. To predict the weather three days from now, we multiply the state transition matrix by itself three times. Simple matrix multiplication allows us to make a plausible future prediction.

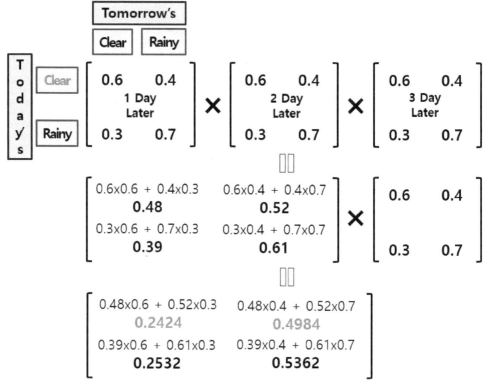

Weather Prediction for 3 Days Later

The state transition matrix after three days is as follows: 0.2424, 0.4984, 0.2532, and 0.5362. Here, the probability of clear weather in three days, given that it's clear today, is 0.2424, while the probability of rain is 0.4984. Therefore, if it's clear today, there is a higher chance of rain three days from now.

Markov Chains are used to represent the state changes of a system over time and consist of a set of states and a state transition matrix. In the weather prediction example, we expressed conditional probabilities in a matrix form. Now, let's look at a system (or environment) represented in a network form to explore the Markov Chain in more depth.

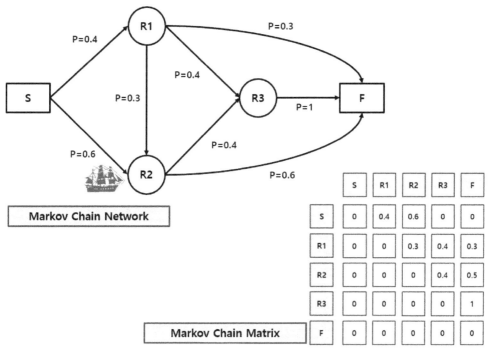

	S	R1	R2	R3	F
S	0	0.4	0.6	0	0
R1	0	0	0.3	0.4	0.3
R2	0	0	0	0.4	0.5
R3	0	0	0	0	1
F	0	0	0	0	0

Various Representations of a Markov Chain

In the figure, you can see a system where a path from the starting point (S) to the destination (F) passes through routers (R). The arrows indicate possible directions, and each arrow has an associated probability. The probability of moving from S to R1 is 0.4, and the probability of moving to R2 is 0.6. All the options from S add up to 1.

The Markov Chain can be represented as a network (left) or in matrix form (right), depending on the problem being solved. Suppose we move one step per time unit and want to determine the probability of reaching the destination (F) in exactly three time units from the start (S). Moving one step per time unit is also called a timestep.

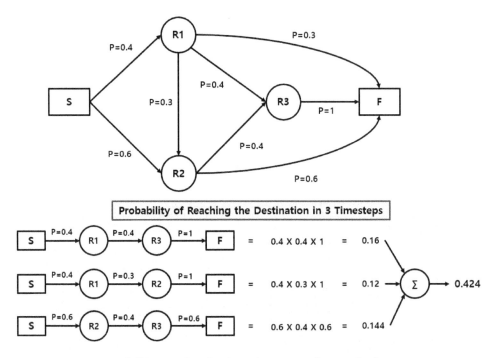

Probability Calculation in a Markov Chain

Let's identify all possible routes from the starting point to the destination in exactly three timesteps (excluding arrival in two timesteps). There are three possible routes: (S, R1, R3, F), (S, R1, R2, F), and (S, R2, R3, F). This series of consecutive state changes is called an "episode." In this example, there are three types of episodes leading to the destination in three timesteps. The probabilities for each route are multiplied due to the conditional probabilities involved, and summing these values gives the probability of reaching the destination in three timesteps (0.424). The purpose of using a Markov Chain is to determine the probability of an event.

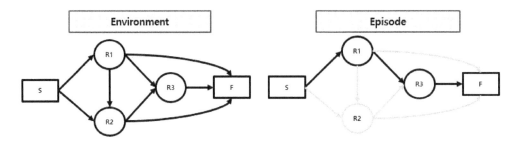

Environment and Episode in Reinforcement Learning

Markov Chains are widely applied in practice. They are notably popular in baseball statistics, as illustrated in the 2011 movie *Moneyball*, where the protagonist uses Markov Chains to predict baseball outcomes. By analyzing past baseball data, average scoring probabilities for each player were obtained, and models were created to estimate expected scores for the next game, helping decide which players to field. The Markov Chain is a simple concept, yet its application in baseball opened an era of scientific analysis in sports.

The purpose of using Markov Chain theory is to calculate the probability of an event occurring. This event could be the batting average of the fourth hitter three days from now or the projected sales of a department store three years later. Based on the calculated probabilities, teams can select players for upcoming games or strategize department store sales.

2.4 Markov Reward Process (MRP)

The Markov Reward Process (MRP) is an extension of the Markov Chain that includes a reward and a discount factor, denoted by gamma (γ), which represents the depreciation of future rewards over time. While a Markov Chain consists of states (S) and a state transition matrix (P), an MRP consists of a set of states (S), a state transition matrix (P), a reward function (R), and a discount factor (γ). In a Markov Chain, only the transition probability between states is given, without indicating the value of state changes. However, by using MRP, we can calculate the value of these state changes. MRP was first introduced in a book by Ronald Arthur Howard, published in 1971.

Now, we'll introduce a bit of mathematical concept, so let's explore it step-by-step without worry; it's simpler than it seems. First, we can mathematically express the elements of the Markov Chain process as follows:

· S : Set of States

· P : State Transition Matrix ⎫

$$P_{ss'} = P[S_{t+1} = s' \mid S_t = s]$$ ⎬ Markov Chain

⎭

· R : Reward Function

$$R_s = E[R_{t+1} \mid S_t = s]$$

· γ : Discount Factor

$$\gamma \in [0, 1]$$

Components of an MRP (Markov Reward Process)

The set of states (S) represents the various states that the environment can take. In an MRP, the states must be finite (i.e., a defined number). Here, the environment refers to the system or problem being dealt with. If you want to predict stock prices, various factors necessary for this prediction make up the environment. Likewise, if predicting department store sales, customer data, sales data, and financial data form the environment.

As explained earlier, P is the state transition matrix, representing the conditional probabilities of transitioning from one state to another in matrix form. Mathematically, this can be shown as the probability that the state will change from s at time t to s' at time t+1.

R represents the reward function. The reward function can be expressed in the form of the expectation (E) of probability, meaning the expected reward received at time t+1 when the state is s at time t.

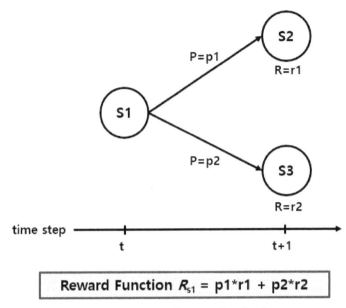

Reward Function R_{s1} = p1*r1 + p2*r2

Reward Function Calculation

If state s at t+1 has two possible next states with probabilities p1 and p2, and rewards r1 and r2 associated with each transition, the value of the reward function is p1×r1+p2×r2. When the state is s at time t, the reward obtained through the reward function only calculates the immediate reward (this will become clearer when we discuss the concept of return later). So, when is the reward for state s calculated? It is calculated at t+1. At time t, the state is s, and at t+1, it transitions to state s′. The reward for state s is thus calculated as time progresses to t+1 and the state moves to s′.

A Quick Note
• Expected Value of Probability
The expected value is the sum of each possible outcome's gain multiplied by the probability of that outcome occurring. It represents the average value of a probabilistic event. (Wikipedia)

Expected Value of a Discrete Probability Distribution	$E(X) = \sum xf(x)$

In a discrete probability distribution, f(x) represents the probability of event x occurring. It is the sum of each event's value (gain) multiplied by its probability.

Expected Value of a Continuous Probability Distribution
$$E(X) = \int_{-\infty}^{\infty} xf(x)dx$$

For a die, the possible values of each outcome range from 1 to 6, with each outcome having a probability of 1/6. By considering all possible outcomes and their probabilities, the expected value can be calculated. Multiplying each possible die value by its probability and summing the results yields the average of the die's values. Thus, the expected value of probability is equivalent to finding the average value of each outcome.

Expected Value of a Die
$$1 \cdot \frac{1}{6} + 2 \cdot \frac{1}{6} + 3 \cdot \frac{1}{6} + 4 \cdot \frac{1}{6} + 5 \cdot \frac{1}{6} + 6 \cdot \frac{1}{6} = 3.5$$

In a continuous probability distribution, f(x) is the probability density function. While individual values can be calculated in discrete settings, continuous settings require integration to account for each possible value. Integration is used to determine the area under the curve represented by a given graph, corresponding to the total probability.

Gamma (γ) represents the discount factor, which can take values between 0 and 1. In general, a discount factor is the rate used to determine the depreciation of value over time. For example, when evaluating the price of a 2-year-old and a 3-year-old car with an annual discount rate of 0.8, we multiply the original price by 0.8×0.8=0.64 for the 2-year-old car and 0.8×0.8×0.8=0.5120 for the 3-year-old car.

The discount factor is also used to calculate the future value of unreceived rewards. Receiving payment for goods delivered today differs in perceived value from receiving the same amount a year later. For instance, 10 million won today has more value than 10 million won a year from now. If we assume a discount factor of 0.9, the present value of 10 million won to be received a year later is 9 million won.

The purpose of MRP is to calculate value. This value calculation involves evaluating the overall value of an entire episode or environment rather than calculating a single momentary value using the reward function. This value must be calculated as the present value. To determine the entire episode value, several timesteps must pass until the episode ends. The discount factor is thus necessary, as it converts the future value into the present value to estimate the episode's value from the current perspective.

The discount factor reflects the relationship between the current and future rewards. When γ is 0, it indicates no consideration for future rewards, while a γ of 1 implies that current and future rewards are valued equally.

$$G_t = R_{t+1} + R_{t+2} + \dots = \sum_{k=0}^{\infty} \gamma^k R_{t+k+1}$$

Return

A new concept, the return (G), is introduced. The return is the cumulative reward calculated at timestep t. This cumulative reward is calculated with a discount factor applied. The return is usually calculated on an episode basis, rather than the entire environment, allowing us to evaluate an episode's efficiency or value based on the return. Designing an environment to maximize the return is one purpose of MRP.

A unique point in the return calculation is that state transition probabilities are not considered. The return calculates the total reward for a chosen path (episode) without needing transition probabilities, as the path is already determined.

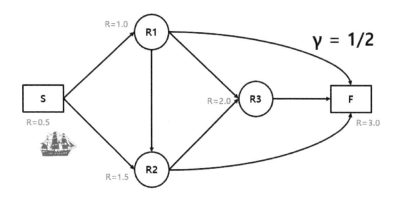

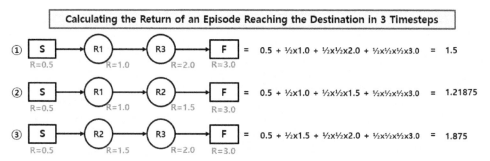

Return Calculation

Assume the discount factor is set at 1/2. There are three episodes that reach the destination in three timesteps. Each node has a defined reward, and the discount factor is multiplied with each reward as time progresses. Summing these values yields the return for each episode. The third episode has the highest efficiency calculated through return.

$$v(s) = E[G_t \mid S_t = s] \qquad ①$$

$$= E[R_{t+1} + \gamma R_{t+2} + \gamma^2 R_{t+3} + .. \mid S_t = s\,] \qquad ②$$

$$= E[R_{t+1} + \gamma(R_{t+2} + \gamma R_{t+3} + ..) \mid S_t = s\,] \qquad ③$$

$$= E[R_{t+1} + \gamma G_{t+1} \mid S_t = s\,] \qquad ④$$

$$= E[R_{t+1} + \gamma v(s_{t+1}) \mid S_t = s\,] \qquad ⑤$$

State Value Function

Let's explore the state value function (v). If the return (G) measures the value of a single episode, the state value function measures the value of the entire environment. As the term "function" suggests, the state value function considers the state transition probabilities.

	Measurement Target	Feature	Discount Factor(γ)	State Transition Probability(P)
G : Return	Episode	Total	Used	Unused
v : State Value Function	Environment	Expected Value	Used	Used

Return and State Value Function

Formula (1) represents that when the state at timestep ttt is sss, the state value function can be obtained as the expectation of the return. For example, if there are two possible states to which state sss can transition, we calculate the return for each possible state in the next timestep (g1, g2), multiply each by its conditional probability (p1, p2), and sum them as v(s)=p1×g1+p2×g2.

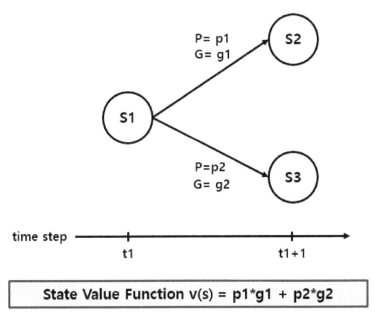

State Value Function v(s) = p1*g1 + p2*g2

State Value Function Using Equation 1

Formula (2) is derived by inserting the return formula, while formula (3) groups the returns of the next timestep using the discount factor. Formula (4) substitutes the return of the next

27

timestep back into the equation. Finally, in formula (4), we replace the return with the state value function. Let's generalize this formula to make it programmable.

$$v(s) = \mathbf{E}[R_{t+1} + \gamma v(S_{t+1}) \mid S_t = s] \qquad ①$$
$$= R_{t+1} + \gamma \mathbf{E}[v(S_{t+1}) \mid S_t = s] \qquad ②$$
$$= R_{t+1} + \gamma \sum_{s' \in S} P_{ss'} v(s') \qquad ③$$

Bellman Equation for the State Value Function

In reinforcement learning, the Bellman equation, named after the American mathematician Richard Ernest Bellman, is commonly used to calculate values through programming.

The Bellman equation typically expresses the expectation as a summation series with the current state related to the next state. Formula (1) is the conceptual state value function we've covered; formula (2) simplifies this by removing a constant, which has no effect in expectations. Formula (3) then expresses the expectation as a sum of a series and the state value function of the next state, known as the Bellman equation.

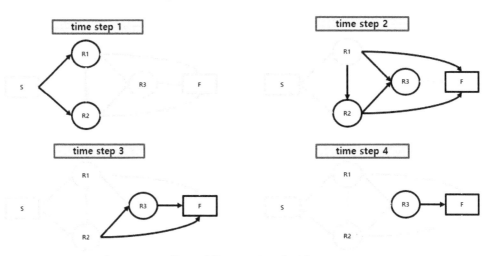

States to Consider at Each Timestep

Applying the Bellman equation directly may be challenging. The purpose of using the Bellman equation is to solve problems through programming. In a simple network-based routing problem, sequential returns can be calculated to determine the state value function. Since MRP serves as a foundational step in understanding reinforcement learning, instead of calculating every state value function, it is sufficient to understand the meaning of the state value function and its representation with the Bellman equation.

Chapter 3

Basic Algorithms of Reinforcement Learning

3. Basic Algorithms of Reinforcement Learning

Reinforcement learning algorithms start with the Markov Decision Process (MDP). Probability and the Markov Reward Process (MRP) were relatively easy to understand, but with MDP, the difficulty suddenly increases due to the introduction of Action and Policy concepts, which are absent in MRP.

However, without properly understanding MDP, it is impossible to grasp advanced reinforcement learning algorithms like Q-learning, REINFORCE, A2C, and PPO. MDP is essential as a theoretical foundation. Make sure to understand this chapter.

3.1 Markov Decision Process (MDP) Concept

The MDP is an extension of the Markov Reward Process (MRP) with added Action (A) and Policy (π). While the goal of MRP is to calculate the overall value of an episode or environment, MDP aims to determine a policy that maximizes the value of the environment. Though it may not be clear now, remember the term "policy decision" for now.

MRP	The agent moves naturally over time steps according to state transition probabilities
MDP	The agent selects actions based on a policy at each time step and moves influenced by state transition probabilities

Agent Movement in MRP and MDP

In MDP, the concept of an agent is introduced. We previously explained Brownian motion by observing the movement of pollen particles in a stochastic process. This pollen corresponds to an agent in MDP. While an agent could be used to explain concepts in stochastic processes and MRP, it wasn't necessary. In stochastic processes and MRP, the state (S: State) of the environment changes naturally over time due to the state transition probability (P). This introduces a passive meaning to the environment. However, in MDP, the agent's actions and the state transition probabilities together affect the environment's state. The agent actively decides actions according to the policy, giving MDP an active meaning that influences its application fields compared to MRP.

The term agent means an actor or entity that takes actions. In MDP, the agent acts based on the policy (π), and the state (S: State) changes based on the actions taken by the agent and the state transition probabilities (P).

- S : Set of States
- P : State Transition Matrix

$$P^a_{ss'} = P[S_{t+1} = s' \mid S_t = s, A_t = a]$$

- R : Reward Function

$$R^a_s = E[R_{t+1} \mid S_t = s, A_t = a]$$

- γ : Discount Factor

$$\gamma \in [0, 1]$$

- A : Set of Actions
- π : Policy Function

MRP

Components of MDP

In MDP, the state transition matrix (P) represents the conditional probability that, given the state s at time t and action a, the state will be s' at time t+1. The reward function (R) is the expected reward at time t+1 when action a is taken in state s at time t. MDP adds action as a condition to the state transition matrix and reward function, meaning actions (A: Set of Actions) must be considered along with these components. Actions influence the next state, and just like states, the number of actions in MDP is finite.

$$\cdot\ \pi = P[A_t = a \mid S_t = s]$$

MDP Policy

In MDP, a policy represents the probability of choosing actions, similar in structure to the state transition matrix. If there are four types of actions, the sum of probabilities for each action in a given state should equal 1. Since policies are probabilistic, following a policy does not always mean taking the highest-probability action but rather that higher-probability actions are more likely to be chosen.

For example, if a policy assigns a 60% probability to action A and a 40% probability to action B, the agent does not always choose action A just because its probability is higher. Instead, action A has a 60% likelihood of being chosen, with the remaining 40% for action B. Similar to real-world decisions, MDP allows for unpredictability in the agent's behavior. This concept is closely related to the exploration problem discussed later.

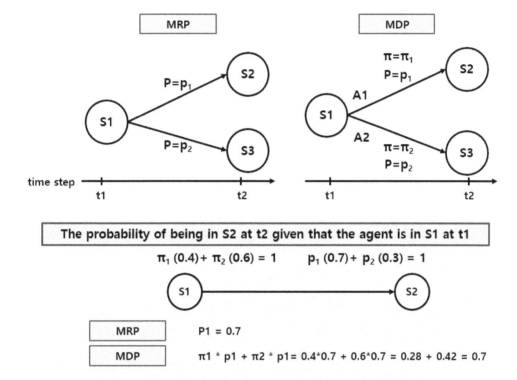

Comparison of MRP and MDP Examples

The sudden appearance of actions and policies might seem confusing, but examining examples should make this clearer. The MRP environment is relatively simple. In timestep t1, the state is S1, and at t2, the states are S2 and S3, with state transition probabilities of 0.7 and 0.3, respectively. The probability of being in S2 at t2 equals the state transition probability.

In an MDP environment, the probability of being in S2 is more complex. In state S1, the available actions are A1 and A2. Action A1 leads to state S2, and action A2 leads to state S3. The agent's policy assigns probabilities of 0.4 and 0.6 for choosing A1 and A2, respectively. Even if the agent selects A1 per the policy, transition to

S2 isn't guaranteed due to the influence of state transition probabilities. In an MDP environment, the agent resembles a captain steering a ship, while transition probabilities are like ocean currents and wind, affecting movement independently of the agent's intentions. To compute probabilities in MDP, multiply each action probability by its respective transition probability and sum the results.

In this example, we see that the probability of moving from S1 to S2 is the same in both MRP and MDP. However, MDP introduces the new element of policy, requiring a more complex formula to account for this. Nonetheless, this complexity adds new functionality.

In MDP, the agent's actions are solely determined by the policy, which does not change over time. Additionally, MDP assumes the Markov property, meaning the policy depends only on the current state, not past states.

$$P_{ss'}^{\pi} = \sum_{a \in A} \pi(a|s) P_{ss'}^{a}$$

$$R_{s}^{\pi} = \sum_{a \in A} \pi(a|s) R_{s}^{a}$$

Considering Policy in State Transition Matrix and Reward Function

In MDPs, policy is an important factor, so we should recreate the state transition matrix (P) to account for policy. The state transition matrix represents the conditional probability of changing state (State) within an environment (Environment) in matrix form. In MDPs, actions (Action) are introduced, and policy (π) is the only determinant of actions. Policy itself is a conditional probability matrix. Therefore, in MDPs, changes in state are influenced by both the original state transition matrix and policy. By calculating the expected value (mean) of the policy-based action and the state transition probability, we can derive a state transition matrix that considers policy.

Similarly, the reward function, taking policy into account, can be represented by calculating the expected value (mean) of the reward function for each action based on policy, just like the state transition matrix.

$$\boxed{\text{MRP}} \quad v(s) = \mathbf{E}[\ R_{t+1} + \gamma v(S_{t+1}) \mid S_t = s\ ] \qquad \text{①}$$

$$= R_{t+1} + \gamma \mathbf{E}[\ v(S_{t+1}) \mid S_t = s\ ] \qquad \text{②}$$

$$= R_{t+1} + \gamma \sum_{s' \in S} P_{ss'} v(s') \qquad \text{③}$$

$$\boxed{\text{MDP}} \quad v_\pi(s) = \mathbf{E}_\pi[R_{t+1} + \gamma v_\pi(S_{t+1}) \mid S_t = s\ ] \qquad \text{①}$$

$$= \sum_{a \in A} \pi(a \mid s)\, (R_s^a + \gamma \sum_{s' \in S} P_{ss'}^a v_\pi(s')\,) \qquad \text{②}$$

$$= \underbrace{\sum_{a \in A} \pi(a \mid s)\, R_s^a}_{\text{③-1}} + \underbrace{\gamma \sum_{a \in A} \pi(a \mid s) \sum_{s' \in S} P_{ss'}^a v_\pi(s')}_{\text{③-2}} \qquad \text{③}$$

State Value Function in MDP

Just as in MRP, a state value function (State Value Function) can be calculated in MDP. From now on, the formulae will become slightly more complex. However, by analyzing them step-by-step, they should be understandable. (1) The general formula is similar to that of MRP, but policy (π) is considered. (2) Policy is a probability for choosing an action, and the sum of probabilities for all actions in a state equals 1. Therefore, to calculate the expected value considering policy, we need to multiply the conditional probability (policy) by each possible action and sum them. (3)-1 calculates the immediate reward in state S by considering the policy. (3)-2 requires the use of both policy and the state transition matrix, so summations ($\sum$) are used twice: the first for policy per action, the second for transition probability per state.

$$v(s) = v_\pi(s)$$

Relationship Between State Value Functions in MRP and MDP

A common mistake here is thinking that v(s) and vπ(s) are different values. Both functions ultimately calculate the same state value, but vπ(s) considers an additional policy factor when calculating value.

The state value function is used to evaluate how valuable a given state is.

$$v_\pi(s) = R^\pi + \gamma P^\pi v_\pi \qquad \textcircled{1}$$

$$v_\pi(s) = (1 - \gamma P^\pi)^{-1} R^\pi \qquad \textcircled{2}$$

Matrix Form

$$\begin{bmatrix} v(1) \\ \cdot \\ \cdot \\ \cdot \\ v(n) \end{bmatrix} = \begin{bmatrix} R_1 \\ \cdot \\ \cdot \\ \cdot \\ R_n \end{bmatrix} + \gamma \begin{bmatrix} P_{11} & \cdots & P_{1n} \\ \cdot & & \cdot \\ \cdot & & \cdot \\ \cdot & & \cdot \\ P_{1n} & \cdots & P_{nn} \end{bmatrix} \begin{bmatrix} v(1) \\ \cdot \\ \cdot \\ \cdot \\ v(n) \end{bmatrix} \qquad \textcircled{3}$$

Simplified Form of State Value Function (Matrix Form)

The state value function can be represented in a simplified form. For various algorithms, a simplified expression may be more useful than a detailed one. (1) The direct reward is calculated by following policy π, so it can be represented as Rπ. For the reward received in the next time step, we must consider the reward expected by following policy π, the state transition probability, and the discount rate. (2) To calculate the state transition probability using only policy, reward, state transition probability, and discount rate, γPπvπ must be moved to the left side, factored out as vπ, and then both sides should be divided accordingly.

There is a slight oddity here, however. In (1), the reward for the next time step should be calculated as v(s')π rather than simply as v(s)π. Yet, here, v(s)π is used directly. The reason for this is (3) it is presented in matrix form. Calculations are performed for every state (s ∈ S) based on the transition probability per state, so using the same v(s)π yields the same calculation results. Both s and s' are subsets of the entire state set S.

3.2 MDP Action-Value Function

Previously, it was mentioned that the goal of an MDP is to determine a policy that maximizes the value of the environment. So, what is a policy? A policy is the probability that determines an action. Therefore, a policy that maximizes value can be thought of as the policy that yields the best outcome for the value function when followed. The state-value function evaluated value based on states rather than actions. To evaluate a policy, a function that evaluates value based on actions is needed. This is known as the Action-Value Function (Q: Action Value Function), also called the Q-function.

$$v_\pi(s) = \mathbb{E}_\pi[R_{t+1} + \gamma v_\pi(S_{t+1}) \mid S_t = s]$$

$$= \underbrace{\sum_{a \in A} \pi(a|s) R_s^a}_{\text{(1)-1}} + \gamma \underbrace{\sum_{a \in A} \pi(a|s) \sum_{s' \in S} P_{ss'}^a v_\pi(s')}_{\text{(1)-2}} \quad \text{①}$$

$$q_\pi(s, a) = \mathbb{E}_\pi[R_{t+1} + \gamma q_\pi(S_{t+1}, A_{t+1}) \mid S_t = s, A_t = a] \quad \text{②}$$

$$= R_s^a + \gamma \sum_{s' \in S} P_{ss'}^a \pi(s', a') q_\pi(s', a') \quad \text{③}$$

MDP Action-Value Function (Q-function)

The Action-Value Function (Q-function) is a function that calculates the value when one of several possible actions is selected. Equation (1) restates the state-value function. In the action-value function, since the action has already been chosen, there is no need to find an expectation. Therefore, it can be described as Equation (3) without parts (1)-1 and (1)-2. A notable point here is the addition of π(s', a'), as to accurately calculate the reward in the next state, one must multiply the probability matrix (policy) for selecting actions with the state transition probability matrix.

$$v_\pi(s) = \sum_{a \in A} \pi(a|s) q_\pi(s, a) \quad \text{①}$$

$$q_\pi(s, a) = R_s^a + \gamma \sum_{s' \in S} P_{ss'}^a v_\pi(s') \quad \text{②}$$

Relationship Between Action-Value Function and State-Value Function

The action-value function is a function that calculates the value of a chosen action, while the state-value function calculates the value of a specific state. In an MDP, to move from one state to another, both the state transition matrix and the probability of selecting an action (policy) must be considered. Therefore, to derive the state-value function using the action-value function, an expected value, or average, of the policy is required. The action-value function calculates the value of an action (a) as the sum of the immediate reward that can be received in the current state and the future rewards. Future rewards depend on the state reached by taking the action, which in turn depends on the chosen action and the state transition matrix values of the environment. Therefore, the discount rate, the state transition matrix, and the future state value function values are taken into account to calculate the action-value function. The key to understanding this equation lies in P^{a}ss', which considers only one action rather than all actions in the state transition matrix.

As previously mentioned, the goal of an MDP is to determine a policy that maximizes the value of the environment. The action-value and state-value functions studied so far are all functions to calculate value. The purpose of calculating value is to evaluate a policy to find the policy that maximizes value (Optimal Policy). This is the fundamental concept of reinforcement learning.

3.3 Optimal Value Function of MDP

Now, let's discuss the Optimal Value Function to achieve the ultimate goal of MDP. The Optimal Value Function can be divided into the Optimal State-Value Function and the Optimal Action-Value Function.

$$v^*(s) = \max_{\pi} v_{\pi}(s) \qquad ①$$

$$q^*(s,a) = \max_{\pi} q_{\pi}(s,a) \qquad ②$$

Optimal State-Value Function and Optimal Action-Value Function

(1) The Optimal State-Value Function (v*(s)) is defined as the state-value function that follows the policy with the highest value when there are multiple state-value functions following different policies. Similarly, (2) the Optimal Action-Value Function (q*(s,a)) is the

action-value function that follows the policy with the highest value among the various action-value functions.

Knowing the Optimal Action-Value Function in an MDP is equivalent to knowing the policy that allows for the selection of the most efficient action. Therefore, if the Optimal Action-Value Function can be found, the MDP problem can be solved.

$$\pi^* : \pi^* \geq \pi, \; \forall \pi \qquad \text{①}$$

$$v_{\pi^*}(s) = v^*(s) \qquad \text{②}$$

$$q_{\pi^*}(s) = q^*(s) \qquad \text{③}$$

Characteristics of the Optimal Policy

We can now naturally define the Optimal Policy (π^*). The Optimal Policy is a policy that allows actions to maximize the optimal value. The Optimal Policy has several characteristics: (1) the value of the Optimal Policy is greater than that of any other policy. Since a policy determines the probability of action selection, having a greater value implies a higher probability. (2) The value of the state-value function obtained by using the Optimal Policy is equal to the value of the Optimal State-Value Function. (3) The value of the action-value function obtained by using the Optimal Policy is also equal to the value of the Optimal Action-Value Function.

$$\pi^*(a|s) = \begin{cases} 1 & \text{if } a = \text{argmax}_{a \in A} \, q * (s, a) \;\; \text{①} \\ 0 & otherwise \qquad\qquad\qquad\quad \text{②} \end{cases}$$

A Method to Represent the Optimal Policy

Let's look at one way to represent the Optimal Policy in an MDP. (1) If an action (a: Action) is the same as the action that returns the maximum value of the Optimal Action-Value Function, the policy for that action is 1; otherwise, the policy for the action is 0. Since the policy is the probability of selecting an action, the policy in state s will always select the action set to a probability of 1.

3.4 Terminology Used in Reinforcement Learning

3.4.1 Policy Evaluation and Policy Control

Various terms are used in reinforcement learning. While they may seem straightforward once understood, they can hinder comprehension of other concepts if unknown. Let's look at a few key terms.

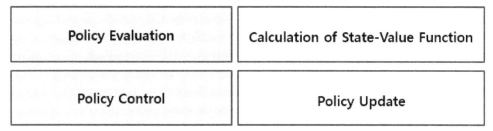

| Policy Evaluation | Calculation of State-Value Function |
| Policy Control | Policy Update |

Policy Evaluation and Policy Control

In MDP, evaluating a policy is equivalent to finding the state-value function. The significance of the state-value function in MDP lies in calculating the total rewards when following a policy (π). Calculating the state-value function indicates the reward that reflects the policy's effectiveness. Thus, the larger the state-value function value, the better the policy.

Policy control involves changing the policy. If evaluating the policy reveals that the set policy yields too little or too much reward, adjustments are necessary. Since the ultimate goal of an MDP is to find a policy that maximizes value, the optimal policy can be discovered through iterative policy control.

Policy evaluation and policy control work complementarily. The policy is evaluated to check its adequacy, and through policy control, it is updated to a new policy, which can then be evaluated for its effectiveness again.

How policy evaluation and policy control are specifically applied will be explored in dynamic programming later on.

3.4.2 Model-Based and Model-Free

Model Based	When all information about the environment is known
Model Free	When only partial information about the environment is known

Model-Based and Model-Free

When studying reinforcement learning algorithms, the terms model-based and model-free are frequently encountered. Simply put, model-based implies having full knowledge of the environment. The environment refers to all the surrounding states in which the MDP operates. The environment generally consists of the state, state transition probability, reward, action, and discount factor. If everything is illustrated in a diagram like the examples examined earlier, it can be considered model-based. Conversely, an environment represented as a black box, where new states and rewards are returned depending on the input action and state, is model-free.

The major difference between model-based and model-free in reinforcement learning is the ability to predict the next state. In the example above, each current state is connected by arrows to possible future states in the next time step, allowing for straightforward verification of the next state without complex algorithms. This is model-based reinforcement learning. In a model-free scenario, the agent cannot predict the state it can move to in the next time step, necessitating complex algorithms to determine it. Most problems that reinforcement learning aims to solve exist in model-free environments.

3.5 Dynamic Programming

Dynamic programming is a representative algorithm that leverages optimization theory to simplify problem-solving. Optimization problems like MDPs are often set in complex environments. While it may be feasible to find a solution in the example we've examined with a few calculations, solving the problem becomes significantly harder when dealing with hundreds of nodes in a network.

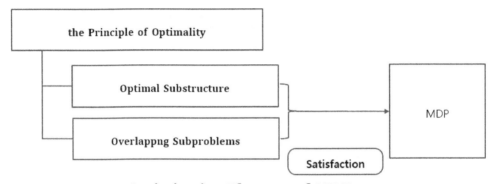

Optimization Theory and MDP

There are two conditions under which a problem can be broken down using optimization theory (the Principle of Optimality). The first is the Optimal Substructure. This means that by dividing a large problem into smaller ones and finding the optimal solutions for these smaller problems, the solution for the larger problem can be constructed. The second is Overlapping Subproblems, which means that small problems recur repeatedly, allowing solutions found once to be reused continuously. MDP satisfies both con...

Now, let's look at dynamic programming, a representative method for solving MDP problems in model-based environments by breaking them into smaller units.

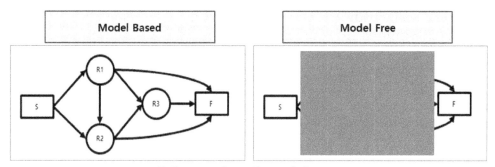

Model-Based and Model-Free

First, let's divide a routing example into model-based and model-free. In a model-based environment, all information regarding actions and states is known. In a model-free environment, however, only the information at the start and end is known, with no prior knowledge of the next state resulting from an action. It's only by taking action that the next state is revealed.

Dynamic Programming (DP) is a model-based method in reinforcement learning, assuming full knowledge of the environment. In DP, <S, A, P, R, γ> is known, and vπ, v*, and π* can be computed. DP first calculates vπ through policy evaluation, then calculates v* and π* through policy control, and updates the policy accordingly.

Let's solve an MDP using dynamic programming.

First, perform policy evaluation. The value function in an MDP consists of two parts: the solution to the initial timestep and the solutions for subsequent steps summed together. In policy evaluation, a fixed policy is used to calculate the value function by considering only the next timestep, and the value of the current timestep is updated. Repeating this process allows calculating the value of each state. If this process is repeated infinitely, the true value function of the MDP can be calculated, which i...

Policy control involves greedily selecting a policy that maximizes the current policy by updating it based on the value function calculated from the fixed policy. Iterative policy evaluation and policy control enable finding the optimal policy.

Now, let's look at an example of gridworld to understand this in more detail. Gridworld is a game where an agent navigates a grid-like environment to reach a destination. The example game has 16 states. The agent is randomly placed in one of the 14 states (excluding the destinations), with the goal of establishing a policy that guides the agent to the destination in the shortest path.

- **State Transition Probability: Assumed to be 1 for all transitions.**
- **Reward: -1 per timestep.**
- **Initial Policy: Random (Up/Down/Left/Right: 0.25 each).**

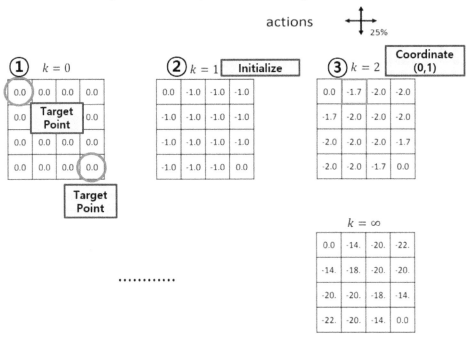

Gridworld Example

Assume a state transition probability of 1, and a reward of -1 is received as each timestep progresses. There are four actions (up, down, left, right), and the initial policy is evenly set to 0.25 for each action. The game has 16 states, with (1) the top-left and bottom-right being the destinations. (2) All states (except the destinations) reset to -1 as each timestep progresses. (2) In timestep 2, the value of state (0,1) is -1.75.

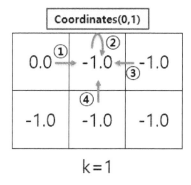

Coordinates(0,1)

$k=1$

$$-1.0 + (0.0*0.25 + -1.0*0.25 + -1.0*0.25 + -1.0*0.25) = -1.75$$

Value of ① ② ③ ④
the current state

Calculating State Value

At timestep k=2, let's directly calculate the state value for (0,1). With an initial policy assigning a probability of 0.25 for each action, the value of the state at the next timestep can be calculated by summing up the policy-weighted values from each state. Repeating this process continuously updates the state values.

Policy Update

Policy evaluation is repeatedly performed to sufficiently calculate the value for each grid. The initially uniform policy (0.25 for each action) is then updated. This is called policy control. Policy control involves setting new probabilities for actions on the grid, and if a greedy approach is used, the policy is set to move toward the grid with the highest value. In the example above, the grid with a value of -14 has the highest value, so the probabilities for moving to it are set equally at 0.5, and the probabilities for moving to other grids are set to 0. Dynamic programming ultimately allows finding the optimal value and policy through sufficient iterations of policy evaluation and policy control.

While understanding dynamic programming fully based on this explanation is challenging, it's not essential for studying reinforcement learning, so we'll conclude with this overview.

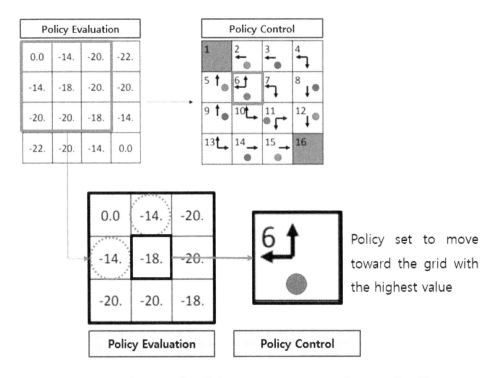

3.6 Monte Carlo Method (MC: Monte-Carlo Method)

In dynamic programming, policy evaluation and control are performed under the assumption that the model is known (Model-Based). When the model is known, the next state can be predicted, allowing the problem to be broken down into smaller units and calculated sequentially to find the optimal policy.

However, in situations where the model is unknown (Model-Free), the reward function (R) and state transition probability (P) are not available, and particularly, the next state is unpredictable. Thus, methods like dynamic programming cannot be used to solve the problem. In such cases, Monte Carlo Prediction is needed.

In dynamic programming, the value of each state is updated by running through all states once, but in Monte Carlo Prediction, the algorithm runs until an episode is completed, accumulating experiences and calculating the value function based on those experiences.

The Monte Carlo method (MC) is one of the most commonly used approaches when there is insufficient information about the environment. Instead of precise mathematical calculations, the Monte Carlo method estimates values statistically using probabilistic techniques. It is typically used to obtain approximate results when calculating an exact value is too complex.

The name "Monte Carlo" originates from Polish-American mathematician Stanislaw Ulam, who named it after the famous gambling city in Monaco. The Monte Carlo method is well-suited for computer simulations, making it useful in the development of atomic and hydrogen bombs and still widely applied in various fields today.

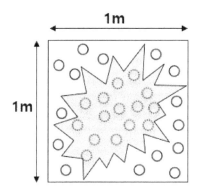

Square Area : 1m x 1m = 1m^2

Number of Balls Inside the Square: 30

Number of Balls Inside the Polygon: 15

Monte Carlo Method: 1m^2 : x ≒ 30 : 15

Polygon Area ≒ 0.5m^2

Monte Carlo Method

For example, calculating the area of a polygon like the one above can be difficult mathematically. Using the Monte Carlo method, we can proceed as follows: First, draw a square that surrounds the polygon. Suppose we draw a square with each side measuring 1 meter. The area of the square is easily calculated by multiplying the width and height, resulting in 1 m^2. Now, let's scatter round balls inside the square. Suppose 30 balls are thrown, and 15 fall inside the polygon. Using the ratio of the total number of balls in the square to those inside the polygon, we can estimate the polygon's area to be 0.5 m^2. This is the essence of the Monte Carlo method.

In this approach, the polygon's area is estimated based on the ratio of balls, rather than through precise measurement. In reinforcement learning, the Monte Carlo method can approximate values effectively in cases where complete information about the environment is unavailable.

There is one prerequisite for using the Monte Carlo method in reinforcement learning: the environment in which the agent operates must have a defined beginning and end. This type of environment is called episodic. For example, in games, MMORPGs like Lineage do not have clear episode boundaries, while games like Diablo progress in episodic units. The Monte Carlo method can be applied only to cases that can be divided into episodes, such as the latter.

The Monte Carlo method involves executing an episode to its end and using the result to estimate a value. For example, to calculate the value function, the Bellman equation is used, which sums the value obtained in the current timestep with all future discounted values. When all information about the environment is available, the next state can be predicted, allowing for precise calculation, as in dynamic programming. However, in the absence of complete information, the next state is unknown. Therefore, the agent must operate through the episode, gathering information based on the chosen policy and the state transition probabilities provided by the environment, and calculate the value function by accumulating this information.

When the agent completes its first episode, there may be a significant difference between the calculated value function and the true value function (which can only be computed if all environmental information is known and is unattainable in a model-free environment). However, by averaging the values obtained over many episodes, the estimated value function will approach the true value function. This approach is known as the Monte Carlo method.

$$\boxed{\text{MDP}} \quad v_\pi(s) = E_\pi[G_t \mid S_t = s] \qquad \text{①}$$

$$= E_\pi[R_{t+1} + \gamma v_\pi(S_{t+1}) \mid S_t = s]$$

$$= \sum_{a \in A} \pi(a|s)\,(R_s^a + \gamma \sum_{s' \in S} P_{ss'}^a v_\pi(s'))$$

$$= \underbrace{\sum_{a \in A} \pi(a|s)\, R_s^a}_{\text{②-1}} + \gamma \underbrace{\sum_{a \in A} \pi(a|s) \sum_{s' \in S} P_{ss'}^a v_\pi(s')}_{\text{②-2}}$$

$$\boxed{\text{MC}} \quad v_\pi(s) = V(s) \quad \text{when } N(s) \to \infty \qquad \qquad \text{③}$$

Accumulated Count : $N(s) \leftarrow N(s) + 1$ (Single Episode Execution) ④

Accumulated Return : $S(s) \leftarrow S(s) + G_t$ ⑤

Average Return : $V(s) \leftarrow S(s) / N(s)$ ⑥

Solving MDP with the Monte Carlo Method

To solve an MDP using the Monte Carlo (MC) method, let's express it mathematically. Recall that in an MDP, the state-value function is defined as (1) the expected value of the return (G). This means that to calculate the value, all possible actions and all possible states (2)-1 and (2)-2 must be considered under a fixed policy. This is possible in a Model-Based environment, where all information about the environment is known.

Now, let's calculate the state-value function using MC. In MC, (3) the average of the returns is used as the state-value function. (4) First, run the agent until the end of an episode. When an episode ends, increment the count (N: accumulated count) by one. (5) Gather all the returns collected during the episode and store them in the variable S (accumulated returns). In contrast to MDP, this approach only considers the actions taken by the agent and the states visited during the episode, without accounting for all actions and states. (6) Finally, divide the accumulated returns by the accumulated count to obtain the average, which gives the state-value function. This calculated state-value function can be used to evaluate the fixed policy.

$$\mu_k = \frac{1}{k} \sum_{j=i}^{k} x_j \qquad \text{①}$$

$$= \frac{1}{k} \left(xk + \sum_{j=i}^{k-1} x_j \right) \qquad \text{②}$$

$$= \frac{1}{k} \left(x_k + \left(\frac{k-1}{1} \right) \underbrace{\left(\frac{1}{k-1} \right) \sum_{j=i}^{k-1} x_j}_{\text{③-1}} \right) \qquad \text{③}$$

$$= \frac{1}{k} \left(x_k + (k-1)\mu_{k-1} \right) \qquad \text{④}$$

$$= \mu_{k-1} + \frac{1}{k} \left(xk - \mu_{k-1} \right) \qquad \text{⑤}$$

$$\doteqdot \mu_k + \frac{1}{k} \left(xk - \mu_k \right) \qquad \text{⑥}$$

Modified for Mathematical Convenience
from k-1 to k

Incremental Mean

Incremental Mean provides a method to quickly update the overall average when a new value arrives by using the previously calculated average up to the last timestep. xj represents a continuously occurring value. (1) To calculate the overall average of continuously occurring xxx values, add all xxx values together and divide by the number of occurrences.

(2) Separate the most recent x value as xk and group the sum of values up to the previous timestep as a sequence.

(3) For ease of calculation in programming, multiply by k−1 and then divide. This adjustment is made for convenience in computation.

(3)-1 This part represents the sum of data up to k−1 since only values up to k−1 are summed.

(4) This can be viewed as the average calculated up to the previous timestep, represented as μk−1.

(5) Transform the equation once more for calculation purposes.

(6) Finally, convert it into a form that's easier to program. While the precise formula should use μk−1, it's acceptable to replace it with μk for convenience.

| MC | $v_\pi(s) = V(s)$ when $N(s) \to \infty$ |

> Accumulated Count : $N(s) \leftarrow N(s) + 1$ (Execution one episode)
>
> Accumulated Return : $S(s) \leftarrow S(s) + G_t$
>
> Average Return : $V(s) \leftarrow S(s) / N(s)$ ①
>
> **Incremental Mean Return** : $V(s) \leftarrow V(s) + \frac{1}{N(s)}(G_t - V(s))$ ②

MC Using Incremental Mean

Now, let's use the incremental mean to transform MC into a form that can be programmed. (1) In the previous formula, the average was calculated by dividing the accumulated return by the accumulated count. To calculate values this way, information from all past episodes must be stored, which burdens the system and slows down computation.

(2) By using the incremental mean, we can simplify this formula: subtract the average return up to the previous timestep, V(s), from the latest return Gt, and divide by the episode count. Adding this result to the average return up to the previous timestep provides the state-value function.

A unique point in this formula is that if Gt and V(s) are equal, the equation becomes V(s)=V(s), meaning the state-value function no longer changes. This state is known as the true value function. In reinforcement learning, the goal is to find a policy that minimizes the difference between Gt and V(s).

| MC | $V(s) \leftarrow V(s) + \frac{1}{N(s)}(G_t - V(s))$ ① |

Change from $\frac{1}{N(s)}$ **to** $\propto$

$$V(s) \leftarrow V(s) + \propto(G_t - V(s))$$ ②

MC for Programming

Now, let's replace 1/N(s) in formula (1) with $\propto$ to create a new formula (2). Changing to $\propto$ makes this value a fixed constant rather than one that changes over time. Typically, $\propto$ is a value between 0 and 1. Transforming to a fixed constant simplifies programming considerably. Replacing elements from the complete mathematical formula for ease of programming is feasible because MC is an empirical method that approaches a solution statistically through experience rather than precise measurement.

3.7 TD (Temporal Difference Learning) and SARSA

3.7.1 TD

MC has one drawback: the state-value function is calculated after the episode is completed, which slows down learning. To address this, a new concept called Temporal Difference Learning (TD) was introduced.

$$\boxed{\text{MC}} \quad V(s_t) \leftarrow V(s_t) + \propto(G_t - V(s_t)) \qquad\qquad \text{①}$$

$$\boxed{\text{TD}} \quad V(s_t) \leftarrow V(s_t) + \propto(R_{t+1} + \gamma V(s_{t+1}) - V(s_t)) \quad \text{②}$$

$$\text{from } G_t \text{ to } R_{t+1} + \gamma V(s_{t+1})$$

Temporal Difference Learning (TD)

(1) The Gt (Return) used in MC is a value obtained at the end of an episode. For more efficient learning, this value can be replaced by the value obtained when a single timestep is completed. (2) It can be replaced by the value obtained immediately in the next timestep (Rt+1) and the value obtained by calculation (or estimation) ($\gamma V(st+1)$).

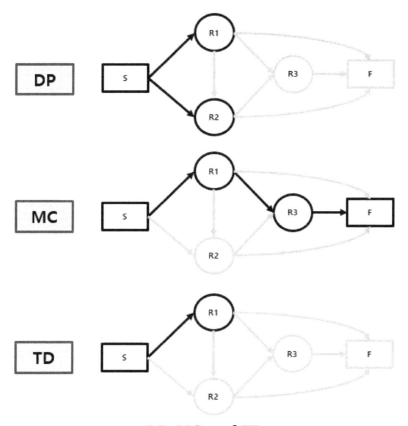

DP, MC, and TD

To aid understanding of Temporal Difference (TD), let's visualize Dynamic Programming (DP), Monte Carlo (MC), and TD. In Dynamic Programming, all possible future states from a given state are considered to calculate value, and the policy is immediately evaluated (value is updated). This process is repeated continuously. In MC, values are calculated by following an episode, and the policy is evaluated all at once when the episode ends. In contrast, TD considers only the value obtained from a single chosen action and evaluates the policy immediately, repeating this process continually. TD combines the frequent, short updates of Dynamic Programming with the single-action execution of MC.

TD can calculate the value function even before an episode is fully completed, so it can be used not only in episodic (Terminating) environments like MC but also in non-terminating environments.

Before exploring policy control in MC and TD, let's look at how policy control is achieved in Dynamic Programming. In DP, the policy is first evaluated, and the value function for several states accessible from the chosen action is calculated. The policy is then updated to take actions that lead to the state with the highest value function. A critical point here is that Dynamic Programming is only possible in a model-based environment where all information about the model is known, allowing us to calculate which state yields the highest value function.

However, since MC and TD operate in model-free environments, they lack sufficient information about the environment. Consequently, the next state cannot be predicted, nor can we know which state would yield the highest value function. Nevertheless, the Q-function can be used to evaluate good actions. Because the Q-function represents the value of a specific action, it can be evaluated even without complete information about the next state.

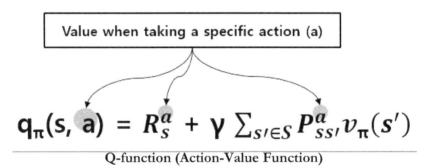

$$q_\pi(s, a) = R_s^a + \gamma \sum_{s' \in S} P_{ss'}^a v_\pi(s')$$

Q-function (Action-Value Function)

Let's revisit the Q-function formula from MDP. The Q-function measures the reward obtained by selecting a single action in the state-value function. To derive the Q-function from the state-value function, the expected value of the state-value function for all states that can be reached from a single action (a) and the state transition probability must be calculated.

Returning to TD, in TD, after going one timestep forward and calculating the value based on a policy (initially set to random values), this value is subtracted from the previous timestep's value. To update the randomly set policy in Dynamic Programming, the state-value function for all states in the next timestep is calculated, and the policy is modified to take actions leading to the state with the highest value. However, in TD, the agent neither knows the possible states in the next timestep nor what those s...

$$\pi'(s) = \operatorname*{argmax}_{a \in A} Q(s,a)$$

Policy Control in Model-Free Environments

In TD, the only information available is the actions possible in the current state. Therefore, if each action is attempted and the action yielding the highest Q-function (Action-Value Function) is found, the policy can be adjusted to perform the related action.

3.7.2 SARSA

In TD, the state-value function was used for policy evaluation, while the Q-function (Action-Value Function) was used only for policy control. However, both policy evaluation and control can be conducted using the Q-function since it contains values for both actions and states.

| TD | $V(s_t) \leftarrow V(s_t) + \propto(R_{t+1} + \gamma V(s_{t+1}) - V(s_t))$ |

| SARSA | $Q(S,A) \leftarrow Q(S,A) + \propto(R_{t+1} + \gamma Q(S',A') - Q(S,A))$ |

$$(S_t, A_t, R_{t+1}, S_{t+1}, A_{t+1}) \rightarrow S\,A\,R\,S\,A$$

SARSA

The Q-function receives a reward Rt+1 after taking action At in state St. Then, in the next state St+1, the process repeats with action At+1, creating a continuous sequence of S, A, R, S, A. This sequence gives the algorithm its name: SARSA.

Looking back at TD, the agent in the environment moves one timestep based on its policy and then calculates the state-value function. The original state-value function involves calculating the expected value of actions and states according to the policy, meaning all actions and states should be considered. However, in MC and TD, only one action based on the policy is chosen to calculate the value, which is not entirely accurate.

Thus, the SARSA algorithm becomes the appropriate formula for policy evaluation in model-free environments. In SARSA, policy control is also updated to select the action that maximizes the Q-function, similar to MC and TD.In the Q-function, when in state St, action At is taken, and reward Rt+1 is received. The action At+1 is taken in the next state St+1, repeating the previous sequence. This sequence of S, A, R, S, A is called SARSA.

Revisiting TD, the agent calculates the state-value function after moving one timestep based on the policy. The original state-value function involves calculating the expected values of actions and states based on the policy, meaning all actions and states should be considered. However, in MC and TD, th...

Thus, the SARSA algorithm becomes the formula for policy evaluation in model-free environments, which we aim to obtain. In SARSA, policy control is updated to select actions that maximize the Q-function, as in MC and TD.

3.8 Q-Learning

3.8.1 On-Policy and Off-Policy

All the content we have studied so far pertains to on-policy. This is because the policy used for evaluation (π) and the policy used for control (π) are the same. In on-policy learning in TD, one more timestep is taken to calculate the state-value function to evaluate the policy, and the policy is modified in a greedy manner in the Q-function, choosing the action with the highest Q-value. This process is repeated continuously. There are two issues here: first, experiences used once for evaluation are no...

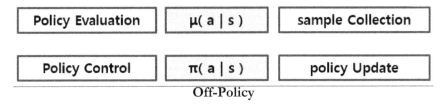

Policy Evaluation	μ(a | s)	sample Collection
Policy Control	π(a | s)	policy Update

Off-Policy

To address the issues of experience reuse and applying various policies, the off-policy algorithm was introduced. In off-policy, the policy used for evaluation and the policy used for control are separately applied.

3.8.2 Importance Sampling

Importance Sampling refers to generating the expected value of f(x) under probability distribution p(x) when it is challenging to sample from p, by instead sampling from a distribution q(x) from which it is relatively easy to obtain samples. This method calculates the expectation of f(x) in p(x) using samples from q(x).

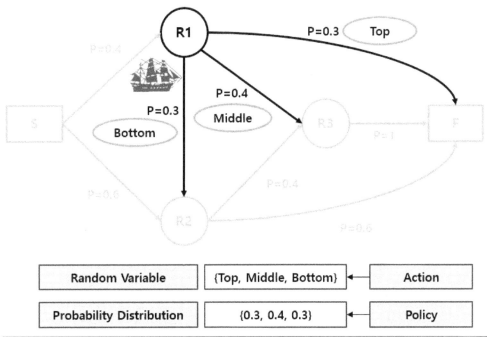

Random Variable	{Top, Middle, Bottom}	Action
Probability Distribution	{0.3, 0.4, 0.3}	Policy

Probability Distributions and Probability Density Function

A random variable, simply put, represents the types of actions (A: Set of Actions), and a probability distribution can be considered as the policy (π: Policy). In the figure above, there are three types of actions: high, medium, and low. The policy for each action is 0.3, 0.4, and 0.3, respectively. To obtain a relatively accurate expected value, the agent must observe many actions taken as it transitions from state R1 to the next state (samples) and calculate the average. If we think of it as finding a new navigation route, samples may not be available, so it is necessary to utilize existing data.

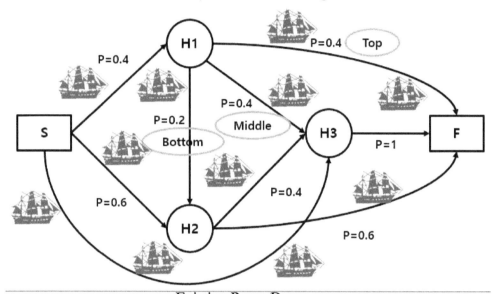

Existing Route Data

By using existing route data, not only can the random variable and probability distribution be obtained, but a large number of samples can also be acquired. This allows us to apply the theory of Importance Sampling to calculate an appropriate expected value for a new route.

$$\sum P(X)f(X) = \sum Q(X) \left[\frac{P(X)}{Q(X)} f(X) \right]$$

P(X)	Probability Distribution P of Variable X in a Given Environment
Q(X)	Probability Distribution Q of Variable X in a Different Environment
f(X)	Function of X (any function is possible, e.g., sin, cos, 2x+1, etc.)
$\sum P(X)f(X)$	Expected Value of the Function f(X) of Variable X under Probability Distribution P

Importance Sampling

To solve problems using importance sampling, it is necessary to know the probability distribution (Q) of the data-rich environment and the probability distribution (P) of the environment we want to target. The expected value of Q and variable x is then calculated, multiplied by the ratio of Q to P. This concept has been mathematically proven, and it's recommended to approach reinforcement learning with this level of understanding.

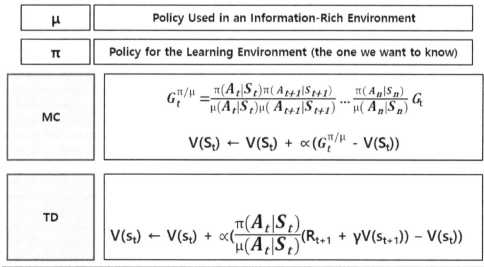

μ	Policy Used in an Information-Rich Environment
π	Policy for the Learning Environment (the one we want to know)
MC	$G_t^{\pi/\mu} = \frac{\pi(A_t\|S_t)\pi(A_{t+1}\|S_{t+1})}{\mu(A_t\|S_t)\mu(A_{t+1}\|S_{t+1})} \cdots \frac{\pi(A_n\|S_n)}{\mu(A_n\|S_n)} G_t$ $V(S_t) \leftarrow V(S_t) + \propto (G_t^{\pi/\mu} - V(S_t))$
TD	$V(s_t) \leftarrow V(s_t) + \propto (\frac{\pi(A_t\|S_t)}{\mu(A_t\|S_t)}(R_{t+1} + \gamma V(S_{t+1})) - V(s_t))$

Importance Sampling in MC and TD

MC and TD can be modified using importance sampling. Here, μ represents a policy from an information-rich environment with extensive experience. This policy is likely to be well-trained and can provide samples easily. π\pi$\pi$ is the policy we aim to learn, but obtaining samples for this policy is difficult. When we want to train policy π using MC, we can use policy μ to obtain samples and train π\pi$\pi$ through importance sampling.

In MC, samples continue to be generated until an episode ends, so importance sampling must be repeatedly multiplied to calculate the expected value. In TD, only a single timestep is executed and its value calculated, requiring just one instance of importance sampling.

In MC, the continuous multiplication of importance sampling can lead to severe value distortion. Therefore, practically, using importance sampling in MC is infeasible.

MC and TD can be modified using importance sampling. μ is the policy from an information-rich environment with many experiences. This policy would be relatively well-trained and provide samples easily. π is the policy we want to train but is difficult to sample from. To train policy π using MC, samples can be obtained through policy μ, and π is trained through importance sampling.

In MC, importance sampling continues to be multiplied because samples are generated until the end of an episode, whereas in TD, ...

MC uses continuous multiplication of importance sampling, which may distort the values significantly. Thus, using importance sampling in MC is impractical.

3.8.3 Q-Learning

Earlier, we explained that the Q-function is used to control policies in MC and TD. In environments where MC and TD are applied, all information about the model is not available (Model-Free), meaning the next state is unknown. Therefore, it is not possible to use the state-value function to find the optimal policy.

However, by using the action-value function (Q-function), we can calculate the value for each possible action (A) in the current state (s), even without knowing the next state. This allows policy control by updating the policy to choose the action that returns the highest value.

SARSA is an extension of TD that replaces the state-value function with the action-value function (Q-function) for policy evaluation and control. In TD, a single action (a) is taken in state (s) based on the policy, and its value is calculated, so strictly speaking, using the Q-function is a more accurate approach. Therefore, SARSA replaces the state-value function with the Q-function.

Both TD and MC use the same policy π for policy evaluation and control, making them examples of on-policy learning methods.

So far, this covers what we've studied. Now, let's explore Q-learning, which allows for more efficient learning. As previously mentioned, Q-functions are used for policy control in MC and TD. In environments where MC and TD are applied, complete information about the model is lacking (Model-Free), making it impossible to know the next state. Therefore, using the state-value function to determine the optimal policy is not feasible.

SARSA	$Q(S,A) \leftarrow Q(S,A) + \propto(R_{t+1} + \gamma Q(S',A') - Q(S,A))$

Q-Learning	$Q(S,A) \leftarrow Q(S,A) + \propto(R_{t+1} + \gamma \max_{a'} Q(S', a) - Q(S,A))$

However, by using the action-value function (Q-function), it is possible to determine the value of each possible action (A) in the current state (s), allowing the policy to be updated to sel...

TD and MC used the same policy π for policy evaluation and policy control, thus falling under the category of on-policy learning.

Up to this point, we have covered the concepts learned so far. Now let's look at Q-learning, which allows for more efficient learning.

In SARSA, experience is accumulated by calculating the Q-value based on the policy (π) to determine the next action. However, in Q-learning, the next action is selected to maximize the Q-value rather than following the policy. This is the key difference between SARSA and Q-learning.

Q-learning does not use importance sampling; however, it is considered an off-policy method because the policy used for evaluation (max) is different from the policy used for control (π). Generally, Q-learning shows better pe...

Let's examine the issues of policy evaluation and policy control in Q-learning, as previously discussed. In the SARSA algorithm, policy evaluation involves calculating the Q-function. Actions are chosen based on a fixed policy, values are calculated, and the Q-function is updated. Policy control modifies the policy to select the action with the highest Q-function calculated during policy evaluation.

Q-learning, on the other hand, does not use a fixed policy. In the policy evaluation process, the action wit...

The algorithms we have studied so far are the foundational theories of reinforcement learning. Dynamic Programming, MC, TD, and Q-learning are not frequently used in practical applications. Starting with DQN, which we will examine next, we'll cover algorithms widely used in practice. However, it is essential to thoroughly understand the early reinforcement learning algorithms because it is nearly impossible to understand advanced algorithms without grasping these foundational ones.

Chapter 4
Artificial Intelligence Concepts

4. Artificial Intelligence Concepts

Most reinforcement learning algorithms use artificial neural networks internally, making it impossible to fully understand reinforcement learning algorithms without a basic understanding of neural networks. However, this doesn't mean that neural networks are inherently difficult to understand. The concept of neural networks is straightforward, although achieving good performance is challenging.

In this chapter, we will explore the theoretical aspects of artificial intelligence, beginning with machine learning and moving into neural networks. The difficulty level is not high, so you can read through it comfortably, and you'll find that the concepts of AI will be organized in your mind before you know it.

4.1 Machine Learning

Machine Learning is an AI technology that learns and continuously improves performance without explicit programming. Machine learning algorithms establish a mathematical model for a specific field and complete this model by training with data, enabling them to predict outcomes or make decisions.

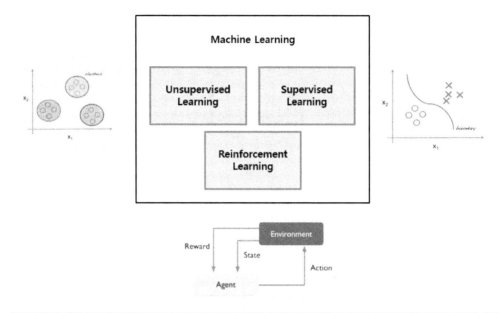

Concept of Machine Learning

Machine learning techniques include unsupervised learning, supervised learning, and reinforcement learning.

Unsupervised learning groups data with similar characteristics based on data features. There is no reference data regarding the learning objective in unsupervised learning. For example, when classifying customer segments based on purchasing data, unsupervised learning can find groups of customers with similar purchasing patterns. Since there is no data indicating which customers are valuable and which are not, a business expert would need to analyze the categorized groups to distinguish valuable from non-valuable customers. In other words, unsupervised learning performs the initial classification, and a business expert conducts a secondary evaluation.

A representative algorithm used in unsupervised learning is the k-means algorithm. Here, k represents the number of groups to classify, so if k=5, the algorithm classifies customers into five groups. The group center (k) is set arbitrarily, and members are regrouped continuously until the average distance between each member and the center is minimized.

Supervised learning is a technique where data with clear outcomes (targets) is used to complete a mathematical model, which then predicts results when new data is introduced. For example, suppose we want to create a model that predicts stock prices. The data required for training would include factors that affect stock prices on each date and the stock prices themselves. The goal of the training is to predict the price for an unknown date given influencing factors, hence the term "supervised learning." After completing the model, we can input basic data to predict the stock price for the following day.

The classic example of supervised learning is the problem of classifying images as dogs or cats. If we want to create a model that can identify whether an image is a dog or a cat, we must train it on millions of labeled images. Once trained, the model will classify new images as either dogs or cats on its own.

Reinforcement learning differs somewhat from supervised and unsupervised learning in concept. Reinforcement learning uses rewards based on the agent's actions and state. Although this was explained earlier, let's review the concept briefly.

Consider a baby learning to walk. The baby doesn't learn from anyone else. If the baby shifts weight onto the left leg and tries to stand up on the right side but falls painfully, they may try to stand up on the left side next time. When standing successfully, the baby receives praise and a broader view, which is a reward for standing correctly. Although the baby can't get up easily the first time, they may stand a bit more easily, motivated by the sense of achievement.

The same goes for walking. If lifting the left foot while shifting weight off the right leg results in pain from falling, the baby will try supporting the right leg when lifting the left. The goal is to avoid pain and reach the destination quickly. Through falling, hurting, and being praised, the baby learns to walk.

Reinforcement learning models this process mathematically. The most fundamental concept is MDP (Markov Decision Process). Reinforcement learning theory is based on MDP, so understanding MDP is essential to understanding reinforcement learning. We will cover reinforcement learning and MDP in more detail shortly.

Since the goal of this book is to understand reinforcement learning, we will focus on supervised learning, which is more closely related to reinforcement learning, and omit an extensive discussion of unsupervised learning.

4.2 Linear Regression Analysis

To understand the concept of machine learning, let's examine simple one-dimensional linear regression analysis. Linear regression analysis is a type of supervised learning used to create a predictive model that can forecast outcomes for unknown data.

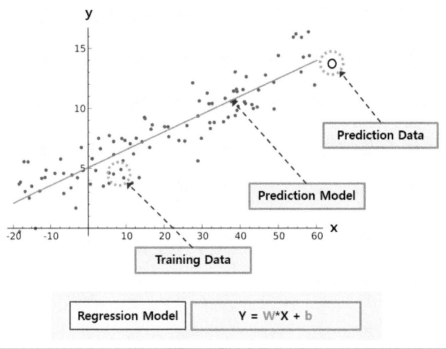

Linear Regression Analysis

In the figure, the training data consists of two-dimensional (x, y) data. The goal is to create a model that can predict the value of y when an x value that isn't in the training data is given. While the data doesn't follow a perfect one-dimensional linear distribution, identifying a linear equation that approximates the data can provide an estimated value for y, even with some error.

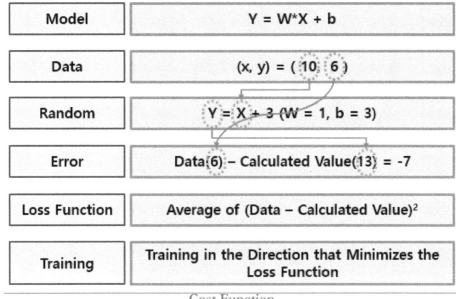

Model	Y = W*X + b
Data	(x, y) = (10, 6)
Random	Y = X + 3 (W = 1, b = 3)
Error	Data(6) – Calculated Value(13) = -7
Loss Function	Average of (Data – Calculated Value)^2
Training	Training in the Direction that Minimizes the Loss Function

Cost Function

As shown in the figure, the model takes the form of a linear equation, requiring only the values of the coefficient W and the intercept b. In machine learning, W is called the weight, and b is called the bias. The goal of one-dimensional linear regression analysis is to find the values of W and b that best describe the data.

Let's see how to find W and b. Start by assigning arbitrary values to W and b. For example, if W=1 and b=3, using the known data point (x, y) = (10, 6) in the model yields y=13. The calculated value of 13 differs from the known value of 6 by approximately -7. This difference between the known and calculated values is called the cost or loss.

To find the values of W and b that minimize the difference between actual and calculated values, we define a loss function (or cost function). Since the sign of the difference (positive or negative) doesn't matter, we square it.

The remaining question is how to adjust W and b. This is where gradient descent comes in.

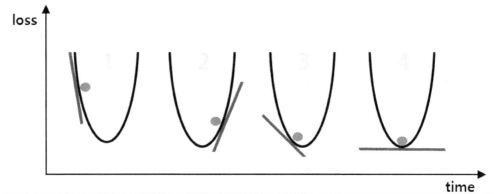

Gradient Descent

By taking the partial derivative of the loss function defined above and adjusting W and b in the direction that reduces the gradient, we can eventually reach the point of minimum error. This algorithm is called gradient descent. This book doesn't delve deeply into the specifics of gradient descent, but it is essential to know that it minimizes the error function.

If gradient descent finds that the optimal values of W and b are (0.15,5) then the model becomes Y=0.15×X+5Y = 0.15. Now, the model can calculate the value of y for unknown x values.

4.3 Classification Analysis

Let's explore binary classification analysis, which categorizes data into two types. Classification analysis is also a type of supervised learning. Here, we'll examine simple two-dimensional (X, Y) data. On the graph, multiple Xs are located at the top, and multiple Os are at the bottom. The goal of binary classification is to use known X and O data to determine the category of unknown data.

First, we need to identify a linear function that separates the boundary between X and O. The objective is to find the values of W and b that satisfy Y=W×X+b. The technique is similar to the concept of linear regression discussed earlier. Finding a linear function that separates the categories is not particularly challenging.

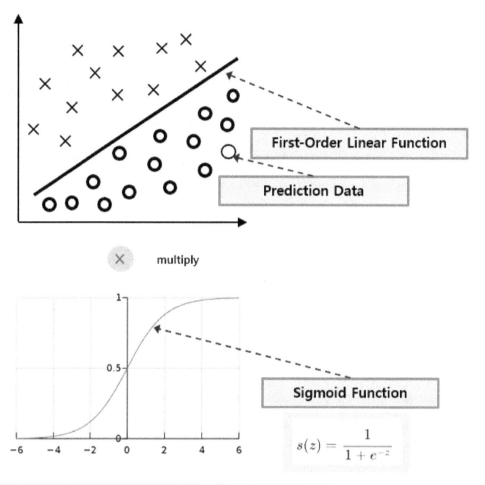

multiply

$$s(z) = \frac{1}{1 + e^{-z}}$$

Classification Analysis

The question is how to apply this linear function to binary classification. This is where the activation function comes in. A common activation function is the sigmoid function. The sigmoid function is a simple concept that converts input data into values between 0 and 1 based on a certain threshold. It's widely used in machine learning because it transforms linear data into non-linear data. Here, if the known value y is greater than the calculated y^ from the linear function, it is converted to 1; otherwise, it is converted to 0.

When first encountering machine learning, one may feel overwhelmed by various mathematical expressions. However, for **Developers**, understanding the basic principles and usage of machine learning is more relevant. Basic knowledge of arithmetic operations, logarithms, and matrix operations is sufficient to grasp fundamental concepts. Rather than focusing on the equations, it may be helpful to observe the shape of the graphs that these equations represent.

Binary Classification Function	$Y = \text{sigmoid}(W*X + b)$

Binary Classification Function

A binary classification function can be mathematically represented as shown above. Besides the sigmoid function, other activation functions such as ReLU and tanh are also used. The concepts introduced in classification analysis form the foundation for understanding neural networks, which will be covered next. By approaching machine learning and deep learning concepts gradually, starting with the basics, anyone can master them without feeling overwhelmed.

4.4 Deep Learning

Neurons (nerve cells) are the cells that make up the nervous system. They send and receive electrical signals to communicate with other neurons, playing a key role in distributing and storing information. The human brain is composed of hundreds of billions of neurons, allowing us to remember, make decisions, and experience emotions. While neurons consist of various components, we will focus only on the elements relevant to building artificial neural networks.

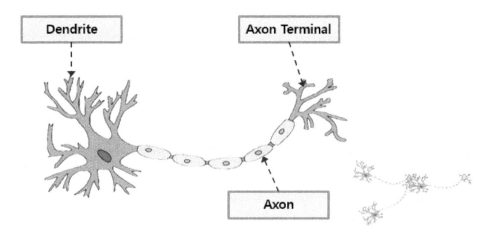

Neuron

In the context of artificial neural networks, a neuron is composed of dendrites, an axon, and an axon terminal. Dendrites receive information from other neurons and send it to the axon. The axon is a chain-like structure made up of multiple segments. The signal received by the dendrites is processed as it travels through the axon, sometimes increasing, decreasing, or disappearing. The processed signal from the axon is then transmitted to other neurons through the axon terminal.

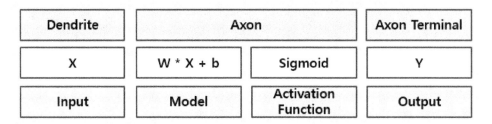

Dendrite	Axon		Axon Terminal
X	W * X + b	Sigmoid	Y
Input	Model	Activation Function	Output

Neuron and Artificial Neural Network

Let's explain neural networks using the binary classification model discussed earlier. The input received by the dendrites corresponds to the input in a linear model. The signal processed through the axon represents the model. The signal processing involves weights (W) and bias (b), and the signal that passes through the model is shaped by an activation function to produce a specific result. The axon terminal, which sends signals to other neurons, corresponds to the output.

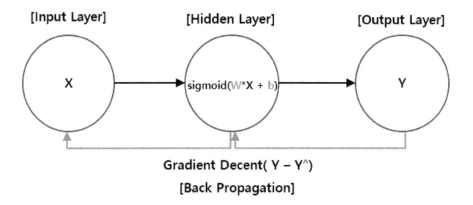

[Input Layer]   [Hidden Layer]   [Output Layer]

X   sigmoid(W*X + b)   Y

Gradient Decent(Y – Y^)
[Back Propagation]

Single Artificial Neural Network

Using the linear regression and binary classification concepts learned earlier, we can build a simple neural network. A neural network consists of an Input Layer, Hidden Layer, Output Layer, and Back Propagation. The Input Layer, Hidden Layer, and Output Layer are similar to the concepts already discussed. Back Propagation is a method that applies the theory of minimizing the mean squared error between actual and predicted values. The difference is that errors propagate from the Output Layer back toward the Input Layer. This may not have a significant effect in a single-layer neural network but has remarkable effects in deep neural networks (those with multiple hidden layers).

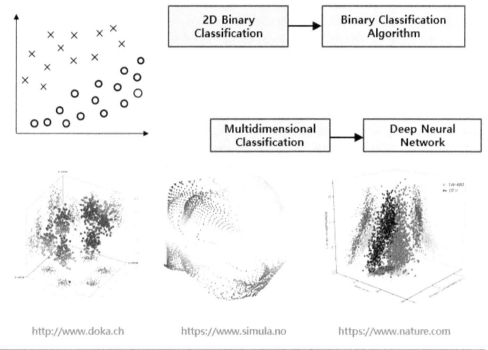

http://www.doka.ch   https://www.simula.no   https://www.nature.com

Multidimensional Classification Problem

Let's tackle a more complex problem: multidimensional classification instead of binary classification. A simple model cannot classify multidimensional data. Solving this problem requires tackling equations with hundreds or thousands of dimensions, for which deep neural networks are used, also known as deep learning.

To create a binary classification model, we first applied a linear model to make a primary prediction and then used an activation function to convert the prediction into non-linear data. Deep neural networks use this principle by dividing hidden layers into multiple nodes (models) that allow data to be classified through a combination of various non-linear functions. While the specific model choice is up to the analyst, the algorithm of the deep neural network automatically identifies weights and biases. With hundreds or thousands of hidden layers, astonishing results can be achieved.

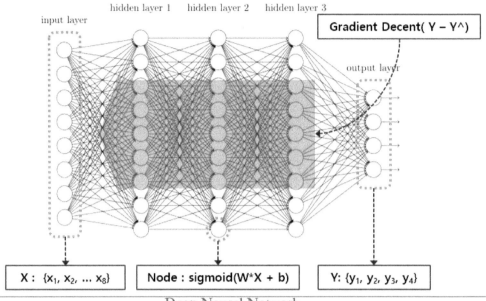

hidden layer 1   hidden layer 2   hidden layer 3

input layer

Gradient Decent(Y – Y^)

output layer

| X : {x₁, x₂, ... x₈} | Node : sigmoid(W*X + b) | Y: {y₁, y₂, y₃, y₄} |

Deep Neural Network

In deep neural networks, the input X may contain multiple values. For example, in a model that learns from images, an 800x600 image could be used as an input matrix of the same dimensions. In some deep learning algorithms, only a portion of the image is used as input.

In machine learning, inputs (X) and outputs (Y) can be processed in matrix form to handle various data types. Any data type, such as numbers, images, or audio, can be converted into matrices, and training is carried out through matrix operations.

The Hidden Layer consists of layers and nodes. Layers increase to the right, while nodes (circles) increase downward. The number of layers and nodes is determined by the analyst, largely depending on the performance of the computer used. As the number of layers and nodes increases, the computational power required grows, so it's advisable to choose a level that does not hinder learning.

The most frequently used mathematical concepts in AI are basic arithmetic, logarithms, sequences, and matrix operations. Of course, those writing academic papers or conducting professional research will need to study mathematics more deeply, but for general AI learning, a high school level understanding of math is sufficient.

High school math can be challenging, but you don't need to master calculus in detail. If you encounter difficulties, a quick online search for key concepts will usually suffice.

4.5 Setting Up the Development Environment

To program for reinforcement learning, you'll need to install several programs. In data analysis, installing Anaconda provides most of the required programs by default, making it convenient. However, here we'll go through the process of setting up the development environment step-by-step, starting with installing Python.

https://www.python.org/downloads/windows	Python 3.7.7

- Python 3.7.7 - March 10, 2020

  Note that Python 3.7.7 *cannot* be used on Windows XP or earlier.

  - Download Windows help file
  - Download Windows x86-64 embeddable zip file
  - Download Windows x86-64 executable installer
  - Download Windows x86-64 web-based installer
  - Download Windows x86 embeddable zip file
  - Download Windows x86 executable installer
  - Download Windows x86 web-based installer

Downloading the Python Installer

There are various Python versions available, but this book uses Python 3.7.7. Installing a different version could lead to errors when running examples, so it's recommended to install this specific version. Download the executable file that matches your operating system: for a 64-bit OS, download the Windows x86-64 executable installer, and for a 32-bit OS, download the Windows x86 executable installer. Since most PCs today use 64-bit Windows 10, downloading the x86-64 file should work. However, it's wise to check your Windows version using "My PC" before proceeding.

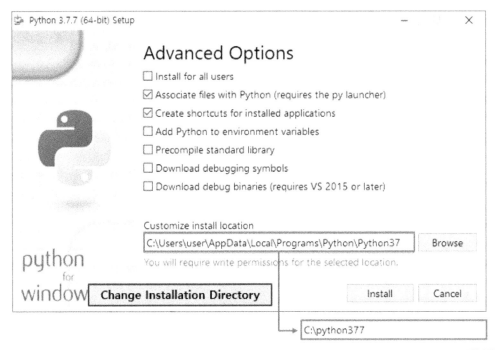

Changing the Installation Directory

Double-click the downloaded installer to start installing Python. While most steps can be followed as prompted, it's advisable to change the installation location. Create a "Python377" directory under the C drive, then click the Browse button on the installation screen to specify the location.

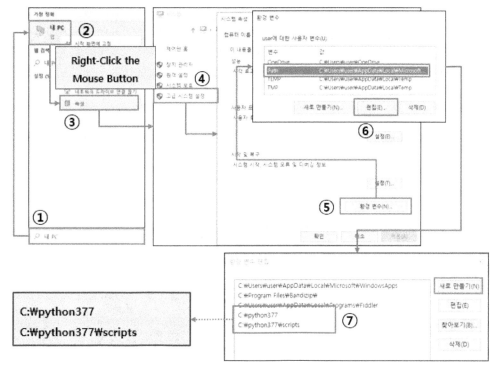

Registering Environment Variables

After installing Python, set up the environment to run Python. Start by typing "My PC" in the Windows search bar to find the program. Once "My PC" appears in the search results, right-click it and select Properties to access system properties. Then, choose "Advanced System Settings" and click the "Environment Variables" button at the bottom. In the Environment Variables window, select the "Path" entry and click Edit. Click "New" and add two folder paths: "C:\python377" and "C:\python377\scripts."

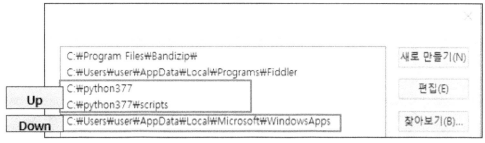

WindowsApps Environment Variable Location

In the environment variable editing screen, if the WindowsApps-related environment variable is above the Python environment variable, Windows will search WindowsApps before Python. Ensure that the Python environment variable is placed above WindowsApps.

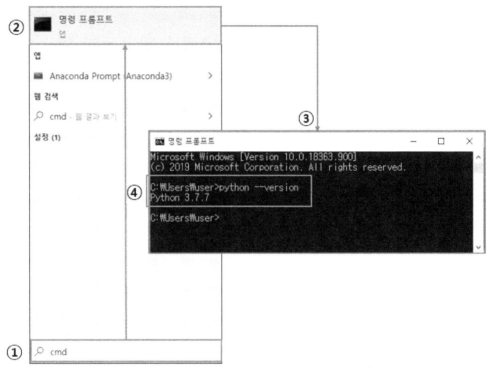

Verifying the Python Installation

To verify that Python has been installed correctly, open Command Prompt by typing "cmd" in the Windows search bar. Run the command "python --version," and it should display "Python 3.7.7." If it doesn't and instead opens a Windows application search window, go back to the environment variable setup steps and carefully review the installation.

Upgrading pip

Python includes pip, a package manager that simplifies handling packages. Before using pip, upgrade it to the latest version by running the command "python -m pip install --upgrade pip."

Installing Jupyter Notebook

To develop Python programs, you need an editor. While Python's default editor, IDLE, is installed, other popular editors include PyCharm and Spyder. However, in AI, Jupyter Notebook is the most commonly used tool. Install it by running the command "pip install notebook."

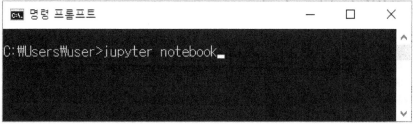

Running Jupyter Notebook

To launch Jupyter Notebook, enter "jupyter notebook" in Command Prompt. Note that you cannot access directories higher than the one from which you start Jupyter Notebook. For example, if you start in the "C:\User\user" directory, you won't be able to open programs in "C:\User\test" in Jupyter. To open a program, move to the desired directory or at least a parent directory before running Jupyter Notebook.

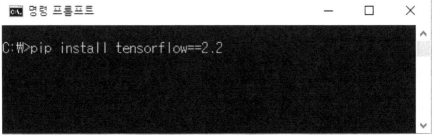

Installing TensorFlow 2.0

Google's deep learning package, TensorFlow, can be easily installed using pip. Run "pip install tensorflow" to install the latest version. You can specify a version, such as 2.2, by adding "==version."

```
C:\RL>pip uninstall numpy
Found existing installation: numpy 1.19.4
Uninstalling numpy-1.19.4:
  Would remove:
    c:\python377\lib\site-packages\numpy-1.19.4.dist-info\*
    c:\python377\lib\site-packages\numpy\*
    c:\python377\scripts\f2py.exe
Proceed (y/n)? y
  Successfully uninstalled numpy-1.19.4

C:\RL>pip install numpy==1.19.3
Collecting numpy==1.19.3
  Downloading numpy-1.19.3-cp37-cp37m-win_amd64.whl (13.2 MB)
     |                              | 13.2 MB 128 kB/s
Installing collected packages: numpy
Successfully installed numpy-1.19.3
```

Installing NumPy 1.19.3

Python 3.7.7 includes NumPy version 1.19.4 by default, which can sometimes cause errors with TensorFlow. Downgrade to version 1.19.3 by first uninstalling the current version with "pip uninstall numpy," then installing the lower version with "pip install numpy==1.19.3."

ImportError: Could not find the DLL(s) 'msvcp140_1.dll'. TensorFlow requires that these DLLs be installed in a directory that is named in your %PATH% environment variable. You may install these DLLs by downloading "Microsoft C++ Redistributable for Visual Studio 2015, 2017 and 2019" for your platform from this URL: https://support.microsoft.com/help/2977003/the-latest-supported-visual-c-downloads

Running TensorFlow 2.2 Errors

When running TensorFlow 2.2, you might encounter an error related to msvcp140_1.dll not being installed. Download and install the necessary program from the Microsoft support site: https://learn.microsoft.com/en-us/cpp/windows/latest-supported-vc-redist?view=msvc-170#visual-studio-2015-2017-2019-and-2022.

Architecture	Link	Notes
ARM64	https://aka.ms/vs/17/release/vc_redist.arm64.exe	Permalink for latest supported ARM64 version
X86	https://aka.ms/vs/17/release/vc_redist.x86.exe	Permalink for latest supported x86 version
X64	https://aka.ms/vs/17/release/vc_redist.x64.exe	Permalink for latest supported x64 version. The X64 Redistributable package contains both ARM64 and X64 binaries. This package makes it easy to install required Visual C++ ARM64 binaries when the X64 Redistributable is installed on an ARM64 device.

Downloading the Microsoft Visual C++ Redistributable Package

Download the Microsoft Visual C++ Redistributable Package for Visual Studio 2015, 2017, and 2019. For a 32-bit Windows system, download the vc_redist.x86.exe program, and for a 64-bit system, download vc_redist.x64.exe.

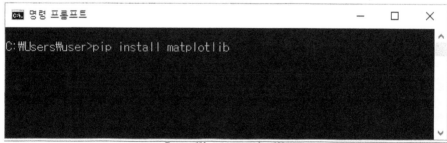

Installing matplotlib

To visualize training results or fine-tune parameters, use a graphing package. While Python has various options, matplotlib is the most straightforward and intuitive. Install it to create graphs easily.

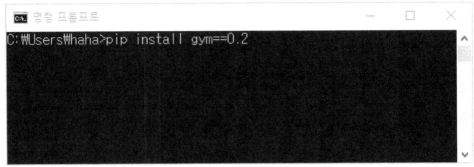

Installing OpenAI Gym

OpenAI, a site providing resources for reinforcement learning, offers test programs packaged as OpenAI Gym. Simply installing the gym package gives access to various reinforcement learning programs.

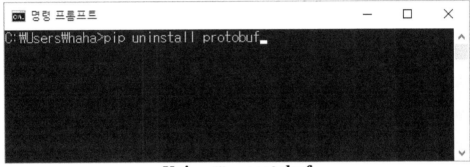

Uninstalling protobuf

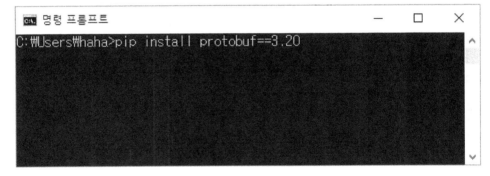

Installing **protobuf**

In recent package installations, it is common to encounter compatibility issues with the protobuf version. As a result, it may be necessary to install a lower version to ensure proper functionality and avoid conflicts.

4.6 TensorFlow

TensorFlow is an open-source software library developed by Google for numerical computations using data flow graphs. It is designed with a structure that makes it ideal for working with neural network-based algorithms. TensorFlow supports GPU acceleration to improve performance and enables visualization of the training process using TensorBoard.

This book uses TensorFlow 2.2. In TensorFlow 1.x, it was necessary to define a graph before executing tasks, then build the graph and run the program within it. This approach, differing significantly from the sequential nature of typical programs, was challenging for beginners to understand. However, TensorFlow 2.x introduced eager execution mode, allowing programs to run sequentially. This makes TensorFlow easier to grasp for newcomers and significantly simplifies its structure.

In TensorFlow 2.x, high-level APIs are unified around tf.keras, consolidating functionalities that were implemented in various ways in TensorFlow 1.0. This simplification resolves the confusion caused by different implementations across various examples found online. TensorFlow 2.x, therefore, offers numerous advantages, notably simplifying its structure. It's time to let go of any preconceptions about TensorFlow being overly complex.

```
import tensorflow as tf                                              ①

mnist = tf.keras.datasets.mnist                                     ②
(x_train, y_train), (x_test, y_test) = mnist.load_data()
print("* shape:", x_train.shape, y_train.shape)

model = tf.keras.models.Sequential([                                ③
    tf.keras.layers.Flatten(input_shape=(28,28)),
    tf.keras.layers.Dense(128, activation='relu'),
    tf.keras.layers.Dense(10, activation='softmax')
])

model.compile(optimazer='adam',                                     ④
          loss='sparse_categorical_crossentropy',
          metrics=['accuracy']
    )

hist= model.fit(x_train, y_train, epochs=5)                         ⑤

model.evaluate(x_test, y_test, verbose=2)                           ⑥
```

Basic Structure of a Program

TensorFlow programs generally follow a similar structure:

1.   Load the TensorFlow package into the program.

2.   Load the dataset for testing—in this case, we use the MNIST dataset, a set of numerical images.

3.   Define the structure of the TensorFlow neural network, deciding on the number of nodes and layers.

4.   Specify the cost function and optimizer for the training process.

5.   Train the model once the neural network structure is defined.

6.   After training is complete, validate the model's performance with test data.

Let's explore each function in more detail.

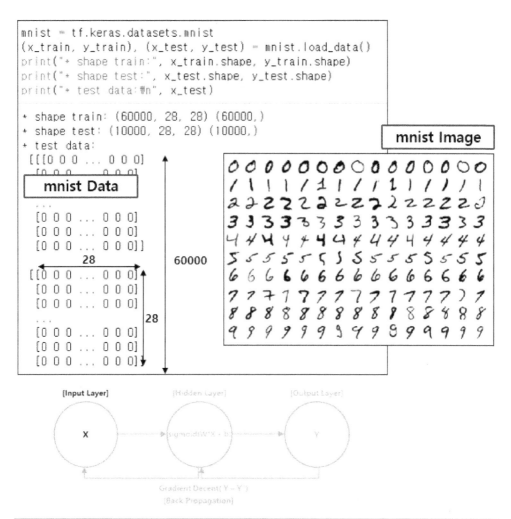

```
mnist = tf.keras.datasets.mnist
(x_train, y_train), (x_test, y_test) = mnist.load_data()
print("+ shape train:", x_train.shape, y_train.shape)
print("+ shape test:", x_test.shape, y_test.shape)
print("+ test data:#n", x_test)

+ shape train: (60000, 28, 28) (60000,)
+ shape test: (10000, 28, 28) (10000,)
+ test data:
 [[[0 0 0 ... 0 0 0]
```

Loading Training Data

The first step is to load the training data. The Keras package provides various datasets, and here we use the MNIST dataset of numerical images. MNIST consists of 70,000 data points, with 60,000 for training and 10,000 for testing. When loaded, the data is split into training and test sets by default.

Training and Testing Data

A Quick Note
• **Training and Testing Data**

Train and test data are the same type of data. We split the data to avoid skewed results that would occur if the model were evaluated using the same data it trained on—similar to practicing problems that appear unchanged on an exam. For this reason, many datasets provided for neural network studies include predefined splits for training and testing, with 70-80% allocated to training and the remainder to testing.

The training data is a 28x28x60,000 multidimensional array. Each image is represented as a 28x28 array, and there are 60,000 such arrays in total. This is similar to defining XXX in the Input Layer in a single-layer neural network.

```
model = tf.keras.models.Sequential([
    tf.keras.layers.Flatten(input_shape=(28,28)),
    tf.keras.layers.Dense(128, activation='relu'),
    tf.keras.layers.Dense(10, activation='softmax')
])
```

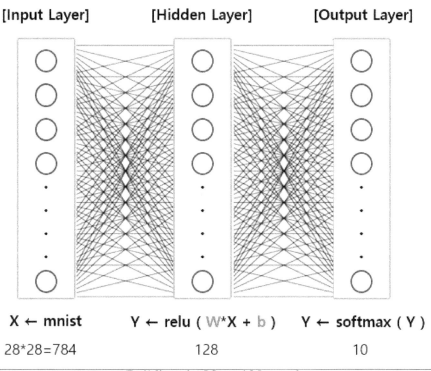

[Input Layer]   **[Hidden Layer]**   **[Output Layer]**

X ← mnist   Y ← relu (W*X + b)   Y ← softmax (Y)

28*28=784   128   10

Building the Neural Network

With the MNIST dataset downloaded, we can now build the neural network for training. We use the Sequential class provided by Keras, which links layers sequentially. The Input Layer is set to receive one image at a time, defined as a 28x28 input. Since TensorFlow requires inputs to be one-dimensional arrays, the 28x28 array is flattened to a 1D array of 784 elements.

Next, we configure the Hidden Layer with 128 nodes and specify the ReLU activation function. ReLU, like the sigmoid function, transforms linear data into non-linear data. The choice of the number of nodes is up to the programmer, and tuning this number may require iterative learning to find the optimal configuration.

The Output Layer is configured based on the types of data in the dataset. Since MNIST classifies numbers 0 through 9, it has 10 output nodes. Here, we use the softmax activation function, which normalizes output values to lie between 0 and 1, with their sum equal to 1, providing probability estimates for each output.

```
model.compile(optimazer='adam',
          loss='sparse_categorical_crossentropy',
          metrics=['accuracy']
   )
```

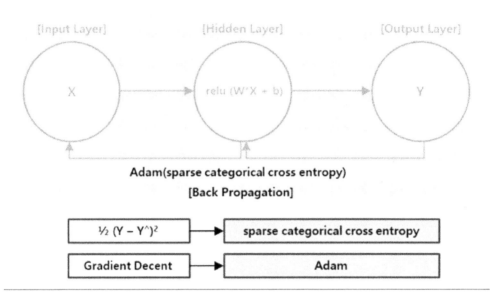

Setting Up the Training Environment

Now, we configure the training environment. The optimizer, which minimizes error, is chosen here as Adam rather than Gradient Descent (commonly used in early AI). Adam is a more efficient algorithm, though we won't delve into its details here.

The error is calculated using sparse categorical cross entropy instead of MSE (Mean Squared Error). Sparse categorical cross entropy is simply another method of defining error. We use accuracy as the metric to assess training quality. Higher accuracy means the neural network and training environment are well-configured.

```
hist= model.fit(x_train, y_train, epochs=5)

Train on 60000 samples
Epoch 1/5
60000/60000 [==============================] - 8s 133us/sample - loss: 0.1850 - accuracy: 0.9839
Epoch 2/5
60000/60000 [==============================] - 7s 121us/sample - loss: 0.1829 - accuracy: 0.9844
Epoch 3/5
60000/60000 [==============================] - 8s 127us/sample - loss: 0.2034 - accuracy: 0.9845
Epoch 4/5
60000/60000 [==============================] - 8s 133us/sample - loss: 0.1866 - accuracy: 0.9850
Epoch 5/5
60000/60000 [==============================] - 7s 119us/sample - loss: 0.1925 - accuracy: 0.9850
```
Training the Model

The completed neural network is stored in a model variable as a
Sequential object, which supports the fit function for training.
Provide the training dataset and specify the number of repetitions
(epochs). If set to 5, the 60,000 training data points are used for
training five times. While training, the screen will display updates
on the loss and accuracy for each epoch. Lower loss and accuracy
values closer to 1 are ideal.

```
model.evaluate(x_test, y_test, verbose=2)

10000/1 - 1s - loss: 0.5757 - accuracy: 0.9646

[1.1514647204219093, 0.9646]
```
Validating the Model

Model accuracy can be determined using test data not involved in
training. Using the MNIST test dataset (x_test, y_test) in the
evaluate function provides accuracy metrics. The verbose parameter
in evaluate controls the output detail level, typically set to 2 in
Jupyter Notebook environments.

In this chapter, we covered the basics of AI and how to create and
train a neural network using TensorFlow. Since most reinforcement
learning algorithms rely on neural networks, becoming proficient
with packages like TensorFlow is essential. Reinforcement learning
algorithms are theoretical, while programming languages bring
them to life, with neural networks at the core. As TensorFlow is
widely used, studying it in depth will benefit your understanding.
Proficiency with neural network packages is crucial to quickly and

accurately implementing algorithms; without it, there is a risk of coding in the wrong direction.

Chapter 5

Function Approximation

5. Function Approximation

Function approximation serves as a bridge between reinforcement learning and artificial neural networks. By using function approximation, neural networks can be applied to reinforcement learning, which has led to a significant advancement in reinforcement learning theory.

To understand function approximation, it is essential to understand the concept of artificial neural networks explained in the previous chapter. If you are not clear on what a neural network is, I recommend revisiting the earlier content.

Studying function approximation requires knowledge of various mathematical concepts. However, this chapter explains essential mathematical theories step by step, so even beginners will find it easy to understand.

5.1 Derivatives (Differentiation)

A derivative finds the rate of change of a function at any given point. Before discussing the rate of change, let's understand the concept of change rate. The rate of change represents the amount of change, including average change rates and instantaneous change rates.

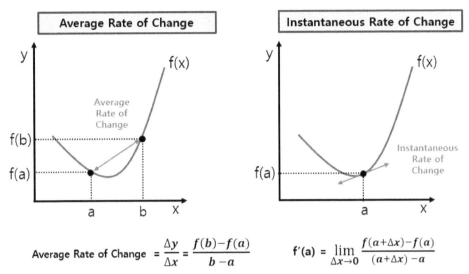

Average Rate of Change

Instantaneous Rate of Change

$$\text{Average Rate of Change} = \frac{\Delta y}{\Delta x} = \frac{f(b) - f(a)}{b - a} \qquad f'(a) = \lim_{\Delta x \to 0} \frac{f(a + \Delta x) - f(a)}{(a + \Delta x) - a}$$

Average Rate of Change vs. Instantaneous Rate of Change

Consider a function f(x) that represents data distributed similarly to the above diagram. 'f' stands for function, and 'x' is the variable used as input. For example, if f(x) = 2x² + x + 3, increasing the value of 'x' and calculating the function (y) values would yield a similar graph as shown above.

Now, if the value of 'x' changes from 'a' to 'b', how much does the function output (y) change in proportion to 'x'? This change is found using the average rate of change. The symbol Δ (delta) used in the formula represents the change amount, where Δy indicates the change in 'y' and Δx indicates the change in 'x'. The average rate of change is obtained by dividing these two values.

If we consider a car traveling over time and create a function from the data of the car's distance, with 'x' as time and 'y' as the distance traveled, the average rate of change between time 'a' and time 'b' would represent the car's speed.

The concept of instantaneous rate of change, which means differentiation, is a bit more challenging compared to the average rate of change. While average rate of change is calculated over a clearly distinguishable interval (from 'a' to 'b'), instantaneous rate of change calculates the rate of change at a single point.

To make it easier, let's use Δx to indicate the change in 'x'. In the average rate of change, Δx is relatively large, but for the instantaneous rate of change, Δx is extremely small. As Δx becomes close to zero (lim: limit), the value of the instantaneous rate of change can be found.

For example, speed cameras measure the speed of a car as it passes a certain point, not between two points ('a' and 'b'), but at a specific location. In this case, differentiation is used. By making the measurement range close to zero, the speed can be calculated at a particular point.

$$(c)' = 0$$

$$(x^n)' = nx^{n-1}$$

| Differentiation Formulas | $\{f(x) \cdot g(x)\}' = \{f(x)' \cdot g(x)\} + \{f(x) \cdot g(x)'\}$ |

$$f(g(x))' = f'(g(x))g(x)'$$

$$(a^x)' = a^x \ln a$$

Differentiation Formula

There may be times when we want to know the result of differentiating at any point, not just a specific point. In such cases, differentiating the function and expressing the differentiation result as another function would be useful. While it's too lengthy to explain the principle here, only the basic formulas are provided. There are various differentiation formulas for different functions, but only the ones used in reinforcement learning are summarized above. Since this is not a mathematics test, use the formulas as reference whenever needed.

5.2 Partial Derivative

A partial derivative is a type of differentiation. The function we looked at earlier had one variable (x). A partial derivative, on the other hand, applies when a function has two or more variables. For instance, if a function is f(x, y), where the value of the function depends on the input values 'x' and 'y', then differentiating with respect to just one variable is called partial differentiation. For example, $f(x, y) = 2x^2 + 3y + 4$ is a function with two variables that can be partially differentiated.

$$\boxed{\begin{array}{c} \textbf{Partial} \\ \textbf{Derivative} \end{array}} \qquad f_x(x, y) = \frac{\partial f}{\partial x}$$

Partial Differentiation

When differentiating with respect to 'x', 'y' is considered constant and is unaffected by differentiation. The symbol ∂, pronounced "partial," is placed in front of both the function and the variable to indicate partial differentiation.

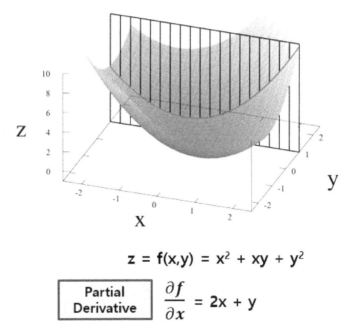

$$z = f(x,y) = x^2 + xy + y^2$$

$$\boxed{\begin{array}{c} \textbf{Partial} \\ \textbf{Derivative} \end{array}} \qquad \frac{\partial f}{\partial x} = 2x + y$$

Application of Partial Derivative (Cited from Wikipedia)

The function $x^2 + xy + y^2$, consisting of variables (x, y), represents a three-dimensional surface. Partially differentiating this function with respect to 'x' yields $2x + y$. When $x = 1$ and $y = 1$, the result is 3, which represents the rate of change at that point. Since this is partial differentiation with respect to 'x', the value of 'y' is fixed (in this case, set to 1), and we observe how the rate of change varies with changing 'x'.

5.3 Scalar and Vector

Let's first look at the concepts of scalar and vector. Scalars are quantities with only magnitude and no direction, like weight, exam scores, or height. Vectors, on the other hand, have both magnitude and direction, like magnetic force, velocity, and acceleration.

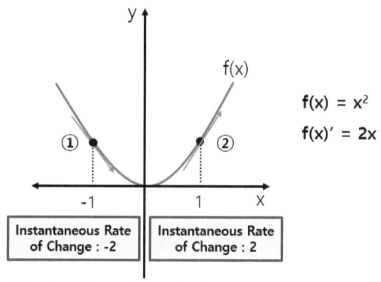

Application of Partial Derivative (Cited from Wikipedia)

The quadratic function $f(x) = x^2$ has pairs of values (x, y) that are scalars. For instance, (x, y) = (-1, 1) or (x, y) = (1, 1). Differentiating function f(x) yields f'(x) = 2x, which can be used to find the rate of change at a particular point. The concept of rate of change implies direction. At x = -1, the rate of change is -2, indicating a decrease, while at x = 1, the rate of change is 2, indicating an increase. Scalars, when differentiated or partially differentiated, become vectors with direction.

5.4 Gradient

A gradient represents the slope in a space. Earlier, we used partial differentiation with respect to 'x' to see how the slope changes along the x-axis on a three-dimensional graph while keeping 'y' constant. A gradient, however, involves finding the partial derivatives for all variables and representing them in matrix form.

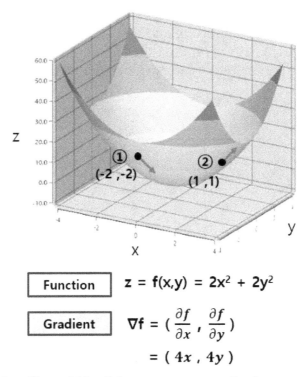

Function	$z = f(x,y) = 2x^2 + 2y^2$
Gradient	$\nabla f = (\dfrac{\partial f}{\partial x} , \dfrac{\partial f}{\partial y})$
	$= (4x , 4y)$

Gradient (Cited from www.syncfusion.com)

Consider the function $f(x, y) = 2x^2 + 2y^2$, which represents a three-dimensional plane. To find the rate of change on the surface, each variable is partially differentiated, yielding 4x and 4y, respectively. These partial derivatives can then be combined into matrix form.

If at point (x, y) = (-2, -2), the gradient is (-8, -8), meaning both 'x' and 'y' are decreasing with a magnitude of 8. At point (x, y) = (1, 1), the gradient is (4, 4), meaning both 'x' and 'y' are increasing with a magnitude of 4.

The symbol for gradient, ∇, is called the nabla or del operator.

5.5 Gradient Descent

Gradient descent is an optimization algorithm used to find the local minimum of a differentiable function through iterative computation. Conversely, an algorithm that finds the local maximum is called gradient ascent.

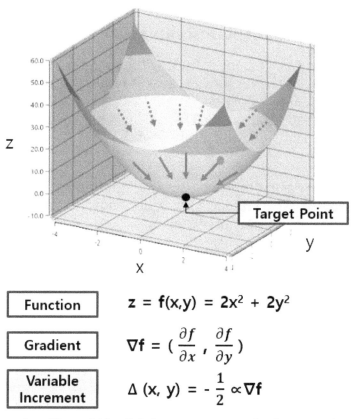

Function	$z = f(x,y) = 2x^2 + 2y^2$
Gradient	$\nabla f = (\frac{\partial f}{\partial x} , \frac{\partial f}{\partial y})$
Variable Increment	$\Delta (x, y) = -\frac{1}{2} \propto \nabla f$

Gradient (Cited from www.syncfusion.com)

Consider the function that creates a three-dimensional plane, representing errors that may occur at coordinates 'x' and 'y'. The goal is to find the point with the lowest value, which would be the optimal value on the plane. If our objective is to find the coordinates of the target point, we would solve it as follows.

First, find the partial derivative of function f(x, y) for each variable (x, y). To make small adjustments rather than large changes, multiply by the step size variable alpha (α). The value 1/2 is used for mathematical convenience, and the minus sign (-) indicates the direction of decreasing values.

Thus, using the formula $-1/2\alpha\nabla f$, adjust the value of the variable (x, y) incrementally in the direction of decreasing values to find the minimum value of the function.

5.6 Stochastic Gradient Descent (SGD)

Gradient descent is efficient at finding the target point, but it has the disadvantage of being slow because it requires training on the entire dataset before adjusting variable increments. To address this, stochastic gradient descent (SGD) was developed, which updates values more quickly by using a subset of the data instead of the entire dataset.

Let's learn the concept of stochastic gradient descent without delving into specific formulas, and explore how it can be applied to future reinforcement learning theories.

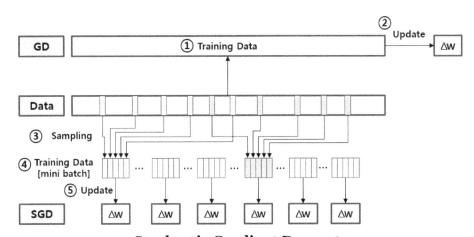

Stochastic Gradient Descent

Gradient Descent (GD) updates Δw by learning from the entire dataset at once. This approach takes a long time per training iteration, but has the advantage of requiring fewer updates overall. In contrast, Stochastic Gradient Descent (SGD) updates Δw by using only a subset of the entire dataset (data sampling) to create a training set. Since it trains with smaller datasets, it requires less time per iteration, but more iterations overall compared to GD, due to the use of sampled data.

Aside from its faster speed, SGD also offers the convenience of using sampling, which is particularly beneficial in reinforcement learning. In the upcoming sections, you will see how various algorithms use SGD to simplify reinforcement learning equations.

5.7 Notations for Partial Derivative and Gradient Descent in Reinforcement Learning

Partial derivatives and gradient descent are expressed in various ways across different books and online sources, depending on the author's choices of function notation and variables. However, regardless of the different notations, the underlying concepts remain consistent.

Many reinforcement learning materials are based on the lecture notes by Professor David Silver. It is advantageous for learners of reinforcement learning to become familiar with the notations used in Silver's lecture materials.

| General Formula: Partial Derivative | $\nabla f(x, y) = (\frac{\partial f}{\partial x}, \frac{\partial f}{\partial y})$ |
| Reinforcement Learning: Partial Derivatives | $\nabla_w J(w) = (\frac{\partial J(w)}{\partial w_1}, \cdots, \frac{\partial J(w)}{\partial wn})$ |

| General Formula: Gradient Descent | $\Delta (x, y) = -\frac{1}{2} \propto \nabla f$ |
| Reinforcement Learning: Gradient Descent | $\Delta w = -\frac{1}{2} \propto \nabla_w J(w)$ |

Notation in Reinforcement Learning

In the formulas explained earlier, only variables 'x' and 'y' were used, but reinforcement learning materials often generalize the variables by using 'w'. The variable 'w' represents all parameters used by the system, from w1 to wn. Additionally, the function is denoted as J, and it is expressed as J(w) when paired with the variable 'w'.

5.8 Function Approximation

All value functions (Value Function) derived so far can be represented as arrays. The state and the actions taken in each state have fixed numerical values that can be managed programmatically.

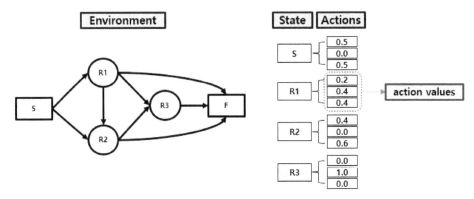

Representing the Navigation Environment as an Array

Let's revisit the navigation environment we studied earlier. The islands accessible by the boat are four in number, excluding the terminal state. Each island has up to three possible routes, which means three actions per state. The action-value function (Q function) for each state-action pair can therefore be represented as an array, with a total of 12 elements to capture the environment.

The policy is embedded within the action-value function. If we use a greedy algorithm, the policy is determined by selecting the action with the highest value in the action-value function (argmax).

Now, consider a scenario where the agent needs to learn how to navigate while walking. The movement of a robot's joints cannot be represented as integers but must be expressed as real numbers. Since real numbers have too vast a range to be represented as an array, we need a function approximation. Using a function approximation, states, actions, policies, and other elements can be expressed.

In reinforcement learning, artificial neural networks are often used as function approximators. Neural networks allow us to incorporate complex state, action, and policy representations that cannot be handled with simple arrays.

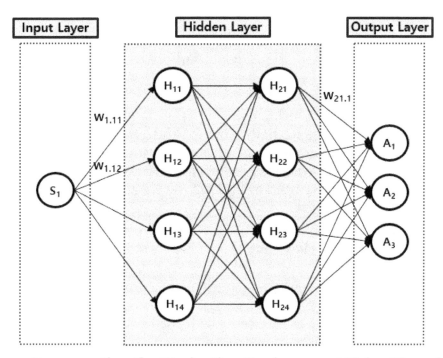

Representing the Navigation Environment Using Neural Networks

Consider representing the navigation environment using a neural network, as shown above. The input is the state (S), and the output is the value of each action (action-value function, Q function). Since we have been using the Q function to determine policies, the action-value function is set as the output, but we can also directly set the policy (π) as the output. Neural networks can theoretically represent any data, allowing the output to be policy (π), state value (V), action value (Q), or any required element. However, the neural network must learn the appropriate weights (w) and biases (b) to represent the data correctly.

Let's understand function approximation through mathematical expressions.

|

$$\hat{v}(s, \ w) \ \doteq \ V_\pi(s)$$

$$\hat{q}(s, \ a, \ w) \ \doteq \ q_\pi(s, \ a)$$

Function Approximation Using Neural Networks

The equations on the right-hand side are the state-value and action-value functions we have studied so far. On the left-hand side are equations that approximate state-value and action-value functions using neural networks with weights (w) and biases (b). To calculate the exact value, what we need to find are the weights and biases that define the neural network.

Mean Squared Error

$$\text{MSE} = \frac{1}{n} \sum_{i=i}^{n} (v - \hat{v})^2 \quad \text{①}$$

$$= E\left[(v - \hat{v})^2\right] \quad \text{②}$$

$$v = \begin{bmatrix} v_1 \\ \cdot \\ \cdot \\ \cdot \\ v_n \end{bmatrix}$$

Mean Squared Error (MSE)

Before diving into function approximation, let's understand the concept of Mean Squared Error (MSE). If we have a variable 'v' that can be represented as an array of size 'n', and an approximation function 'v^', the mean squared error is calculated by finding the difference between the two values, squaring it, and finding the average. MSE can be represented as a sequence sum or as an expectation. Squaring the difference ensures that the magnitude of the value, not its direction (positive or negative), is emphasized.

MSE is one of the most commonly used measures for evaluating the accuracy of predicted values in the field of artificial intelligence. In the reinforcement learning we will study, the target function will be expressed in MSE form, and learning will proceed in the direction that minimizes MSE using SGD (Stochastic Gradient Descent).

①-1　　　①-2

| Goal(MSE) |

$$J(w) = E_\pi \left[(v_\pi(s) - \hat{v}(s, \ w))^2 \right]$$

| Gradient Decent |

$$\Delta w = -\frac{1}{2} \propto \nabla_w J(w) \quad \text{②-1}$$

$$= \propto E_\pi \left[(v_\pi(s) - \hat{v}(s, \ w)) \nabla_w \hat{v}(s, \ w) \right] \quad \text{②-3}$$

| Stochastic Gradient Decent |

$$\Delta w = \propto (v_\pi(s) - \hat{v}(s, \ w)) \nabla_w \hat{v}(s, \ w) \quad \text{③}$$

| Differentiation Formulas |

②-2

$$y = (a - x)^2$$
$$y' = 2(a - x)(a - x)'$$
$$= -2(a - x) \nabla_w x$$

Function Approximation

Now, let's take a closer look at function approximation. Suppose we have an extremely accurate value function (vπ) known only to the omniscient, and we want to approximate it using a neural network represented by parameter 'w'. We can determine the correct value of the approximate function by minimizing the MSE.

Equation (2)-1 represents the gradient descent (GD) for the function J(w). By substituting the value function and the neural network into J(w), we derive equation (2)-3, which shows that gradient descent is expressed in terms of the value function, the neural network, and expectations.

However, since expectations are difficult to compute during the reinforcement learning process, an alternative value must be found. This is where stochastic gradient descent (SGD) comes in. Expectation refers to the mean, which means computing the expected value would require running all possible cases and summing up the results. Since this is practically impossible, we use a Monte Carlo method, which finds an approximation through sampling. By using SGD instead of expectation, we eliminate the need to calculate expectations, which is similar to the Monte Carlo (MC) or Temporal Difference (TD) methods studied earlier.

Ultimately, using SGD results in equation (3).

| Stochastic Gradient Decent | $\Delta w = \propto (v_\pi(s_t) - \hat{v}(s_t,\ w))\ \nabla_w \hat{v}(s_t,\ w)$ | ① |

| MC | $\Delta w = \propto (G_t - \hat{v}(s_t,\ w))\ \nabla_w \hat{v}(s_t,\ w)$ | ② |

| TD | $\Delta w = \propto (R_{t+1} + \hat{v}(s_{t+1},\ w) - \hat{v}(s_t,\ w))\ \nabla_w \hat{v}(s_{t+1},\ w)$③ |

Using MC and TD for Function Approximation

The value function vπ we have studied so far is the true value function, calculated with complete knowledge of the environment. However, in a model-free environment where complete information about the environment is not available, we cannot compute the true value function.

Function approximation can also be done using MC and TD methods. Instead of vπ, we replace it with the return Gt for a full episode or the one-step return Rt+1 − V^(st+1, w).

Using the equations above, we can now compute MC and TD using neural networks for function approximation.

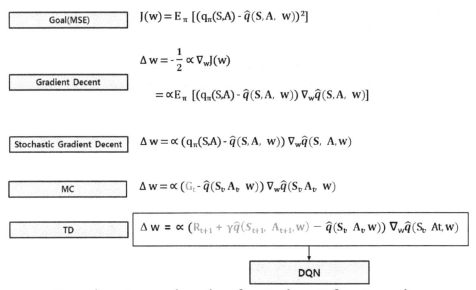

| Goal(MSE) | $J(w) = E_\pi\ [(q_\pi(S,A) - \hat{q}(S,A,\ w))^2]$ |

$$\Delta w = -\frac{1}{2} \propto \nabla_w J(w)$$

| Gradient Decent | $= \propto E_\pi\ [(q_\pi(S,A) - \hat{q}(S,A,\ w))\ \nabla_w \hat{q}(S,A,\ w)]$ |

| Stochastic Gradient Decent | $\Delta w = \propto (q_\pi(S,A) - \hat{q}(S,A,\ w))\ \nabla_w \hat{q}(S,\ A,w)$ |

| MC | $\Delta w = \propto (G_t - \hat{q}(S_t,A_t,\ w))\ \nabla_w \hat{q}(S_t,A_t,\ w)$ |

| TD | $\Delta w = \propto (R_{t+1} + \gamma \hat{q}(S_{t+1},\ A_{t+1},w) - \hat{q}(S_t,\ A_t,w))\ \nabla_w \hat{q}(S_t,\ At,w)$ |

| DQN |

Function Approximation for Action-Value Function (Q Function)

The action-value function (Q function) can also be represented using function approximation, just like the value function. Here, we can also use MC and TD to simplify the equations. Using neural networks to represent the Q function is referred to as Deep Q Learning (DQN), which was once a widely used reinforcement learning algorithm.

Chapter 6

Value-Based Reinforcement Learning and DQN Algorithm

6. Value-Based Reinforcement Learning and DQN Algorithm

In this chapter, we will explore the DQN (Deep Q Learning) algorithm, which is the most frequently mentioned value-based reinforcement learning algorithm on the internet. The reason why there is so much material on DQN is that it not only demonstrated impressive performance at the time of its release, but also because it is easy to understand. The difficulty will significantly increase from the next chapter when we start studying policy-based algorithms. Before that, I hope you enjoy understanding reinforcement learning through the DQN algorithm.

6.1 DQN Algorithm

Until now, we have mainly covered the theory. From DQN (Deep Q Learning) onward, we will look at how reinforcement learning works through actual code. Based on what we have learned, we can approximate the action-value function using a neural network with parameter w, and by using gradient descent to minimize the difference between the true action-value function and the approximated action-value function, we can find a neural network that is very close to the true action-value function.

| Goal(MSE) | $J(w) = E_{\pi}\,[(q_{\pi}(S,\ A) - \hat{q}(S,\ A,\ w))^2]$ | ① |

$$\Delta w = \alpha\,(\underbrace{R_{t+1} + \gamma\,\hat{q}(S_{t+1},\ A_{t+1},\ w) - \hat{q}(S_t,\ A_t,\ w)}_{\text{②-1}})\,)\,\nabla_w\hat{q}(S_t,\ At,\ w)\ ②$$

| TD | (above equation) |

$$ERR = \underbrace{R_{t+1} + \gamma\,\hat{q}(S_{t+1},\ A_{t+1},\ w)}_{\text{③-1}} - \underbrace{\hat{q}(S_t,\ A_t,\ w)}_{\text{③-2}} \qquad ③$$

| Prediction Error | (above equation) |

③-1	③-2
Action-value function obtained by executing the agent	Action-value function predicted by the neural network

DQN Prediction Error Function

Let's take another look at the objective function of the neural network approximation. ① The objective function measures how much the neural network that approximates the action-value function deviates from the true action-value function. ② The best outcome here is for the neural network and the true action-value function to match, so we keep adjusting the parameter w in the direction that minimizes this value.

Now, let's look at Equation ②-1. The front part of the equation substitutes the true action-value function in the temporal difference (TD) with the value function obtained through actions, while the back part represents the value function modeled by the neural network. When the difference between the two values is zero, we have found the optimal parameter w that determines the neural network, regardless of the partial derivative with respect to the neural network in the latter part.

Therefore, we can derive the prediction error function that we need to minimize as shown in Equation ③. ③-1 represents the action-value function obtained by the agent, while ③-2 represents the action-value function predicted by the neural network. The goal of DQN is to find a neural network that minimizes the result of Equation ③.

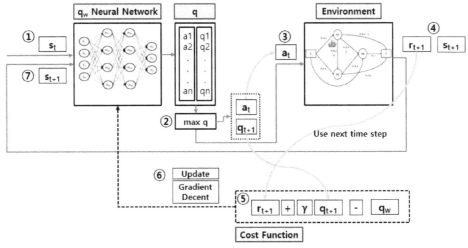

DQN Logic

Now, let's examine the DQN logic step by step. To perform actions, the agent needs a policy for selecting actions. In Q-learning, the policy selects the action with the highest Q-value. Instead of creating a separate policy, Q-learning calculates the Q-value and selects the action with the highest Q-value, effectively replacing the policy.

To select an action, the first thing that Q-learning must do is calculate the Q-value. The Q-value is held in the neural network, and ① when the state is input, it returns the Q-values for each action a in matrix form. From here, ② we identify the action with the highest Q-value, and ③ the agent performs the action accordingly. After the agent performs the action, the environment returns the reward (r_{t+1}) and the next state (s_{t+1}).

Since we now have the Q-value and reward (r) of the current state, ⑤ we can calculate the cost function. The reward used in the cost function is obtained from the previous time step (t), not the next time step (t+1). ⑥ The neural network is trained in the direction that minimizes the cost function. Once the training is complete, ⑦ the next state is input into the neural network to continue training the agent.

Some readers might be confused about where the qw in the cost function ⑤ suddenly comes from. To clarify, the qw used here is the output of the neural network during the training process. It is not something that the programmer manually calculates and inputs into the equation. The programmer only needs to calculate the value of rt+ γqt+1 and provide it to the neural network, which then calculates qw internally.

The neural network models the action-value function that we are trying to find using parameter w. Therefore, if we determine the exact value of w, we can obtain the true action-value function. To find the precise w, the neural network repeatedly trains using gradient descent to minimize the cost function.

6.2 Cartpole

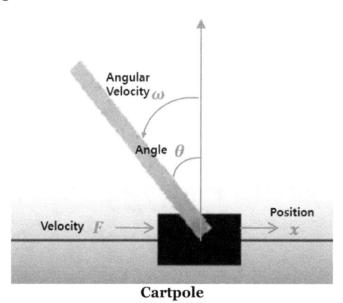

Cartpole

OpenAI (https://gym.openai.com/docs) provides various examples for reinforcement learning, including Cartpole, which we will implement directly using DQN. Cartpole is a game in which a cart with a pole attached is moved left or right to keep the pole from falling. The pole is not fixed to the cart and can move to either side. It is similar to a game where you try to balance a stick on your palm without letting it fall, except that here you move a cart instead of your palm.

In Cartpole, the agent can perform one of two actions: move left or move right. In reinforcement learning, the state refers to the environment as perceived by the agent. The agent recognizes the cart's position (x), the cart's velocity (F), the pole's angle (θ), and the pole's angular velocity (ω). These four values are all the agent needs to operate. Therefore, the state of the agent is represented by four variables: position, cart velocity, pole angle, and pole angular velocity.

6.3 Exploration and Exploitation

One of the most commonly discussed issues in reinforcement learning is Exploration vs. Exploitation. Reinforcement learning makes decisions to maximize cumulative rewards, and this decision-making approach is called a greedy policy. If a policy is determined greedily in the early stages of learning, it results in the agent not learning in various ways, because the policy is still immature at the beginning of learning.

| Epsilon-Greedy Policy | if random value $> \varepsilon$
    argmax(a)
else
    random(a) |

Epsilon-Greedy Policy

To solve this issue, the epsilon-greedy policy was introduced. An epsilon value ($0 < \square < 1$) is chosen (by the learner), and if a randomly chosen number (between 0 and 1) is greater than epsilon, the agent chooses an action according to the greedy policy; otherwise, it chooses an action randomly. By using an epsilon-greedy policy, the agent can explore various states, thus improving learning performance.

As the learning progresses and the accuracy of the policy improves, the epsilon value should decay. This increases the probability that the agent will act according to the policy. The rate at which epsilon decays is something the learner must decide.

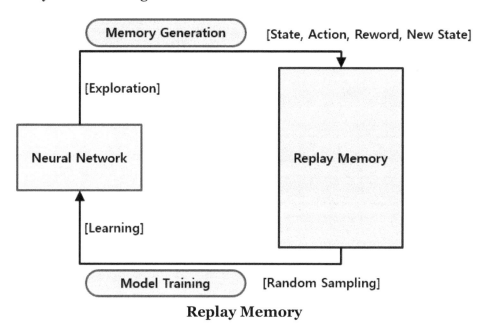

Replay Memory

If the training data in reinforcement learning has temporal correlations, it can cause problems in training. If recently collected data is used continuously for training, the agent may keep learning bad data when it enters an unfavorable environment. Therefore, using older data that had good training can be helpful.

Replay Memory is a technique introduced to solve this problem. Replay memory separates the learning process into two stages: generating replay memory and training using replay memory. In the replay memory generation stage, the model is not trained; instead, data is collected by executing the agent and stored in replay memory. Since replay memory has a limited size, if the collected data exceeds the memory capacity, the oldest data is deleted.

After generating replay memory, the model is trained using randomly sampled data from the replay memory. This process helps remove the temporal correlation in the training data.

6.4 Basic Structure of the DQN Algorithm

Now, let's explore the concept of DQN through code. First, we'll create an Agent class that provides DQN functionality. The Agent class consists of eight functions in total, and we will go over the role of each function.

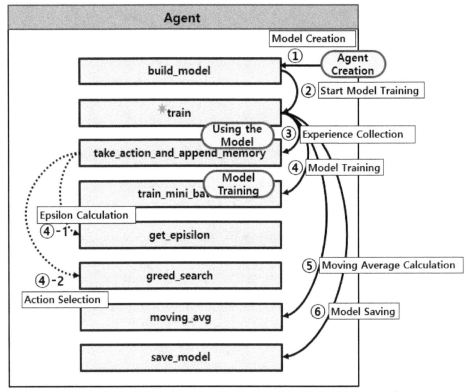

Features of the Agent Class in the DQN Algorithm

When the Agent class is created to train a DQN model, the first function called is ① build_model, which constructs the neural network. Next, calling ② the train function initiates the actual model training process.

Within the train function, four main operations are performed. First, ③ the take_action_and_append_memory function is called to execute actions repeatedly until the program ends and to store the experience in Replay Memory. The take_action_and_append_memory function uses the neural network model, which approximates the Q-function, to select actions according to the policy. The ③-1 get_epsilon function returns an epsilon value used to adjust the degree of exploration.

The ③-2 greed_search function determines whether to choose an action randomly or use the neural network model based on the epsilon value, and returns the selected action.

Next, ④ the train_mini_batch function is called to retrieve data from replay memory and train the model. The neural network model is trained repeatedly inside the train_mini_batch function. During the number of episodes specified by the learner (episode_num), the take_action_and_append_memory function and the train_mini_batch function are repeatedly called to run the Cartpole program, and the results are stored in replay memory. Data is then randomly selected from the stored replay memory for training. Logs are recorded intermittently to check whether the model is training properly.

⑤ The moving_avg function calculates the average number of executions of Cartpole over the last 20 runs, providing evidence of whether the model is training correctly.

⑥ The save_model function saves the variables and the model used by the neural network to a file once the training is complete, so that the model's performance can be tested later.

6.5 Reviewing the Entire DQN Algorithm Code

Let's take a look at the overall code and then examine each function in detail. The code may seem unfamiliar at first, but since the structure will be reused, repeated execution will help you become familiar with it. Once you understand the structure, the remaining process will be easier to comprehend.

```
import tensorflow as tf
```

```python
from tensorflow.keras.layers import Input, Dense
from tensorflow.keras.optimizers import Adam
import gym
import numpy as np
import random as rand
class Agent(object):
    def __init__(self):
        self.env = gym.make('CartPole-v1')
        self.state_size = self.env.observation_space.shape[0]
        self.action_size = self.env.action_space.n

        self.node_num = 12
        self.learning_rate = 0.001
        self.epochs_cnt = 5
        self.model = self.build_model()

        self.discount_rate = 0.97
        self.penalty = -100

        self.episode_num = 500

        self.replay_memory_limit = 2048
        self.replay_size = 32
        self.replay_memory = []

        self.epsilon = 0.99
        self.epsilon_decay = 0.2
        self.epsilon_min = 0.05

        self.moving_avg_size = 20
        self.reward_list= []
        self.count_list = []
        self.moving_avg_list = []

    def build_model(self):
        input_states = Input(shape=(1,self.state_size), name='input_states')
        x = (input_states)
        x = Dense(self.node_num, activation='relu')(x)
        out_actions = Dense(self.action_size, activation='linear',
                            name='output')(x)
        model = tf.keras.models.Model(inputs=[input_states],
                                      outputs=[out_actions])
        model.compile(optimizer=Adam(lr=self.learning_rate),
              loss='mean_squared_error'
              )
        model.summary()
        return model

    def train(self):
        for episode in range(self.episode_num):
            state = self.env.reset()
            Q, count, reward_tot = self.take_action_and_append_memory(episode,
                                                                      state)
```

```python
            if count < 500:
                reward_tot = reward_tot-self.penalty

            self.reward_list.append(reward_tot)
            self.count_list.append(count)

            self.moving_avg_list.append(self.moving_avg(self.count_list,self.moving_avg_size))

            self.train_mini_batch(Q)

            if(episode % 10 == 0):
                print("episode:{}, moving_avg:{}, rewards_avg:{}".format(episode,
                                self.moving_avg_list[-1], np.mean(self.reward_list)))
        self.save_model()

    def take_action_and_append_memory(self, episode, state):
        reward_tot = 0
        count = 0
        done = False
        episilon = self.get_episilon(episode)
        while not done:
            count+=1
            state_t = np.reshape(state,[1, 1, self.state_size])
            Q = self.model.predict(state_t)
            action = self.greed_search(episilon, episode, Q)
            state_next, reward, done, none = self.env.step(action)

            if done:
                reward = self.penalty
            self.replay_memory.append([state_t, action, reward, state_next, done])
            if len(self.replay_memory) > self.replay_memory_limit:
                del self.replay_memory[0]
            reward_tot += reward
            state = state_next
        return Q, count, reward_tot

    def train_mini_batch(self, Q):
        array_state = []
        array_Q = []
        this_replay_size = self.replay_size
        if len(self.replay_memory) < self.replay_size:
            this_replay_size = len(self.replay_memory)

        for sample in rand.sample(self.replay_memory, this_replay_size):
            state_t,action,reward,state_next,done = sample
            if done:
                Q[0, 0, action] = reward
            else:
                state_t= np.reshape(state_next,[1,1,self.state_size])
                Q_new = self.model.predict(state_t)
                Q[0, 0, action] = reward + self.discount_rate * np.max(Q_new)
            array_state.append(state_t.reshape(1,self.state_size))
```

```python
            array_Q.append(Q.reshape(1,self.action_size))
        array_state_t = np.array(array_state)
        array_Q_t = np.array(array_Q)
        hist = self.model.fit(array_state_t, array_Q_t,
                              epochs=self.epochs_cnt, verbose=0)

    def get_episilon(self, episode):
        result = self.epsilon * ( 1 - episode/(self.episode_num*self.epsilon_decay) )
        if result < self.epsilon_min:
            result = self.epsilon_min
        return result

    def greed_search(self, episilon, episode, Q):
        if episilon > np.random.rand(1):
            action = self.env.action_space.sample()
        else:
            action = np.argmax(Q)
        return action

    def moving_avg(self, data, size=10):
        if len(data) > size:
            c = np.array(data[len(data)-size:len(data)])
        else:
            c = np.array(data)
        return np.mean(c)

    def save_model(self):
        self.model.save("./model/dqn")
        print("*****end learing")

if __name__ == "__main__":
    agent = Agent()
    agent.train()
```

Cartpole_DQN.py

It is recommended to test the example using the Jupyter Notebook that was installed earlier. With other Python programs, you would need to run the entire code at once, but Jupyter Notebook allows the code to be divided into cells and executed in parts. This is one of the reasons why Jupyter Notebook is widely used in data analysis.

6.6 Detailed Structure of the DQN Algorithm

From now on, let's look closely at the Agent class of the DQN algorithm. The properties of the Agent class are as follows:

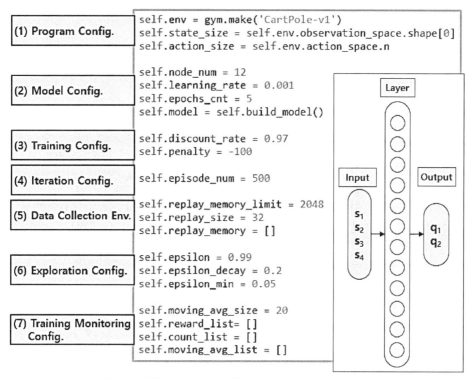

| (1) Program Config. | ```
self.env = gym.make('CartPole-v1')
self.state_size = self.env.observation_space.shape[0]
self.action_size = self.env.action_space.n
``` |
| (2) Model Config. | ```
self.node_num = 12
self.learning_rate = 0.001
self.epochs_cnt = 5
self.model = self.build_model()
``` |
| (3) Training Config. | ```
self.discount_rate = 0.97
self.penalty = -100
``` |
| (4) Iteration Config. | ```
self.episode_num = 500
``` |
| (5) Data Collection Env. | ```
self.replay_memory_limit = 2048
self.replay_size = 32
self.replay_memory = []
``` |
| (6) Exploration Config. | ```
self.epsilon = 0.99
self.epsilon_decay = 0.2
self.epsilon_min = 0.05
``` |
| (7) Training Monitoring Config. | ```
self.moving_avg_size = 20
self.reward_list= []
self.count_list = []
self.moving_avg_list = []
``` |

Properties of the Agent Class in the DQN Algorithm

Program Configuration: This area has three properties—first, there is the env variable that stores the instance of the Cartpole class. The state_size variable stores the number of states that Cartpole has (4), and the action_size variable stores the number of actions that can be taken in Cartpole (2).

Model Configuration: There are four properties in this area. The model variable stores the neural network model, and the node_num variable specifies the number of nodes in the neural network layer (12). The learning_rate variable stores the learning rate (0.001) for the neural network model. The epochs_cnt variable determines how many times to repeat training for each batch.

Training Configuration: This area consists of two properties. The discount_rate variable sets the discount rate for rewards received in the future. The penalty variable sets the negative reward value when the pole falls and the Cartpole game ends. In Cartpole, if the pole does not fall, a reward of 1 is given, and if the pole falls, a reward of -1 is given. By setting an appropriate penalty value, the

117
```

learning can be conducted more effectively.

Iteration Configuration: This area consists of one property, episode_num, which determines how many episodes will be repeated to collect data and conduct training.

Data Collection Environment: This area has three variables. The replay_memory_limit variable specifies the size of the area to store data collected while the agent runs Cartpole using the model. When the amount of data exceeds replay_memory_limit, the oldest data is deleted to store new data. The replay_size variable determines the amount of data to train with mini-batch. It fetches data of the size specified by replay_size from replay memory, which has a relatively large capacity, for training. The replay_memory variable stores the Cartpole execution information collected by the agent up to the size of replay_memory_limit.

A Quick Note
• Learning Rate, Batch, Mini-Batch

1. Learning Rate: The learning rate is the speed of calculation to find the local minimum in gradient descent. A high learning rate may quickly find a local minimum, but it may also miss the actual minimum point, similar to a car moving too fast and missing the destination. A low learning rate may take too long to converge.

2. Batch: Batch refers to training with multiple data points at once. Training one by one is time-consuming and inefficient, so data is collected and trained all at once.

3. Mini-Batch: Mini-batch is training with a portion of the collected training data. Replay memory is a typical use case of mini-batch, where data is stored in memory and a fixed amount is used for batch training to reduce temporal dependency.

Exploration Configuration: This area has three variables. epsilon sets the threshold for selecting actions randomly. If epsilon is 1, all actions are selected randomly; if epsilon is 0, all actions are selected using the model. epsilon_decay determines the rate at which epsilon decreases. As training progresses, more actions should be selected using the model, so epsilon must decrease. If epsilon_decay is set to 0.2, epsilon will reach zero after 20% of the episodes. The closer epsilon_decay is to 1, the more actions are selected randomly. epsilon_min specifies the minimum value of epsilon, ensuring that it does not fall below 0.05 if epsilon_min is set to 0.05.

Training Monitoring: This area has four variables. moving_avg_size determines how many episodes to consider when recording moving average data. reward_list stores the sum of rewards received in each episode. count_list records the number of times Cartpole is executed in each episode. moving_avg_list stores the moving average number of Cartpole executions for the most recent episodes, as determined by moving_avg_size.

```
def build_model(self):

        input_states = Input(shape=(1,self.state_size), name='input_states')
  (1) x = (input_states)

  (2) x = Dense(self.node_num, activation='relu')(x)

  (3) out_actions = Dense(self.action_size, activation='linear', name='output')(x)

  (4) model = tf.keras.models.Model(inputs=[input_states], outputs=[out_actions])

  (5) model.compile(optimizer=Adam(lr=self.learning_rate),

                  loss='mean_squared_error'

                  )

  (6) model.summary()

      return model
```

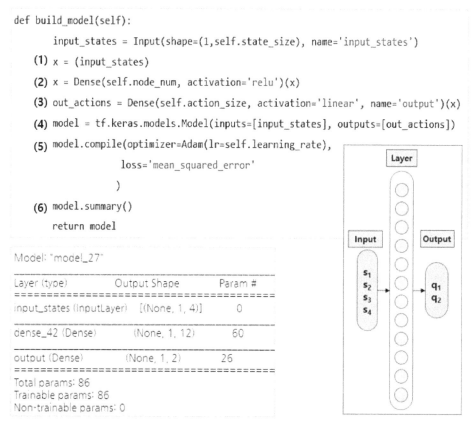

```
Model: "model_27"

_____
Layer (type)            Output Shape         Param #
========================================================
input_states (InputLayer)   [(None, 1, 4)]       0

dense_42 (Dense)            (None, 1, 12)        60

output (Dense)             (None, 1, 2)         26
========================================================
Total params: 86
Trainable params: 86
Non-trainable params: 0
```

Cartpole_DQN: build_model Function

Now, let's look at the functions that make up the Agent class. The build_model function, used to set the model variable in the model configuration, constructs the neural network used for training.

(1) The input shape is set to match the number of state values in Cartpole, creating the input layer of the neural network.

(2) In the example, one layer is used, with nodes equal to node_num (12). The ReLU function, which performs better than sigmoid, is used as the activation function.

(3) The number of output values of the neural network matches the number of actions in Cartpole, and a linear activation function is used to calculate and return the Q-values for each action.

(4) After all settings are complete, the model is finally constructed using the Model class provided by Keras.

(5) When compiling the model, the training environment is set using Adam, which outperforms gradient descent. The learning rate is set to the value assigned to learning_rate.

(6) The summary function can be used to output the constructed model for confirmation, and the model configuration is printed when the program runs.

(7) The newly introduced concepts related to the neural network configuration will be revisited in the chapter on neural network tuning later on. For now, just understand that a more efficient technique than what we know has been used.

```
def train(self):
(1) for episode in range(self.episode_num):
(2)     state = self.env.reset()

(3)     Q, count, reward_tot = self.take_action_and_append_memory(episode, state)

        if count < 500:
            reward_tot = reward_tot-self.penalty

(4)     self.reward_list.append(reward_tot)
        self.count_list.append(count)
(5)     self.moving_avg_list.append(self.moving_avg(self.count_list,self.moving_avg_size))

(6)     self.train_mini_batch(Q)

        if(episode % 10 == 0):
(7)         print("episode:{}, moving_avg:{}, rewards_avg:{}".
                format(episode, self.moving_avg_list[-1], np.mean(self.reward_list)))
(8) self.save_model()
```

Cartpole_DQN: train Function

The train function is the central function of the Agent class, responsible for collecting data and training the model.

(1) A step refers to one execution of Cartpole, and an episode refers to the entire process from when Cartpole first starts until the pole falls due to incorrect cart movement. The number of episodes for which data is collected and the model is trained is determined by the class variable episode_num.

(2) The Cartpole execution environment is stored in the env variable and can be reset using the reset function.

(3) The take_action_and_append_memory function is called to collect data while Cartpole is running, and the collected data is stored in replay_memory.

(4) After each episode ends, information about the collected reward and the number of executions is stored in reward_list and count_list.

(5) To effectively monitor the model training, a moving average is calculated. The example uses the average number of Cartpole executions over 20 episodes.

(6) The train_mini_batch function is called to train the model using data stored in replay_memory of size specified by replay_size.

(7) Training logs are recorded every 10 episodes, displaying the moving average and the average reward received over all episodes.

(8) Once all episodes have been executed, the final trained model is saved to a file, which can later be loaded and used to visually confirm the training results by running Cartpole.

```
     def take_action_and_append_memory(self, episode, state):
         reward_tot = 0
         count = 0
         done = False
(1)      episilon = self.get_epsilon(episode)
(2)      while not done:
             count+=1
(3)          state_t = np.reshape(state,[1, 1, self.state_size])
(4)          Q = self.model.predict(state_t)
(5)          action = self.greed_search(episilon, episode, Q)
(6)          state_next, reward, done, none = self.env.step(action)
             if done:
(7)
                 reward = self.penalty
(8)          self.replay_memory.append([state_t, action, reward, state_next, done])
             if len(self.replay_memory) > self.replay_memory_limit:
(9)              del self.replay_memory[0]
             reward_tot += reward
             state = state_next
         return Q, count, reward_tot
```

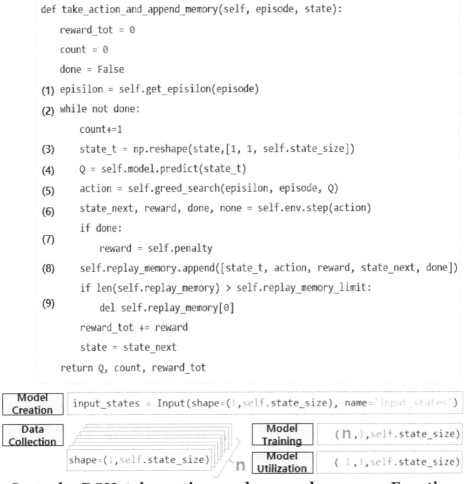

Cartpole_DQN: take_action_and_append_memory Function

The take_action_and_append_memory function is used to execute Cartpole, record the results in memory, and prepare them for later use during training.

(1) First, the get_epsilon function is called to get the epsilon value, which serves as the basis for deciding whether to choose actions based on the model or randomly. Epsilon is designed to decrease as the episodes progress.

(2) One episode continues until the game ends. Using the env.step function, the cart is moved, and the result (whether the pole has fallen) is returned and stored in the done variable. If the cart falls, the done variable stores True.

(3) To use the model, the shape of the data needs to be changed to (1, 1, 4). In the example, the model input is declared as (1, 4), but since data is accumulated and trained in batches (multiple inputs at once) during an episode, the actual input data for the model becomes (n, 1, 4). Therefore, to predict using a single input, the data shape must be changed to (1, 1, 4).

(4) In DQN, the model approximates the Q-value, so the value obtained by inputting the state into the model is the Q-value.

(5) The greed_search function is used to select the action. When the epsilon value obtained earlier and the Q-value from the model are input, the function outputs the next action to take. The detailed operation of the greed_search function will be explained later.

(6) The action output by the greed_search function is input into the env.step function to move the cart. After the cart moves, the information about the state of the pole (state_next), the corresponding reward (reward), and whether the pole has fallen (done) are returned.

(7) If the pole falls, the reward is set to the value of the penalty class variable (-100). Since the penalty value significantly affects model training, it is important to set an appropriate value.

(8) The information used to move the cart, the state of the cart after movement, the reward, and whether the pole has fallen are stored in replay memory (self.replay_memory).

(9) Replay memory is maintained at a certain size, and old information is deleted to keep the data in memory up to date. The

size of replay memory is specified in the class variable replay_memory_limit.

```python
def train_mini_batch(self, Q):
    array_state = []
    array_Q = []
    this_replay_size = self.replay_size
(1) if len(self.replay_memory) < self.replay_size:
        this_replay_size = len(self.replay_memory)
(2) for sample in rand.sample(self.replay_memory, this_replay_size):
(3)     state_t,action,reward,state_next,done = sample
        if done:
            Q[0, 0, action] = reward
        else:
(4)         state_t= np.reshape(state_next,[1,1,self.state_size])
            Q_new = self.model.predict(state_t)
            Q[0, 0, action] = reward + self.discount_rate * np.max(Q_new)
        array_state.append(state_t.reshape(1,self.state_size))
(5)     array_Q.append(Q.reshape(1,self.action_size))
    array_state_t = np.array(array_state)
(6) array_Q_t = np.array(array_Q)
(7) hist = self.model.fit(array_state_t, array_Q_t, epochs=self.epochs_cnt, verbose=0)
```

Cartpole_DQN: train_mini_batch Function

The train_mini_batch function provides the ability to train the model by randomly selecting data from replay memory.

(1) The first step is to determine the size of the data to be used for training. The original data size is specified by the class variable replay_size, but if the data accumulated in replay memory is smaller than the size specified by replay_size, errors may occur in the program logic, so appropriate handling is needed.

(2) Next, training data is repeatedly retrieved from replay_memory using the sample function provided by the random package to randomly select data of a specific size.

(3) The data selected for training is returned in the same format as stored in replay memory by the take_action_and_append_memory function. The training data consists of: state (state_t), action (action), reward (reward), next state (state_next), and completion status (done).

(4) Now the Q-value must be calculated. If the game is over, there is no next state, so the reward can be assigned directly as the Q-value. However, if the game is not over, the Q-value from the next state is calculated, multiplied by the discount rate, and added to the reward obtained from the current state.

(5) The state and Q-value to be used for model training are reshaped into a usable form. The reason for reshaping was explained earlier.

(6) The data structure in which the collected data is stored is a list. TensorFlow internally handles data in numpy format, so the data is converted to numpy.

(7) Finally, the collected data is input for model training. The number of times training is repeated with the same data is determined by the class variable epochs_cnt, and multiple pieces of data are input into the model simultaneously for training.

```
def get_episilon(self, episode):

(1)  result = self.epsilon * ( 1 - episode/(self.episode_num*self.epsilon_decay) )

     if result < self.epsilon_min:
(2)
         result = self.epsilon_min

     return result
```

Cartpole_DQN: get_epsilon Function

The get_epsilon function is responsible for calculating the epsilon value used in the greed_search function to adjust the degree to which actions are chosen randomly.

(1) The formula shows that the epsilon value decreases as the number of current episodes increases. Examining the formula further reveals that the epsilon_decay class variable becomes zero

when it matches the ratio of the total episodes to the current episode. Also, the larger the value of epsilon_decay, the higher the proportion of randomly selected actions, leading to more exploration by the agent.

```
def greed_search(self, episilon, episode, Q):
(1) if episilon > np.random.rand(1):
        action = self.env.action_space.sample()
    else:
(2)     action = np.argmax(Q)
    return action
```

Cartpole_DQN: greed_search Function

The greed_search function takes the input epsilon value as a basis to randomly select an action or to choose one based on the Q-value and returns it.

(1) The np.random.rand(1) function randomly selects and returns a value between 0 and 1. Therefore, if the epsilon value passed as an argument is greater than the random value, an action is selected randomly. Although it is somewhat probabilistic, the closer the epsilon value is to 1, the higher the likelihood of choosing an action randomly.

(2) The Q-value received as an argument is the prediction result obtained by inputting the state into the model before calling the greed_search function. Since the model output is the Q-value, an action with a higher Q-value is considered more valuable. Therefore, the argmax function, which returns the index of the array with the highest Q-value, is used to select the action.

```
def moving_avg(self, data, size=10):
(1) if len(data) > size:
        c = np.array(data[len(data)-size:len(data)])
    else:
        c = np.array(data)
(2) return np.mean(c)
```

Cartpole_DQN: moving_avg Function

The moving_avg function calculates the moving average of the number of executions over the last 20 episodes to effectively monitor the training process. The average of the total reward, which is often used in monitoring logs, has limitations in observing recent training status, while displaying only the number of executions from recent episodes can distort the outcome due to coincidence. Therefore, observing the moving average over about 20 episodes alongside the average of the total reward is important for monitoring the training process.

```
def save_model(self):
    self.model.save("./model/dqn")
    print("*****end learing")
```

Cartpole_DQN: save_model Function

The save_model function saves the model, weights, and biases to a specified directory. The saved model can be loaded later to continue training or to observe its performance during program execution.

6.7 Analysis of DQN Algorithm Training Results

In this program, logs are output to the screen every 10 episodes during training. By examining the logs generated during the training process, we can check whether the training is proceeding normally and assess the performance.

Model: "model_2"

Layer (type)	Output Shape	Param #
input_states (InputLayer)	[(None, 1, 4)]	0
dense_2 (Dense)	(None, 1, 12)	60
output (Dense)	(None, 1, 2)	26

Total params: 86
Trainable params: 86
Non-trainable params: 0

episode:0, moving_avg:12.0, rewards_avg:11.0
episode:10, moving_avg:28.636363636363637, rewards_avg:27.636363636363637

episode:20, moving_avg:27.65, rewards_avg:25.904761904761905
episode:30, moving_avg:23.05, rewards_avg:24.032258064516128
episode:40, moving_avg:19.45, rewards_avg:22.26829268292683
episode:50, moving_avg:19.95, rewards_avg:22.03921568627451
episode:60, moving_avg:19.5, rewards_avg:21.0327868852459
episode:70, moving_avg:14.85, rewards_avg:19.732394366197184
episode:80, moving_avg:11.8, rewards_avg:18.506172839506174
episode:90, moving_avg:10.35, rewards_avg:17.45054945054945
episode:100, moving_avg:10.0, rewards_avg:16.623762376237625
episode:110, moving_avg:9.7, rewards_avg:15.873873873873874
episode:120, moving_avg:11.25, rewards_avg:15.570247933884298
episode:130, moving_avg:36.75, rewards_avg:18.908396946564885
episode:140, moving_avg:71.05, rewards_avg:23.29787234042553
episode:150, moving_avg:62.2, rewards_avg:24.509933774834437
episode:160, moving_avg:74.75, rewards_avg:29.565217391304348
episode:170, moving_avg:110.3, rewards_avg:34.42690058479532
episode:180, moving_avg:109.5, rewards_avg:38.28729281767956
episode:190, moving_avg:92.85, rewards_avg:40.43979057591623
episode:200, moving_avg:84.45, rewards_avg:42.78109452736319
episode:210, moving_avg:86.55, rewards_avg:44.71563981042654
episode:220, moving_avg:99.85, rewards_avg:47.8552036199095
episode:230, moving_avg:118.2, rewards_avg:50.99134199134199
episode:240, moving_avg:121.6, rewards_avg:53.892116182572614
episode:250, moving_avg:115.15, rewards_avg:56.02390438247012
episode:260, moving_avg:101.05, rewards_avg:57.42911877394636
episode:270, moving_avg:69.45, rewards_avg:56.94095940959409
episode:280, moving_avg:31.1, rewards_avg:55.48398576512456
episode:290, moving_avg:15.9, rewards_avg:54.05154639175258
episode:300, moving_avg:65.1, rewards_avg:56.056478405315616
episode:310, moving_avg:118.9, rewards_avg:58.157556270096464
episode:320, moving_avg:128.3, rewards_avg:60.495327102803735
episode:330, moving_avg:112.6, rewards_avg:61.38670694864048
episode:340, moving_avg:55.2, rewards_avg:60.12609970674487
episode:350, moving_avg:17.6, rewards_avg:58.83475783475784
episode:360, moving_avg:18.8, rewards_avg:57.78116343490305
episode:370, moving_avg:20.5, rewards_avg:56.714285714285715
episode:380, moving_avg:18.45, rewards_avg:55.664041994750654
episode:390, moving_avg:16.55, rewards_avg:54.608695652173914
episode:400, moving_avg:12.55, rewards_avg:53.46384039900249
episode:410, moving_avg:9.85, rewards_avg:52.38199513381995
episode:420, moving_avg:9.8, rewards_avg:51.342042755344416
episode:430, moving_avg:9.5, rewards_avg:50.34570765661253
episode:440, moving_avg:9.35, rewards_avg:49.39229024943311
episode:450, moving_avg:9.35, rewards_avg:48.48337028824834
episode:460, moving_avg:9.4, rewards_avg:47.613882863340564
episode:470, moving_avg:9.6, rewards_avg:46.789808917197455
episode:480, moving_avg:12.6, rewards_avg:46.11642411642411
episode:490, moving_avg:12.65, rewards_avg:45.35845213849287

Cartpole_DQN: Results of cartpole_DQN Execution

If the print statement logs every 10 episodes, it looks like this. The
values recorded in the logs include the moving average of the

number of executions over 20 episodes and the average reward. When the moving average is greater than the rewards average over time, it indicates that the model is gradually being trained effectively, with the best scenario being both values gradually increasing simultaneously.

```
    import matplotlib.pyplot as plt
(1) plt.figure(figsize=(10,5))

    plt.plot(agent.reward_list, label='rewards')
(2)
    plt.plot(agent.moving_avg_list, linewidth=4, label='moving average')

(3) plt.legend(loc='upper left')

(4) plt.title('DQN')

(5) plt.show()
```

Cartpole_DQN: Visualization of Results

It is more suitable to visualize the entire data set rather than just viewing the test logs to determine whether training has been successful. Let's use the matplotlib package, which is frequently used for visualization, to plot graphs.

(1) The figure function allows setting properties for the graph. Here, the figsize attribute is used to set the size of the graph.

(2) The plot function provides the functionality to plot data on the graph. The default graph type for the plot function is a line graph. The average reward and moving average data are plotted using a line chart. The label attribute can be used to assign a legend to each graph.

(3) The legend function is used to specify legend properties. The loc attribute is used to set the position to the upper left.

(4) The title function can be used to set the title of the entire graph.

(5) The show function displays the graph on the screen, though in some cases the graph may be displayed even without explicitly calling the show function.

The test was conducted over 500 episodes. This number is a bit insufficient for fully training a reinforcement learning model. However, if the average reward and moving average show an upward trend over time, it indicates that further training with the same parameters over more episodes could potentially improve model performance.

It can also be observed that even when the same parameters and episodes are used, the results vary slightly each time, and sometimes the results differ significantly. This is due to the various random functions used during the model training process.

Let's revisit the concept of probability studied earlier. When rolling a die a few times at the beginning, the numbers rolled do not exactly reflect a 1/6 ratio. However, as the number of rolls increases sufficiently, the proportion of each number approaches 1/6. Thus, a sufficient number of tests is needed for probability to function properly.

The same principle applies to reinforcement learning. If a small number of episodes are trained, it is mostly random, whereas with a sufficiently large number of episodes, it becomes probabilistic. Therefore, if somewhat effective parameters have been found, training with a sufficient number of episodes can help create a more perfect model.

DQN is a relatively early reinforcement learning algorithm. While many newer algorithms with significantly improved performance exist, DQN can still deliver good performance if an appropriate reward system and training environment are designed.

Chapter 7

Policy-Based Reinforcement Learning: REINFORCE Algorithm

7. Policy-Based Reinforcement Learning: REINFORCE Algorithm

In the value-based reinforcement learning we previously studied, the value function was used to derive the policy. For example, in Q-learning, we derived the Q-value and created a policy that selects the action that maximizes the Q-value. However, this approach always seeks the maximum value, which can make optimization challenging.

Now, let's explore policy-based reinforcement learning, where instead of finding a policy through the value function, we learn the policy directly.

7.1 Revisiting Neural Networks

Before diving into policy-based reinforcement learning, let's revisit the concept of neural networks.

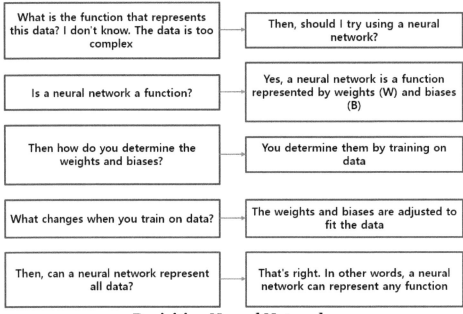

Revisiting Neural Networks

Previously, we explained that a neural network can be used to predict various data, and it becomes complete when the weights and biases within the network are determined through training.

A neural network is essentially a type of function that represents data. Since the form of data is often too varied to be represented by common mathematical functions, we use neural networks. In this chapter, we define a function that represents a policy, but because we do not know the exact form of this function, we use a neural network. If we treat the neural network as a policy function and train it with data that has the properties of a policy function, the neural network will become a function that represents such data. In other words, the weights and biases of the neural network will be adjusted to match the data.

One of the most challenging parts of moving from value-based reinforcement learning to policy-based reinforcement learning is the sudden introduction of a function to represent the policy. However, if you keep the concept of neural networks in mind and read through the subsequent explanations step by step, it will become easier to understand.

7.2 Policy Gradient

In the function approximation method we learned earlier, we created a function J(w) consisting of weights w to approximate the value function. This time, we define a similar function J(θ), composed of parameters θ, to evaluate the policy. The function J(θ) is differentiable with respect to θ, and it is called the policy objective function.

To review, a policy (π) is the probability that an agent selects a specific action. Since the function consisting of θ is expressed as a policy evaluation function, the policy can be represented as πθ (s,a).

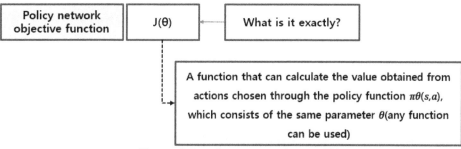

Policy Objective Function J(θ)

What does the policy objective function J(θ) mean? It is a function that calculates the value obtained from actions chosen by the policy function πθ(s,a), which consists of the parameter θ. In function approximation, the mean squared error (MSE) between the true value function and the approximated value function by the neural network was defined as the function J(w). Since J(w) represents the error, gradient descent was used to find the minimum value.

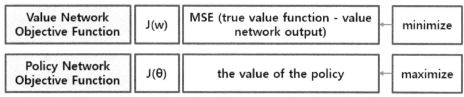

Value Network and Policy Network Evaluation Functions

Can we use gradient descent to find J(θ) just like we did for J(w)?

No, we cannot. While J(w) requires finding the minimum value, J(θ) represents the value of the policy, meaning that we need to find the maximum value. Therefore, we use gradient ascent instead.

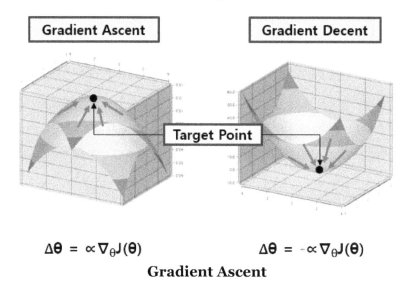

$$\Delta\theta = \propto \nabla_\theta J(\theta) \qquad\qquad \Delta\theta = -\propto \nabla_\theta J(\theta)$$

Gradient Ascent

Gradient descent has already been studied in the context of function approximation. Gradient descent is an algorithm used to find the minimum point by taking the partial derivative of the function J(θ) with respect to parameter θ and updating it in the negative direction by $\propto$. On the other hand, gradient ascent is an algorithm used to find the maximum point. It can be thought of as the opposite of gradient descent. If gradient descent updates in the negative direction, gradient ascent updates in the positive direction. Essentially, you can understand it as simply flipping the sign.

$$\boxed{\text{MDP}}\quad v_\pi(s) = E_\pi[G_t \mid S_t = s] \qquad\qquad ①$$
$$= E_\pi[R_{t+1} + \gamma v_\pi(S_{t+1}) \mid S_t = s] \qquad ②$$
$$= \sum_{a \in A} \pi(a|s)\,(R_s^a + \gamma \sum_{s' \in S} P_{ss'}^a v_\pi(s')) \qquad ③$$
$$= \sum_{a \in A} \pi(a|s)\, R_s^a + \gamma \sum_{a \in A} \pi(a|s) \sum_{s' \in S} P_{ss'}^a v_\pi(s') \;\,④$$

Value Function in MDP

Let's briefly revisit the value function in MDP (Markov Decision Process):

(1) The value function can be expressed as the expected return obtained by following a policy π.

(2) The value function can also be represented as the sum of the immediate reward and the discounted value of the reward received at time t+1, with the discount rate γ.

(3) By multiplying the conditional probability (policy) of each possible action and summing them, we can express the expected value.

Finally, by expanding the equation, we arrive at Equation ④.

Earlier, we mentioned redefining the policy evaluation function J(θ). This redefinition should use a function that makes sense, so we apply the value function from MDP to define J(θ).

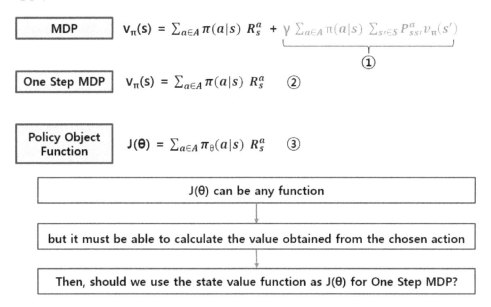

Policy Objective Function for One-Step MDP

Let's create a value function for a one-step MDP, considering only a single time step. Since we consider only one time step, Equation ①

naturally drops out, and only Equation ② remains. By using the value function of a one-step MDP as the policy objective function, we get Equation ③.

Our goal is to find the θ that maximizes the result of the policy objective function, so we must derive an update equation for θ using gradient ascent. This is called the policy gradient.

| Policy Gradient | $\nabla_\theta J(\theta) = \sum_{a \in A} \nabla_\theta \pi_\theta(a|s)\, R_s^a$ | ① |

$$= \underbrace{\sum_{a \in A} \pi_\theta(a|s) \nabla_\theta log\pi_\theta(a|s)}_{②-1}\, R_s^a \quad ②$$

$$= E_{\pi\theta}[\, \nabla_\theta log\pi_\theta(a|s)\, R_s^a\,] \quad ③$$

| Policy Gradient with SGD | $\fallingdotseq \nabla_\theta log\pi_\theta(a|s)\, r$ | ④ |

| Likelihood Ratio | $\nabla_\theta \pi_\theta(a|s) = \pi_\theta(a|s)\, \dfrac{\nabla_\theta \pi_\theta(a|s)}{\pi_\theta(a|s)}$ |
| | $= \pi_\theta(a|s) \nabla_\theta log\pi_\theta(a|s)$ |

Policy Gradient

By applying the concept of the likelihood ratio to the policy objective function obtained earlier (Equation ①), we can rewrite it

as shown in Equation ②. The likelihood ratio is a mathematically

proven concept, so we do not need to delve too deeply into it—just accept it as is. Using the likelihood ratio helps make calculations

more convenient in reinforcement learning. Since Equation ②-1 can be transformed into an expected value, we ultimately obtain Equation ③.

Finally, by using Stochastic Gradient Descent (SGD), we can eliminate the expected value through sampling, resulting in

Equation ④. Here, R changes to r because, to calculate the expected value, we would need to consider the rewards R for all states and actions, but with sampling, we only consider the rewards (r) received while the agent is operating, hence the use of the symbol r.

Equation ④ becomes the objective function of the policy gradient.

By finding the θ that maximizes Equation ④ using gradient ascent, we can find the desired policy. In a one-step MDP, since only a single time step is considered, the reward R (representing the rewards for all states and actions) can be replaced by r, which is the reward received for taking a single action from a single state.

| One Step MDP | $\nabla_\theta J(\theta) = E_{\pi_\theta}[\nabla_\theta log\pi_\theta(a|s) R_s^a]$ |

| Multi Step MDP | $\nabla_\theta J(\theta) = E_{\pi_\theta}[\nabla_\theta log\pi_\theta(a|s) Q^{\pi_\theta}(s,a)]$ |

| MC (REINFORCE) | $\nabla_\theta J(\theta) = E_{\pi_\theta}[\nabla_\theta log\pi_\theta(a|s) G_t]$ |

Various Forms of Cost Functions

When considering multiple time steps (multi-step MDP), we must use the reward R, which represents the rewards for all states and actions. However, R is not easy to compute because it involves considering all states and actions. In such cases, to simplify the calculation, R can be replaced with Q. Since Q calculates the value of a selected action, it is easier to compute than R, which considers all states and actions. The fact that R can be replaced with Q is a proven theory, so we will use it as is without further explanation.

From a programming perspective, calculating Q is still not easy. In such cases, the return (Gt) is more straightforward to calculate from the perspective of executing the agent. We learned how to calculate the return in Monte Carlo (MC), where the return is the sum of the value function obtained by running the agent until the end of an episode. Another advantage of using the MC approach is that, since the agent collects samples while running an episode, there is no need to calculate the expected value. Using the return G becomes the MC approach, and in reinforcement learning, this is called the REINFORCE algorithm.

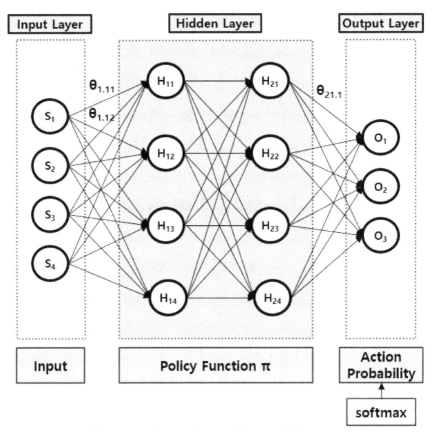

Policy Gradient Using Neural Networks

The policy gradient problem can be solved using a neural network.

If the policy (π) can be represented by a neural network with parameter θ, the output of the neural network can be obtained using the softmax function. As the agent repeatedly interacts with the environment, the neural network is updated until it ultimately learns a policy close to the true value.

The softmax function is a function that outputs a real number between 0 and 1. Since the sum of the softmax function outputs is 1, it can be used as the activation function in the policy network.

7.3 REINFORCE Algorithm Operation

Now, let's explore the most basic Monte Carlo policy gradient algorithm among policy gradient algorithms. This algorithm is also known as the REINFORCE algorithm, and it is more commonly referred to as REINFORCE rather than the Monte Carlo policy gradient.

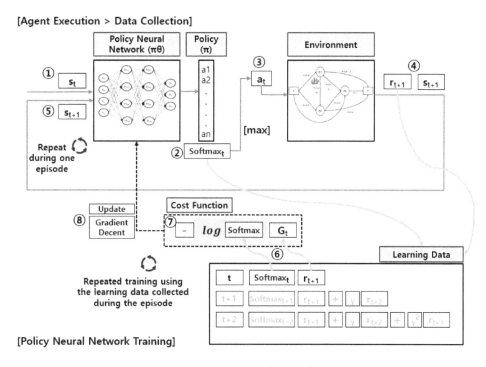

REINFORCE Algorithm

Let's take a detailed look at how the REINFORCE algorithm works. At first glance, the diagram may seem very complicated, but if you follow the numbered steps in sequence, you will realize that it is simpler than it appears. Let's first look at the components required to solve the problem. We have the policy neural network, which represents the policy, and there is the policy itself, which is the output of the policy neural network. This policy consists of the output of the softmax function. There is also an environment in which the actions derived from the policy are executed, and a learning data area (storage) that stores the rewards obtained through the policy and environment. Lastly, there is the cost function, which is used to train the policy neural network.

The REINFORCE algorithm consists of two stages: one stage involves collecting learning data while running the agent until the end of an episode, and the other stage involves training the policy neural network using the collected learning data.

Let's first look at the data collection stage.

(1) The state (st) is input into the neural network to determine the action of the agent. (2) The neural network runs the softmax function to return the result, which represents the policy. The softmax function output is composed of numbers that sum to 1 and are between 0 and 1, indicating probabilities or weights. The number of outputs is equal to the number of possible actions. To make use of the neural network for learning after the episode is over, the output of the neural network is saved in the learning data area.

(3) The action (at) with the highest weight is selected, allowing the agent to act in the environment. (4) The environment returns the reward (rt+1) and the next state(st+1) as a result of the agent's action. The reward is saved in the learning data area for neural network training. (5) If the episode is not yet over, the new state (st+1) is input into the neural network, and the previous process is repeated. This continues until the episode ends.

Once the episode ends, the data stored in the learning data area is used to train the neural network. During the episode, the softmax function output and the return (cumulative reward discounted by the discount factor) would have accumulated for each time step the agent took action.

(6) The softmax function output and return are taken as pairs from the learning data area and input into the cost function to calculate the value. (7) A minus sign is added in front of the cost function at this stage because the policy gradient must find the maximum value

of the policy function represented by the neural network using gradient ascent. Adding a negative sign allows the same goal to be achieved through gradient descent.

(8) Finally, the cost function is minimized through gradient descent, allowing the neural network to learn and represent a more efficient policy.

The REINFORCE algorithm has a disadvantage when the episode length is long, as the waiting time to learn increases. Moreover, since it uses the return, it has the drawback of high variance.

Now, let's look at the REINFORCE algorithm in detail through code.

7.4 Basic Structure of the REINFORCE Algorithm

The basic difference between the REINFORCE algorithm and the DQN algorithm is not only the use of completely different objective functions, but also the fact that the REINFORCE algorithm does not use replay memory and the epsilon-greedy policy.

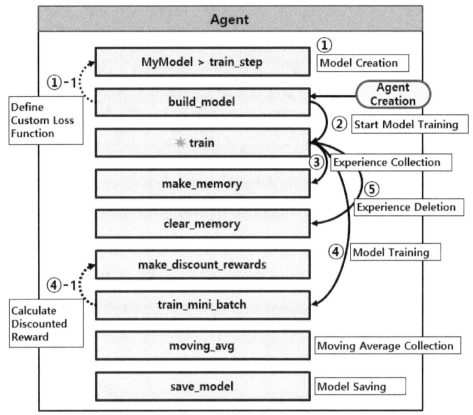

REINFORCE Algorithm Agent Class Features

Let's first look at the structure of the Agent class. Compared to the DQN algorithm, the greed_search and get_epsilon functions related to action selection are not used, and new components such as the MyModel inner class and the make_discount_rewards function are introduced.

In DQN, the epsilon-greedy policy was used to allow the agent to select actions in order to accumulate more diverse experiences. However, in policy-based reinforcement learning, actions are selected probabilistically when choosing a policy, so there is no need for the epsilon-greedy policy. We will look at this more closely in the make_memory function.

(1) When the Agent class is instantiated, the build_model function is called first to create the model. The noteworthy aspect here is that while the DQN algorithm uses the mean squared error (MSE)

as the cost function, the REINFORCE algorithm uses a user-defined cost function instead of a system-provided one. TensorFlow 2.2 offers features that allow the use of various user-defined functions. (1)-1 One approach here is to create a new child class by inheriting from the Model class. Additionally, to incorporate the user-defined cost function into the training process, the train_step function is redefined to include the user-defined cost function.

(2) After creating the Agent class, the train function is called, marking the start of training.

(3) The first step in the train function is to call the make_memory function, which repeatedly runs the CartPole program to gather experiences and collect data.

(4) The collected data is used to train the model after a CartPole episode ends. (4)-1 Before training the model, the rewards collected are processed by applying the discount rate to future rewards.

The process of gathering experience and training the model is repeated for the predetermined number of episodes to complete model training.

7.5 Reviewing the Complete REINFORCE Algorithm Code

The basic structure of the REINFORCE algorithm is similar to that of the DQN algorithm. Let's review the code while keeping the differences between the two algorithms in mind.

```python
import tensorflow as tf
import tensorflow.keras.backend as K
from tensorflow.keras.layers import Input, Dense, Flatten
from tensorflow.keras.optimizers import Adam
import gym
import numpy as np
import random as rand
class Agent(object):
    def __init__(self):
        self.env = gym.make('CartPole-v1')
        self.state_size = self.env.observation_space.shape[0]
        self.action_size = self.env.action_space.n
        self.value_size = 1
```

```python
        self.node_num = 12

        self.learning_rate = 0.0005
        self.epochs_cnt = 5
        self.model = self.build_model()

        self.discount_rate = 0.95
        self.penalty = -10

        self.episode_num = 500

        self.moving_avg_size = 20

        self.states, self.action_matrixs, self.action_probs, self.rewards = [],[],[],[]
        self.DUMMY_ACTION_MATRIX, self.DUMMY_REWARD = \
                np.zeros((1,1,self.action_size)), np.zeros((1,1,self.value_size))

        self.reward_list= []
        self.count_list = []
        self.moving_avg_list = []

    class MyModel(tf.keras.Model):
        def train_step(self, data):
            in_datas, out_actions = data
            states, action_matrix, rewards = in_datas[0], in_datas[1], in_datas[2]
            with tf.GradientTape() as tape:
                y_pred = self(states, training=True)
                action_probs = K.sum(action_matrix*y_pred, axis=1)
                loss = -K.log(action_probs)*rewards
            trainable_vars = self.trainable_variables
            gradients = tape.gradient(loss, trainable_vars)
            self.optimizer.apply_gradients(zip(gradients, trainable_vars))

    def build_model(self):
        input_states = Input(shape=(1,self.state_size), name='input_states')
        input_action_matrixs = Input(shape=(1,self.action_size),
                                    name='input_action_matrixs')
        input_action_probs = Input(shape=(1,self.action_size),
                                    name='input_action_probs')
        input_rewards = Input(shape=(1,self.value_size), name='input_rewards')

        x = (input_states)
        x = Dense(self.node_num, activation='relu')(x)
        out_actions = Dense(self.action_size, activation='softmax',
                                name='output')(x)

        model = self.MyModel(inputs=[input_states, input_action_matrixs,
                                    input_rewards],
                                outputs=out_actions)

        model.compile(optimizer="adam")

        model.summary()
```

```python
    return model

def train(self):
    for episode in range(self.episode_num):
        state = self.env.reset()
        self.env.max_episode_steps = 500
        count, reward_tot = self.make_memory(episode, state)
        self.train_mini_batch()
        self.clear_memory()

        if count < 500:
            reward_tot = reward_tot-self.penalty

        self.reward_list.append(reward_tot)
        self.count_list.append(count)

        self.moving_avg_list.append(self.moving_avg(self.count_list,self.moving_avg_size))

        if(episode % 10 == 0):
            print("episode:{}, moving_avg:{}, rewards_avg:{}".format(episode,
                        self.moving_avg_list[-1], p.mean(self.reward_list)))

    self.save_model()

def make_memory(self, episode, state):
    reward_tot = 0
    count = 0
    reward = np.zeros(self.value_size)
    action_matrix = np.zeros(self.action_size)
    done = False
    while not done:
        count+=1
        state_t = np.reshape(state,[1, 1, self.state_size])
        action_matrix_t = np.reshape(action_matrix,[1, 1, self.action_size])

        action_prob = self.model.predict([state_t, self.DUMMY_ACTION_MATRIX,
                        self.DUMMY_REWARD])

        action = np.random.choice(self.action_size, 1, p=action_prob[0][0])[0]
        action_matrix = np.zeros(self.action_size)
        action_matrix[action] = 1

        state_next, reward, done, none = self.env.step(action)

        if count < 500 and done:
            reward = self.penalty

        self.states.append(np.reshape(state_t, [1,self.state_size]))
        self.action_matrixs.append(np.reshape(action_matrix, [1,self.action_size]))
        self.action_probs.append(np.reshape(action_prob, [1,self.action_size]))
        self.rewards.append(reward)
        reward_tot += reward
```

```
        state = state_next
      return count, reward_tot

  def clear_memory(self):
    self.states, self.action_matrixs, self.action_probs, self.rewards = [],[],[],[]

  def make_discount_rewards(self, rewards):
    discounted_rewards = np.zeros(np.array(rewards).shape)
    running_add = 0
    for t in reversed(range(0, len(rewards))):
      running_add = running_add * self.discount_rate + rewards[t]
      discounted_rewards[t] = running_add

    return discounted_rewards

  def train_mini_batch(self):
    discount_rewards = np.array(self.make_discount_rewards(self.rewards))
    discount_rewards_t = np.reshape(discount_rewards, [len(discount_rewards),1,1])
    states_t = np.array(self.states)
    action_matrixs_t = np.array(self.action_matrixs)
    action_probs_t = np.array(self.action_probs)
    self.model.fit(x=[states_t, action_matrixs_t, discount_rewards_t],
               y=[action_probs_t], epochs=self.epochs_cnt, verbose=0)

  def moving_avg(self, data, size=10):
    if len(data) > size:
      c = np.array(data[len(data)-size:len(data)])
    else:
      c = np.array(data)
    return np.mean(c)

  def save_model(self):
    self.model.save("./model/reinforce")
    print("*****end learing")

if __name__ == "__main__":
  agent = Agent()
  agent.train()
```

cartpole_REINFORCE.py

In the DQN algorithm, the results from multiple episodes were
continuously accumulated in the replay_memory variable, but in
the REINFORCE algorithm, all collected data is deleted at the end
of an episode. Additionally, the REINFORCE algorithm has the
characteristic of probabilistically selecting actions based on the
policy output by the neural network.

7.6 Exploring the Detailed Structure of the REINFORCE

Algorithm

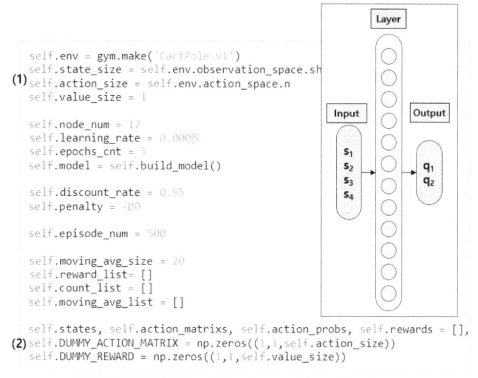

```
    self.env = gym.make('CartPole-v1')
    self.state_size = self.env.observation_space.sh
(1) self.action_size = self.env.action_space.n
    self.value_size = 1

    self.node_num = 12
    self.learning_rate = 0.0005
    self.epochs_cnt = 5
    self.model = self.build_model()

    self.discount_rate = 0.95
    self.penalty = -1.0

    self.episode_num = 500

    self.moving_avg_size = 20
    self.reward_list= []
    self.count_list = []
    self.moving_avg_list = []

    self.states, self.action_matrixs, self.action_probs, self.rewards = [],
(2) self.DUMMY_ACTION_MATRIX = np.zeros((1,1,self.action_size))
    self.DUMMY_REWARD = np.zeros((1,1,self.value_size))
```

REINFORCE Algorithm Agent Class Attributes

The attributes of the Agent class in the REINFORCE algorithm are similar to those in the DQN algorithm. Most of them are alike, but the variables related to replay memory and epsilon-greedy policy have been removed. Let's look at the remaining attributes:

(1) In the program operation setting area, a value_size attribute has been added. This attribute is used to set the size of the reward value used in the program.

(2) In the data collection environment, dummy variables (DUMMY) are declared along with the variables that store the data collected during an episode. These dummy variables are required to match the number of arguments when calling functions, although the actual value of the arguments is not significant.

```
class MyModel(tf.keras.Model):        (1)

    def train_step(self, data):   (2)

        in_datas, out_actions = data
    (3)
        states, action_matrix, rewards = in_datas[0], in_datas[1], in_datas[2]


    (4)  with tf.GradientTape() as tape:
    (5)      y_pred = self(states, training=True)
    (6)      action_probs = K.sum(action_matrix*y_pred, axis=-1)
    (7)      loss = -K.log(action_probs)*rewards


    (8)  trainable_vars = self.trainable_variables
    (9)  gradients = tape.gradient(loss, trainable_vars)
    (10) self.optimizer.apply_gradients(zip(gradients, trainable_vars))
```

```
build_model : Model Creation
```
```
model = self.MyModel(inputs=[input_states, input_action_matrixs, input_rewards],
                     outputs=out_actions)
```
```
train_mini_batch : Training Model
```
```
self.model.fit(x=[states_t, action_matrixs_t, discount_rewards_t], y=[action_probs_t],
               epochs=self.epochs_cnt, verbose=0)
```

cartpole_REINFORCE: MyModel Class

Generally, the tf.keras.Model class is used when constructing a
neural network. However, to use a custom cost function, a new class
must be created by inheriting from the Model class.

(1) The MyModel class is a user-defined class newly constructed by
inheriting from the tf.keras.Model class.

(2) In the tf.keras.Model class, the train_step function is
responsible for training the neural network step by step. The neural
network learns in the direction of minimizing the cost function, and
once the name of the cost function to be used is given when creating
the class, the learning proceeds automatically. Common cost
functions are already defined in the tf.keras.Model class, and you
can specify which cost function to use by name. To use a user-
defined cost function, redefine the train_step function.

(3) The redefinition of the train_step function starts with setting
input variables. The inputs and outputs arguments, passed during

model creation in the build_model function, are grouped as the data argument and passed to the train_step function. The in_datas variable represents the input values, and out_datas represents the output values. The three input values are stored sequentially in the in_datas variable as an array. When training the neural network, the data is received in the order specified when the model was defined, so each value is stored separately in a variable.

(4) TensorFlow provides an automatic differentiation feature. To perform automatic differentiation, operations are recorded in the order they occur, and gradients are calculated by differentiating the recorded data in reverse order. The GradientTape class is used for this purpose.

```
import tensorflow as tf
import tensorflow as tf
import tensorflow.keras.backend as K
import numpy as np
x = tf.constant([1.0, 2.0, 3.0])
with tf.GradientTape() as tape:
    tape.watch(x)
    y = (x*x)
z = tape.gradient(y, x)
print(z)
```
----

tf.Tensor([2. 4. 6.], shape=(3,), dtype=float32)

How GradientTape Works

By declaring the use of the GradientTape class with the with keyword and specifying the variable to monitor using the watch function, all operations are recorded in the GradientTape class.

(5) The state is input into the neural network to output the policy. The policy outputs the probability of each action, which includes the probabilities for left/right actions.

(6) The policy represents the probability of an action. For example, if the policy is [0.6, 0.4], it means that the probability of selecting action 0 is 60%, and the probability of selecting action 1 is 40%. If we always select the action with the highest probability, the policy becomes deterministic, making it identical to Q-learning, which always selects the policy with the highest Q-value. On the other

hand, in the stochastic policy selection method, if the policy is [0.6, 0.4], action 0 is selected with a 60% probability, and action 1 is selected with a 40% probability. Rather than always selecting the action with the highest probability, the chances of selection are increased proportionally. This method is a more realistic way of choosing actions.

```
import tensorflow as tf
import tensorflow.keras.backend as K
import numpy as np

y_pred = np.array([[0.6,0.4], [0.3,0.7]])
action_matrix = np.array([[1,0], [0,1]])

action_probs = K.sum(action_matrix*y_pred, axis=-1)
print("*action_probs:", action_probs)
```
----

*action_probs: tf.Tensor([0.6 0.7], shape=(2,), dtype=float64)

Stochastic Policy Selection

Information about stochastic policy selection is stored in the action_matrix variable. The actions are selected in advance probabilistically, with 1 indicating the selected action and 0 for actions not selected. For example, the values [0, 1] are stored in action_matrix. The exact way of setting these values is discussed in more detail later.

Thus, if the variable y_pred contains [0.6, 0.4] and the action_matrix contains [1, 0], multiplying them along axis=-1 (the last index direction) will leave only 0.6.

(7) To create the cost function, take the log of the policy and multiply it by the return. Also, add a minus sign to convert gradient ascent into gradient descent.

(8) In the tf.keras.Model class, the weights and biases of the neural network are stored in the trainable_variables variable.

(9) Gradients are computed using the cost function, weights, and biases recorded in the GradientTape.

(10) The specified optimization algorithm (adam) is applied to the

input variables using the zip function, which combines several data items of the same length into a single data structure.

---

b= zip([1, 2, 3], [4, 5, 6])

c = list(b)

print(c)

[(1, 4), (2, 5), (3, 6)]

Functionality of the zip Function

```
def build_model(self):
        input_states = Input(shape=(1,self.state_size), name='input_states')
        input_action_matrixs = Input(shape=(1,self.action_size),
(1)
                                     name='input_action_matrixs')
        input_rewards = Input(shape=(1,self.value_size), name='input_rewards')


        x = (input_states)
(2)     x = Dense(self.node_num, activation='relu')(x)
        out_actions = Dense(self.action_size, activation='softmax', name='output')(x)


(3) model = self.MyModel(inputs=[input_states, input_action_matrixs, input_rewards],
                         outputs=out_actions)


    model.compile(optimizer="adam")


    model.summary()
    return model
```

cartpole_REINFORCE: build_model Function

Let's now examine the functions that constitute the Agent class, starting with the build_model function.

(1) The variables required for model training and model usage are defined as input values. The three variables used for model training are states, action_matrixs, and rewards. When predicting with the model, only the states variable is used.

(2) The network is structured in the same way as the DQN algorithm. The only difference is that the output in the DQN algorithm is the Q-value for each action, which is numerical data, whereas the output in the REINFORCE algorithm is the probability of the policy for each action. Thus, the softmax function, which has this output characteristic, is used as the activation function.

(3) When creating the model, the MyModel class, which inherits from the tf.keras.Model class, is used. The input values are the same three variables used to create the cost function: states, action_matrixs, and rewards.

```
def train(self):
    for episode in range(self.episode_num):
        state = self.env.reset()
        self.env.max_episode_steps = 500
(1)     count, reward_tot = self.make_memory(episode, state)
(2)     self.train_mini_batch()
        self.clear_memory() (3)

        if count < 500:
            reward_tot = reward_tot-self.penalty

        self.reward_list.append(reward_tot)
        self.count_list.append(count)
        self.moving_avg_list.append(self.moving_avg(self.count_list,self.moving_avg_size))

        if(episode % 10 == 0):
            print("episode:{}, moving_avg:{}, rewards_avg:{}".
                format(episode, self.moving_avg_list[-1], np.mean(self.reward_list)))

    self.save_model()
```

cartpole_REINFORCE: train Function

The structure of the train function is similar to that of the DQN algorithm. In the DQN algorithm, data is continuously accumulated in the replay memory and randomly sampled for training, while in the REINFORCE algorithm, all the data collected during one episode is used for training.

(1) The make_memory function is used to collect data during an episode and store it in a list format as a class variable.

(2) The train_mini_batch function trains the neural network model using the collected data.

(3) Once the model training is completed, all the collected data is

deleted.

The training result is then stored in a variable, monitoring logs are printed, and the model is saved to a file in a designated location when training is complete.

```python
def make_memory(self, episode, state):
    reward_tot = 0
    count = 0
    reward = np.zeros(self.value_size)
    action_matrix = np.zeros(self.action_size)
    done = False
    while not done:
        count+=1
        state_t = np.reshape(state,[1, 1, self.state_size])
        action_matrix_t = np.reshape(action_matrix,[1, 1, self.action_size])

        (1) action_prob = self.model.predict([state_t, self.DUMMY_ACTION_MATRIX, self.DUMMY_REWARD])

        (2) action = np.random.choice(self.action_size, 1, p=action_prob[0][0])[0]
        action_matrix = np.zeros(self.action_size)
        (3) action_matrix[action] = 1

        state_next, reward, done, none = self.env.step(action)

        if count < 500 and done:
            reward = self.penalty

        self.states.append(np.reshape(state_t, [1,self.state_size]))
        self.action_matrixs.append(np.reshape(action_matrix, [1,self.action_size]))
        self.action_probs.append(np.reshape(action_prob, [1,self.action_size]))
        self.rewards.append(reward)
        reward_tot += reward
        state = state_next
    return count, reward_tot
```

cartpole_REINFORCE: make_memory Function

The make_memory function collects experiences while running the CartPole program. Most of it is similar to the DQN algorithm, but there are a few differences.

(1) When predicting an action with the model (model.predict), only the correct value of the state is provided, while action_matrix and rewards are filled with zeros just to match the shape since they are used only during training.

```
import numpy as np
acton_prob = [0.7, 0.3]
for i in range(10):
    d = np.random.choice(a=2, size=1, p=acton_prob)[0]
    print(d, end=', ')
```

1, 1, 0, 0, 0, 0, 1, 0, 1, 0,

Functionality of random.choice

(2) To select actions probabilistically, the random.choice function from NumPy is used. It takes arguments a, size, and p, where a is the size of the array containing the probabilities, size is the shape of the output variable, and p is the probability that determines the action. In the example, with an array having probabilities of 0.7 and 0.3, when selecting an index using the random.choice function, index 0 is selected with a 70% chance, and index 1 with a 30% chance.

(3) Next, the action matrix to be used in the custom cost function is created. The action matrix is an array consisting of two elements, 0 or 1. It is initially set to [0, 0], and the index corresponding to the probabilistically selected action is set to 1. This is used in the cost function to combine the model output (action selection probabilities, e.g., [0.7, 0.3]) and output only the probability of the selected action among the two policies.

```
def clear_memory(self):
    self.states, self.action_matrixs, self.action_probs, self.rewards = [],[],[],[]
```

cartpole_REINFORCE: clear_memory Function

The various experiences obtained while running CartPole are stored as attributes of the Agent class. Once the model is trained using the stored data at the end of an episode, the data should be deleted to store new experiences.

```
def make_discount_rewards(self, rewards):
    discounted_rewards = np.zeros(np.array(rewards).shape)
    running_add = 0
    for t in reversed(range(0, len(rewards))): (1)
        (2) running_add = running_add * self.discount_rate + rewards[t]
        discounted_rewards[t] = running_add

    return discounted_rewards
```

cartpole_REINFORCE: make_discount_rewards Function

The make_discount_rewards function calculates the discounted return for each time step of the CartPole run. The rewards received during each CartPole run are stored in the rewards variable of the Agent class. This value, along with the discount rate (discount_rate), is used to calculate the discounted return.

(1) To calculate the discounted return, multiply the reward received at the last time step repeatedly by the discount rate. Thus, the built-in reversed function is used to retrieve the rewards from the last index and calculate the return in reverse order.

```
a = [1,2,3,4,5]
for t in reversed(range(0, len(a))):
    print(t, end=', ')
```

4, 3, 2, 1, 0,

Functionality of reversed Function

(2) The return calculated at each point in time is stored in the running_add variable. The return for the next step is calculated by multiplying the running_add by the discount rate and adding the reward received at that step.

```
def train_mini_batch(self):
```
(1) `discount_rewards = np.array(self.make_discount_rewards(self.rewards))`

(2) `discount_rewards_t = np.reshape(discount_rewards, [len(discount_rewards),1,1])`

`states_t = np.array(self.states)`

(3) `action_matrixs_t = np.array(self.action_matrixs)`

`action_probs_t = np.array(self.action_probs)`

(4) `self.model.fit(x=[states_t, action_matrixs_t, discount_rewards_t],`

`y=[action_probs_t], epochs=self.epochs_cnt, verbose=0)`

cartpole_REINFORCE: train_mini_batch Function

The train_mini_batch function trains the model using the collected data.

(1) First, the make_discount_rewards function is used to calculate the discounted return for the rewards collected at each step.

(2) The NumPy reshape function is used to reshape the return data into a trainable form.

(3) Since the attributes of the Agent class store data in list form, it is converted into a NumPy array for model training.

(4) Finally, the fit function is called to train the model. The input variables are state, action_matrix, and discount_rewards, while the target function is the probability for each action.

7.7 Analysis of REINFORCE Algorithm Training Results

Now that we have finished analyzing the program, let's examine the performance by actually running the REINFORCE algorithm. The CartPole program is very simple in structure, so the REINFORCE algorithm runs quickly and performs relatively well. However, keep in mind that the REINFORCE algorithm may have structural weaknesses that could result in decreased performance in more complex environments.

Model: "my_model_7"

Layer (type)	Output Shape	Param #	Connected to
input_states (InputLayer)	[(None, 1, 4)]	0	
dense_7 (Dense)	(None, 1, 12)	60	input_states[0][0]
input_action_matrixs (InputLaye	[(None, 1, 2)]	0	
input_rewards (InputLayer)	[(None, 1, 1)]	0	
output (Dense)	(None, 1, 2)	26	dense_7[0][0]

Total params: 86
Trainable params: 86
Non-trainable params: 0

episode:0, moving_avg:27.0, rewards_avg:26.0
episode:10, moving_avg:20.90909090909091, rewards_avg:19.90909090909091
episode:20, moving_avg:24.2, rewards_avg:23.333333333333332
episode:30, moving_avg:28.75, rewards_avg:24.967741935483872
episode:40, moving_avg:37.95, rewards_avg:29.975609756097562
episode:50, moving_avg:41.0, rewards_avg:30.862745098039216
episode:60, moving_avg:40.8, rewards_avg:33.19672131147541
episode:70, moving_avg:50.75, rewards_avg:36.183098591549296
episode:80, moving_avg:55.5, rewards_avg:38.45679012345679
episode:90, moving_avg:50.3, rewards_avg:39.065934065934066
episode:100, moving_avg:59.45, rewards_avg:42.415841584158414
episode:110, moving_avg:73.85, rewards_avg:45.153153153153156
episode:120, moving_avg:69.45, rewards_avg:46.71900826446281
episode:130, moving_avg:67.25, rewards_avg:48.37404580152672
episode:140, moving_avg:70.1, rewards_avg:49.8936170212766
episode:150, moving_avg:93.05, rewards_avg:54.158940397350996
episode:160, moving_avg:111.1, rewards_avg:57.37267080745342
episode:170, moving_avg:95.45, rewards_avg:58.87134502923977
episode:180, moving_avg:77.15, rewards_avg:59.447513812154696
episode:190, moving_avg:76.6, rewards_avg:60.62303664921466
episode:200, moving_avg:85.35, rewards_avg:61.92537313432836
episode:210, moving_avg:98.5, rewards_avg:64.11848341232228
episode:220, moving_avg:115.95, rewards_avg:66.72398190045249
episode:230, moving_avg:105.45, rewards_avg:67.6103896103896
episode:240, moving_avg:77.0, rewards_avg:67.49377593360995
episode:250, moving_avg:60.35, rewards_avg:66.95219123505976
episode:260, moving_avg:64.9, rewards_avg:67.2183908045977
episode:270, moving_avg:88.75, rewards_avg:68.4870848708487
episode:280, moving_avg:99.5, rewards_avg:69.44483985765125
episode:290, moving_avg:156.4, rewards_avg:74.46048109965636
episode:300, moving_avg:179.75, rewards_avg:76.70764119601328
episode:310, moving_avg:128.95, rewards_avg:77.90032154340837
episode:320, moving_avg:112.25, rewards_avg:78.85981308411215
episode:330, moving_avg:112.85, rewards_avg:79.95166163141994

episode:340, moving_avg:120.75, rewards_avg:81.25806451612904
episode:350, moving_avg:171.9, rewards_avg:85.13390313390313
episode:360, moving_avg:199.8, rewards_avg:87.77008310249307
episode:370, moving_avg:180.25, rewards_avg:90.20754716981132
episode:380, moving_avg:161.25, rewards_avg:91.5748031496063
episode:390, moving_avg:127.15, rewards_avg:92.0460358056266
episode:400, moving_avg:115.75, rewards_avg:92.73067331670823
episode:410, moving_avg:131.75, rewards_avg:93.9294403892944
episode:420, moving_avg:177.2, rewards_avg:96.6959619952494
episode:430, moving_avg:188.3, rewards_avg:98.26218097447796
episode:440, moving_avg:129.9, rewards_avg:98.15646258503402
episode:450, moving_avg:119.9, rewards_avg:99.17738359201773
episode:460, moving_avg:161.8, rewards_avg:100.87418655097613
episode:470, moving_avg:149.95, rewards_avg:101.29087048832272
episode:480, moving_avg:139.4, rewards_avg:102.43451143451144
episode:490, moving_avg:207.3, rewards_avg:105.56822810590631
INFO:tensorflow:Assets written to: ./model/reinforce\assets
*****end learing

cartpole_REINFORCE: Execution Results

The REINFORCE algorithm, like the DQN algorithm, uses random functions throughout the algorithm, including model variable initialization, so the results vary each time it is run. If the example provided in this book does not perform well, try running it multiple times.

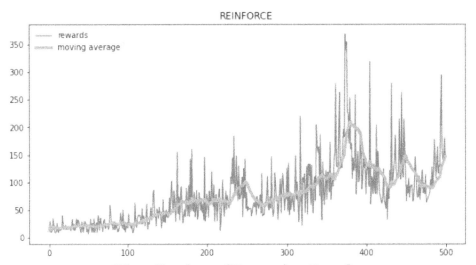

Visualization of Execution Results

When executed in the same state, the REINFORCE algorithm performs slightly better than the DQN algorithm. It improved the performance by probabilistically determining actions rather than always taking the maximum value, which is the biggest drawback of value-based algorithms, and by using discounted rewards.

So far, we have studied the simplest policy-based algorithm, the REINFORCE algorithm. Moving forward, we will study the A2C and PPO algorithms to understand how policy-based algorithms have evolved.

Chapter 8

Policy-Based Reinforcement Learning: A2C Algorithm

8. Policy-Based A2C Algorithm

The DQN and REINFORCE algorithms, which we learned about in the previous chapters, have several theoretical limitations. "Theoretical" means that there are environments where DQN or REINFORCE might still perform well. A2C (Advantage Actor Critic) is a reinforcement learning algorithm that emerged to address these limitations. Although in the CartPole environment, A2C might not outperform the REINFORCE algorithm, it laid down several theoretical foundations before the advent of the PPO algorithm, which is significant in its own right.

8.1 Actor-Critic Algorithm

Before diving into the Actor-Critic (AC) algorithm, let's first revisit the characteristics of DQN and REINFORCE, which are representative algorithms of value-based and policy-based learning, respectively. In DQN, replay memory is used to train on large amounts of data in batches, but it fundamentally employs a one-step TD algorithm, executing and learning at each timestep. In contrast, the REINFORCE algorithm collects data until an episode ends and then performs learning all at once.

The REINFORCE algorithm keeps gathering data until the end of an episode using a single policy, resulting in low bias in the data. However, since the learning data in REINFORCE is the cumulative sum of rewards collected throughout the episode, the variance also accumulates, making it high. On the other hand, in DQN, the bias is high because the entire dataset is estimated (using the Bellman equation) based on the data collected from a single action. However, the variance is low because DQN uses data from individual actions.

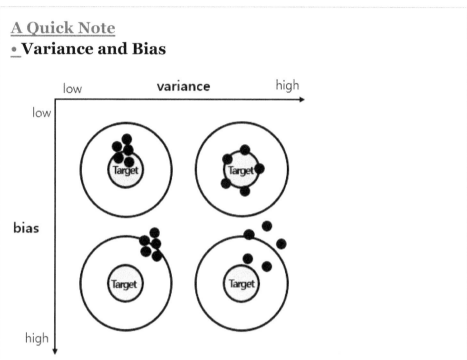
The Actor-Critic algorithm combines the low bias of the REINFORCE algorithm and the low variance of the DQN algorithm, suggesting a more efficient way to find the optimal policy. While REINFORCE and DQN use the same neural network for both policy and value learning, Actor-Critic separates the policy network and value network. The value network is used to evaluate the policy by calculating the value that can be obtained through the policy, and the policy network is used to determine the actions of the agent. The goal is to derive an efficient policy network. The Monte Carlo

approach used in the policy network helps reduce bias, and using the value network's results instead of directly using the returns from the environment helps reduce variance.

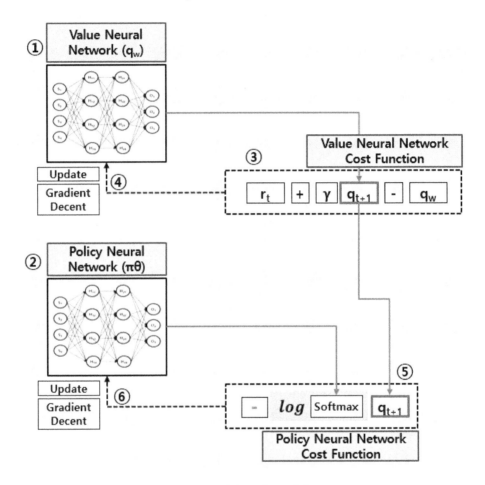

Actor-Critic Algorithm

Let's explore the Actor-Critic algorithm step-by-step through a diagram. The Actor-Critic algorithm utilizes two neural networks:

① a value neural network and ② a policy neural network. The value network is represented by the variable w, and the policy network by the variable θ. The goal of training is to find the variables w and θ that best represent value and policy.

③ The output of the value neural network is the action-value function qt. ④ This qt is used in the cost function to train the neural network. The qt output from the value network is then ⑤ applied in the cost function of the policy network, thus ⑥ contributing to policy network training. In the previous REINFORCE algorithm, the cost function of the policy network used the return r, but here, the action-value function replaces the return. In a one-step MDP environment (considering only a single timestep), the return serves as an unbiased sample of the action-value function. An unbiased sample implies that repeated calculations of the return approximate the action-value function.

The action-value function estimates the value of an agent's actions under a given policy, while the value function assesses the value of one state transitioning to another. Additionally, the return represents the total reward from the environment. In a one-step MDP environment, where only one action can be chosen and only one resulting state exists, repeated sampling (yielding statistical probability) allows the action-value function, value function, and return to serve as unbiased samples of each other.

8.2 Advantage Actor-Critic (A2C)

The Actor-Critic algorithm still has limitations. Although separating the value and policy networks reduces bias and variance, the REINFORCE algorithm used for learning policy still generates a high variance due to continuously collecting data under a single policy until the episode ends.

Advantage Actor-Critic (A2C) was proposed to reduce this variance. In the Actor-Critic (AC) algorithm, the cost function for training the policy network used the action-value function q. However, directly using the action-value function may increase variance due to data collection under unstable policies. To manage this, a baseline is set to reduce fluctuations in values and control data variance.

This leads to the question of what value to use as a baseline, and generally, the value function serves this purpose. Instead of directly using the action-value function in the policy network's cost function, the advantage function is computed by subtracting the value function (baseline) from the action-value function. This is called the advantage.

Using the advantage reduces variance without changing the expected value, a theory proven mathematically. Therefore, we will proceed with this approach without additional explanation.

$$A^{\pi\theta}(s, a) = Q^{\pi\theta}(s, a) - V^{\pi\theta}(s) \qquad ①$$

$$V^{\pi\theta}(s) \fallingdotseq V_v(s) \qquad ②$$

$$Q^{\pi\theta}(s, a) \fallingdotseq Q_w(s, a) \qquad ③$$

$$A(s, a) = Q_w(s, a) - V_v(s) \qquad ④$$

Advantage

Formula ① expresses the general advantage described above, using values attainable under a policy represented by the variable θ.

Using neural networks, we can represent ② the value function and ③ the action-value function, enabling ④ approximation of the advantage through neural networks.

| TD | $V^{\pi\theta}(s) \leftarrow V^{\pi\theta}(s) + \propto (r + \gamma V^{\pi\theta}(s') - V^{\pi\theta}(s))$ | ① |

| Cost Function | $\delta = r + \gamma V^{\pi\theta}(s') - V^{\pi\theta}(s)$ | ② |

| Expected value | $E[\delta^{\pi\theta} |s,a] = E[\underbrace{r + \gamma V^{\pi\theta}(s')|s,a}_{③\text{-}1}] - E[\underbrace{V^{\pi\theta}(s) |s,a}_{③\text{-}2}]$ | ③ |

$$= Q^{\pi\theta}(s,\ a) - V^{\pi\theta}(s) \qquad ④$$

$$= A^{\pi\theta}(s,\ a) \qquad ⑤$$

> **The definition of value function and action-value function**
>
> $v_\pi(s) = \sum_{a \in A} \pi(a|s) q_\pi(s, a)$
>
> $q_\pi(s, a) = R_s^a + \gamma \sum_{s' \in S} P_{ss'}^a v_\pi(s')$

Advantage Calculation

When calculating the value function in TD (Temporal Difference), it corresponds to Equation ①. Since the TD value function has been discussed extensively earlier, we'll move on without further explanation. The cost function in TD is defined as $\delta(\lambda)$, as shown in Equation ②. Now, let's calculate the expected value of the cost function. By taking the expectation of Equation ②, we get Equation ③. Referring to the definition of the action-value function, it's easy to see that Equation ③-1 calculates the action-value function. Likewise, examining Equation ③-2 in the context of the value function's definition, which considers all states and actions, shows that it equates to the value function.

Therefore, calculating the expected value of the cost function reveals that it is equivalent to the advantage. Additionally, as previously discussed, the expected value of the cost function can be approximated by repeatedly collecting samples using the cost function.

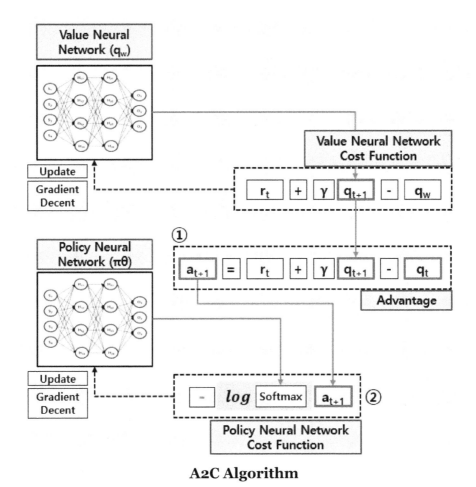

A2C Algorithm

The main difference from the Actor-Critic algorithm lies in

Equations ① and ②. In Equation ①, the advantage is calculated. The advantage is determined using the action-value function derived from the neural network and the action-value function from the previous timestep. Previously, the value function was used for this calculation, but here, the action-value function is used because, in the sampling environment, the value function and the action-value function yield the same result. This advantage obtained in

Equation ① can then be input into Equation ② to determine the cost function for the policy network.

8.3 Basic Structure of the A2C Algorithm

The Agent class in the A2C (Advantage Actor-Critic) algorithm consists of eight functions. A notable characteristic of the A2C algorithm is that it structures the value network and policy network separately and conducts training before the episode ends.

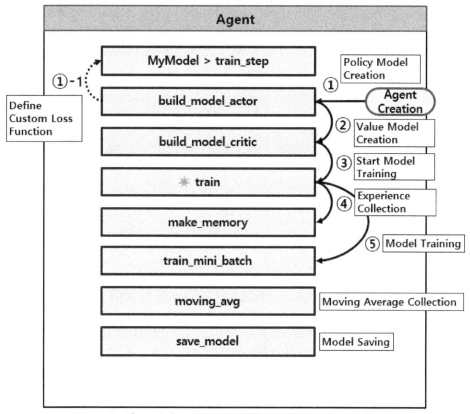

A2C Algorithm Agent Class Functionality

In this example, the learning approach differs by training immediately after each experience, rather than using batch learning after gathering numerous experiences. Although batch learning can be applied in the A2C algorithm, this is explored further in the PPO algorithm.

(1) When creating the Agent class for training, the build_model_actor function is automatically called to set up the policy network.

(2) After constructing the policy network, the build_model_critic function is called to set up the value network.

(3) With the Agent class created, calling the train function initiates training, where the make_memory, train_mini_batch, moving_avg, and save_model functions are executed in sequence.

(4) The first function called for training is make_memory, which gathers state and reward values from running CartPole, then immediately calls train_mini_batch to proceed with training.

(5) The train_mini_batch function trains the model on a single experience, simultaneously training both the policy and value networks.

Now that we've reviewed the basic structure, let's examine the code to understand the detailed operation of each part. This will help clarify how each function contributes to the overall workings of the A2C algorithm.

8.4 Full Code Review of the A2C Algorithm

The main difference between the A2C algorithm and the REINFORCE algorithm is the use of two neural networks. Let's observe how the neural networks are defined separately and how the relationship between the two is structured.

```python
import tensorflow as tf
import tensorflow.keras.backend as K
from tensorflow.keras.layers import Input, Dense, Flatten
from tensorflow.keras.optimizers import Adam
import gym
import numpy as np
import random as rand
class Agent(object):
    def __init__(self):
        self.env = gym.make('CartPole-v1')
        self.state_size = self.env.observation_space.shape[0]
        self.action_size = self.env.action_space.n
        self.value_size = 1

        self.node_num = 12
```

```python
        self.learning_rate = 0.002
        self.discount_rate = 0.95
        self.penalty = -100
        self.epochs_cnt = 1

        self.episode_num = 500

        self.moving_avg_size = 20

        self.model_actor = self.build_model_actor()
        self.model_critic = self.build_model_critic()

        self.reward_list= []
        self.count_list = []
        self.moving_avg_list = []

        self.DUMMY_ACTION_MATRIX, self.DUMMY_ADVANTAGE =
                np.zeros((1,self.action_size)), np.zeros((1,self.value_size))

    class MyModel(tf.keras.Model):
        def train_step(self, data):
            in_datas, out_action_probs = data
            states, action_matrixs, advantages = in_datas[0], in_datas[1], in_datas[2]
            with tf.GradientTape() as tape:
                y_pred = self(states, training=True)  # Forward pass
                action_probs = K.max(action_matrixs*y_pred, axis=-1)
                loss = -K.log(action_probs)*advantages
            trainable_vars = self.trainable_variables
            gradients = tape.gradient(loss, trainable_vars)
            self.optimizer.apply_gradients(zip(gradients, trainable_vars))

    def build_model_actor(self):
        input_states = Input(shape=(self.state_size), name='input_states')
        input_action_matrixs = Input(shape=(self.action_size),
                                        name='input_action_matrixs')
        input_advantages = Input(shape=(self.value_size), name='input_advantages')

        x = (input_states)
        x = Dense(self.node_num, activation='relu')(x)
        out_actions = Dense(self.action_size, activation='softmax', name='output',
                                kernel_initializer='he_uniform')(x)

        model = self.MyModel(inputs=[input_states, input_action_matrixs,
                                        input_advantages], outputs=out_actions)
        model.compile(optimizer=Adam(lr=self.learning_rate))
```

```python
        model.summary()
        return model

    def build_model_critic(self):
        input_states = Input(shape=(self.state_size), name='input_states')

        x = (input_states)
        x = Dense(self.node_num, activation='relu')(x)
        out_values = Dense(self.value_size, activation='linear', name='output')(x)

        model = tf.keras.models.Model(inputs=[input_states], outputs=[out_values])
        model.compile(optimizer=Adam(lr=self.learning_rate),
                loss='mean_squared_error'
                )
        model.summary()
        return model

    def train(self):
        reward_list=[]
        count_list = []
        moving_avg_list = []
        for episode in range(self.episode_num):
            state = self.env.reset()
            self.env.max_episode_steps = 500
            count, reward_tot = self.make_memory(episode, state)

            if count < 500:
                reward_tot = reward_tot-self.penalty

            self.reward_list.append(reward_tot)
            self.count_list.append(count)

            self.moving_avg_list.append(self.moving_avg(self.count_list,self.moving_avg_s
            ize))

            if(episode % 10 == 0):
                print("episode:{}, moving_avg:{}, rewards_avg:{}".
                    format(episode, self.moving_avg_list[-1], np.mean(self.reward_list)))
            self.save_model()

    def moving_avg(self, data, size=10):
        if len(data) > size:
            c = np.array(data[len(data)-size:len(data)])
        else:
            c = np.array(data)
```

```python
        return np.mean(c)

    def clear_memory(self):
        self.states, self.action_matrixs, self.states_next, self.action_probs,
            self.rewards = [],[],[],[],[]

    def make_memory(self, episode, state):
        reward_tot = 0
        count = 0
        reward = np.zeros(self.value_size)
        action_matrix = np.zeros(self.action_size)
        done = False
        while not done:
            count+=1
            state_t = np.reshape(state, [1,self.state_size]) #현재상태
            action_matrix_t = np.reshape(action_matrix, [1,self.action_size])

            action_prob = self.model_actor.predict([state_t,
                          self.DUMMY_ACTION_MATRIX,
                          self.DUMMY_ADVANTAGE])
            action = np.random.choice(self.action_size, 1, p=action_prob[0])[0]

            action_matrix = np.zeros(self.action_size) #초기화
            action_matrix[action] = 1
            state_next, reward, done, none = self.env.step(action)

            if count < 500 and done:
                reward = self.penalty

            self.train_mini_batch(state, state_next, reward,
                                  action_matrix, action_prob, done, count)

            state = state_next
            if done:
                reward = self.penalty

            reward_tot += reward

        return count, reward_tot

    def train_mini_batch(self, state, state_next, reward, action_matrix, action_prob,
                         done, count):

        state_t = np.reshape(state, [1, self.state_size])
        state_next_t = np.reshape(state_next, [1, self.state_size])
```

171

```
reward_t = np.reshape(reward, [1, self.value_size])
action_matrix_t = np.reshape(action_matrix, [1, self.action_size])
action_prob_t = np.reshape(action_prob, [1, self.action_size])

advantage_t = np.zeros((1, self.value_size))
target_t = np.zeros((1, self.value_size))

value_t = self.model_critic.predict(state_t)
value_next_t = self.model_critic.predict(state_next_t)

if(count< 500 and done):
    advantage_t =  reward_t - value_t
    target_t = reward_t
else:
    advantage_t = reward_t + self.discount_rate*value_next_t - value_t
    target_t = reward_t + self.discount_rate * value_next_t

self.model_actor.fit(x=[state_t, action_matrix_t, advantage_t],
                                    y=[action_prob_t], epochs=self.epochs_cnt,
                    verbose=0)
self.model_critic.fit(x=state_t, y=target_t, epochs=self.epochs_cnt, verbose=0)

def save_model(self):
    self.model_actor.save("./model/a2c")
    print("*****end a2c learing")

if __name__ == "__main__":
    agent = Agent()
    agent.train()
```

CartPole_A2C.py

In the A2C algorithm, the policy network for policy representation is created using the build_model_actor function, and the value network for value representation is created using the build_model_critic function. The policy network outputs probabilities using the softmax function, while the value network outputs values using a linear function.

8.5 Examining the Detailed Structure of the A2C Algorithm

```
    self.env = gym.make('CartPole-v1')
    self.state_size = self.env.observation_space.shape[0]
    self.action_size = self.env.action_space.n
    self.value_size = 1

    self.node_num = 12
    self.learning_rate = 0.001
(1) self.epochs_cnt = 1
    self.model_actor = self.build_model_actor()
    self.model_critic = self.build_model_critic()

    self.discount_rate = 0.95
    self.penalty = -20

    self.episode_num = 500

    self.moving_avg_size = 20
    self.reward_list= []
    self.count_list = []
    self.moving_avg_list = []

    self.DUMMY_ACTION_MATRIX = np.zeros((1,self.action_size))
    self.DUMMY_ADVANTAGE = np.zeros((1,self.value_size))
```

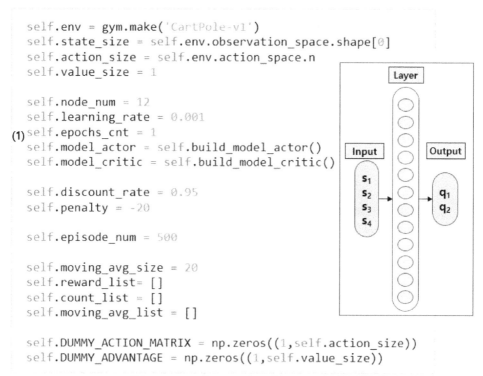

Agent Class Attributes in the A2C Algorithm

The Agent class attributes in the A2C algorithm are mostly similar to those in the REINFORCE algorithm. The main difference is that the A2C algorithm uses two class variables, model_actor and model_critic, to store the policy and value networks.

```
class MyModel(tf.keras.Model):
    def train_step(self, data):
        in_datas, out_action_probs = data
        states, action_matrixs, advantages = in_datas[0], in_datas[1], in_datas[2]
        with tf.GradientTape() as tape:
            y_pred = self(states, training=True)
            action_probs = K.max(action_matrixs*y_pred, axis=-1)
        (1) loss = -K.log(action_probs)*advantages   Cost Function
        trainable_vars = self.trainable_vari  loss = -K.log(action_probs)*rewards
        gradients = tape.gradient(loss, trainable_vars)
        self.optimizer.apply_gradients(zip(gradients, trainable_vars))
```

MyModel Class in cartpole_A2C

The MyModel class in the A2C algorithm is similar in functionality
and structure to the REINFORCE algorithm, but it differs in that it
uses advantages instead of rewards when calculating the cost
function. The advantage must be provided when creating the class
or training the model.

```
def build_model_actor(self): (1) Policy Neural Network Model
    input_states = Input(shape=(self.state_size), name='input_states')
    input_action_matrixs = Input(shape=(self.action_size), name='input_action_matrixs')
    input_advantages = Input(shape=(self.value_size), name='input_advantages')

    x = (input_states)
    x = Dense(self.node_num, activation='relu')(x)
    out_actions = Dense(self.action_size, activation='softmax', name='output')(x)

    model = self.MyModel(inputs=[input_states, input_action_matrixs, input_advantages],
                        outputs=out_actions)
    model.compile(optimizer=Adam(lr=self.learning_rate))

    model.summary()
    return model

def build_model_critic(self): (2) Value Neural Network Model
    input_states = Input(shape=(self.state_size), name='input_states')

    x = (input_states)
    x = Dense(self.node_num, activation='relu')(x)
    out_values = Dense(self.value_size, activation='linear', name='output')(x)

    model = tf.keras.models.Model(inputs=[input_states], outputs=[out_values])
            model.compile(optimizer=Adam(lr=self.learning_rate),
                loss='mean_squared_error'
                )
    model.summary()
    return model
```

build_model Function in cartpole_A2C

The build_model function in the A2C algorithm is implemented in two parts:

(1) build_model_actor: This function constructs the policy network with logic similar to the REINFORCE algorithm. It uses the MyModel class, which inherits from the Keras Model class to define a custom cost function, and applies the softmax activation function to express policies as probabilities.

(2) build_model_critic: This function constructs the value network following the logic of the DQN algorithm, using a linear activation function to express values.

```
def train(self):
    reward_list=[]
    count_list = []
    moving_avg_list = []
    for episode in range(self.episode_num):
        state = self.env.reset()
        self.env.max_episode_steps = 500
        count, reward_tot = self.make_memory(episode, state)

        if count < 500:
            reward_tot = reward_tot-self.penalty

        self.reward_list.append(reward_tot)
        self.count_list.append(count)
        self.moving_avg_list.append(self.moving_avg(self.count_list,self.moving_avg_size))

        if(episode % 10 == 0):
            print("episode:{}, moving_avg:{}, rewards avg:{}"
                .format(episode, self.moving_avg_list[-1], np.mean(self.reward_list)))
    self.save_model()
```

(1) Data Collection

(2) Model Training

```
self.train_mini_batch(state, state_next, reward, action_matrix, action_prob, done, count)
```

train Function in cartpole_A2C

In the A2C algorithm, data collection and training happen
sequentially rather than accumulating data for batch learning. The
make_memory function is called to collect data, and within it, the
train_mini_batch function is called to train the model. Since data is
not stored, the clear_memory function is not needed.

```python
def make_memory(self, episode, state):
    reward_tot = 0
    count = 0
    reward = np.zeros(self.value_size)
    action_matrix = np.zeros(self.action_size)
    done = False
    while not done:
        count+=1
(1)     state_t = np.reshape(state, [1,self.state_size])
        action_matrix_t = np.reshape(action_matrix, [1,self.action_size])

        action_prob = self.model_actor.predict([state_t, self.DUMMY_ACTION_MATRIX,
                                            self.DUMMY_ADVANTAGE])
        action = np.random.choice(self.action_size, 1, p=action_prob[0])[0]

        action_matrix = np.zeros(self.action_size)
        action_matrix[action] = 1
        state_next, reward, done, none = self.env.step(action)

        if count < 500 and done:
            reward = self.penalty

(2)     self.train_mini_batch(state, state_next, reward, action_matrix, action_prob,
                                done, count)

        state = state_next
        reward_tot += reward

    return count, reward_tot
```

make_memory Function in cartpole_A2C

The make_memory function is responsible for collecting experiences and training the model. Instead of accumulating experiences, it immediately uses the experiences gathered from running CartPole to train the model.

(1) Data Formatting for Training: Before using the experience for training, it must be formatted appropriately. Since the A2C algorithm uses only one dataset at a time, it reformats the data to [1, data_size] rather than the [1, 1, data_size] format used in the REINFORCE algorithm, which supports batch learning. In batch learning, large numbers of experiences are entered in the format [number_of_experiences, 1, data_size].

(2) Training the Model: The training itself is handled by the train_mini_batch function, which is called immediately after each

run of CartPole. Although the training logic could be included within the make_memory function, train_mini_batch is kept separate to maintain consistency with other algorithms and program structures.

```python
def train_mini_batch(self, state, state_next, reward, action_matrix, action_prob, done, count)

    state_t = np.reshape(state, [1, self.state_size])
    state_next_t = np.reshape(state_next, [1, self.state_size])
    reward_t = np.reshape(reward, [1, self.value_size])
    action_matrix_t = np.reshape(action_matrix, [1, self.action_size])
    action_prob_t = np.reshape(action_prob, [1, self.action_size])

    advantage_t = np.zeros((1, self.value_size))
    target_t = np.zeros((1, self.value_size))

    value_t = self.model_critic.predict(state_t)          (1) Value Prediction
    value_next_t = self.model_critic.predict(state_next_t)

    if(count< 500 and done):
        advantage_t = reward_t - value_t
        target_t = reward_t                               (2) advantage and target calculation
    else:
        advantage_t = reward_t + self.discount_rate*value_next_t - value_t
        target_t = reward_t + self.discount_rate * value_next_t

    self.model_actor.fit(x=[state_t, action_matrix_t, advantage_t], y=[action_prob_t],
                        epochs=self.epochs_cnt, verbose=0) (3) Model Training
    self.model_critic.fit(x=state_t, y=target_t, epochs=self.epochs_cnt, verbose=0)
```

train_mini_batch Function in cartpole_A2C

The train_mini_batch function trains the model based on experiences collected from running CartPole. The process is similar to REINFORCE, with the following differences for A2C:

(1) Calculating the Advantage: The value of the current state (Q function) and the next state Q function are obtained via the value network.

(2) The advantage is computed by taking the reward plus the discounted Q value of the next state and subtracting the Q value of the current state.

(3) Since two models are used in A2C, both models are trained simultaneously.

8.6 Analyzing A2C Algorithm Training Results

Running the A2C algorithm reveals a slower performance than

REINFORCE because A2C trains the neural network immediately after each experience rather than batching several experiences for learning.

Model: "my_model_3"

Layer (type)	Output Shape	Param #	Connected to
input_states (InputLayer)	[(None, 4)]	0	
dense_6 (Dense)	(None, 12)	60	input_states[0][0]
input_action_matrixs (InputLayer)	[(None, 2)]	0	
input_advantages (InputLayer)	[(None, 1)]	0	
output (Dense)	(None, 2)	26	dense_6[0][0]

Total params: 86
Trainable params: 86
Non-trainable params: 0

Model: "model_3"

Layer (type)	Output Shape	Param #
input_states (InputLayer)	[(None, 4)]	0
dense_7 (Dense)	(None, 12)	60
output (Dense)	(None, 1)	13

Total params: 73
Trainable params: 73
Non-trainable params: 0

---

episode:0, moving_avg:18.0, rewards_avg:17.0
episode:10, moving_avg:21.727272727272727, rewards_avg:20.727272727272727
episode:20, moving_avg:21.9, rewards_avg:20.714285714285715
episode:30, moving_avg:20.9, rewards_avg:20.193548387096776
episode:40, moving_avg:18.75, rewards_avg:19.26829268292683
episode:50, moving_avg:19.95, rewards_avg:19.705882352941178
episode:60, moving_avg:21.75, rewards_avg:19.75409836065574
episode:70, moving_avg:22.45, rewards_avg:20.197183098591548
episode:80, moving_avg:26.25, rewards_avg:21.11111111111111
episode:90, moving_avg:29.5, rewards_avg:22.021978021978022
episode:100, moving_avg:31.05, rewards_avg:22.88118811881188
episode:110, moving_avg:23.65, rewards_avg:22.135135135135137
episode:120, moving_avg:17.9, rewards_avg:21.892561983471076
episode:130, moving_avg:20.3, rewards_avg:21.702290076335878
episode:140, moving_avg:25.25, rewards_avg:22.22695035460993
episode:150, moving_avg:32.25, rewards_avg:22.966887417218544

```
episode:160, moving_avg:30.4, rewards_avg:23.11801242236025
episode:170, moving_avg:32.2, rewards_avg:23.92982456140351
episode:180, moving_avg:39.65, rewards_avg:24.834254143646408
episode:190, moving_avg:38.55, rewards_avg:25.356020942408378
episode:200, moving_avg:47.2, rewards_avg:26.960199004975124
episode:210, moving_avg:52.0, rewards_avg:27.786729857819907
episode:220, moving_avg:48.6, rewards_avg:28.828054298642535
episode:230, moving_avg:47.5, rewards_avg:29.406926406926406
episode:240, moving_avg:46.75, rewards_avg:30.232365145228215
episode:250, moving_avg:52.5, rewards_avg:31.16733067729084
episode:260, moving_avg:49.95, rewards_avg:31.666666666666668
episode:270, moving_avg:51.3, rewards_avg:32.579335793357934
episode:280, moving_avg:58.0, rewards_avg:33.469750889679716
episode:290, moving_avg:88.0, rewards_avg:36.31958762886598
episode:300, moving_avg:129.7, rewards_avg:39.79734219269103
episode:310, moving_avg:205.85, rewards_avg:47.157556270096464
episode:320, moving_avg:278.5, rewards_avg:54.610591900311526
episode:330, moving_avg:222.55, rewards_avg:57.69788519637462
episode:340, moving_avg:197.05, rewards_avg:62.91202346041056
episode:350, moving_avg:243.1, rewards_avg:68.21367521367522
episode:360, moving_avg:222.85, rewards_avg:71.7202216066482
episode:370, moving_avg:176.7, rewards_avg:74.00808625336927
episode:380, moving_avg:207.6, rewards_avg:78.8005249343832
episode:390, moving_avg:233.1, rewards_avg:82.09462915601023
episode:400, moving_avg:164.15, rewards_avg:83.0074812967581
episode:410, moving_avg:75.3, rewards_avg:81.71532846715328
episode:420, moving_avg:27.2, rewards_avg:80.30878859857482
episode:430, moving_avg:29.15, rewards_avg:79.22969837587007
episode:440, moving_avg:164.45, rewards_avg:84.08843537414965
episode:450, moving_avg:397.05, rewards_avg:93.31042128603104
episode:460, moving_avg:500.0, rewards_avg:102.13232104121475
episode:470, moving_avg:381.8, rewards_avg:105.54352441613588
episode:480, moving_avg:192.9, rewards_avg:105.86902286902287
episode:490, moving_avg:131.4, rewards_avg:106.55600814663951
INFO:tensorflow:Assets written to: ./model/a2c\assets
*****end a2c learing
```

Execution Results of cartpole_A2C

Like REINFORCE, the A2C algorithm's results vary due to randomization in model initialization and various random functions in the algorithm. If performance is not optimal, try running the example multiple times.

Although training takes longer than REINFORCE, A2C generally demonstrates better performance. Batch-style training is possible for A2C, which can be easily implemented using GAE from the PPO algorithm, allowing for a batch A2C algorithm.

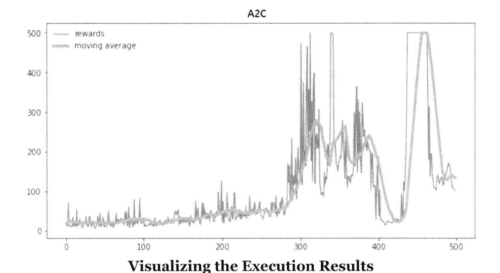

Visualizing the Execution Results

When visualized, the A2C algorithm exhibits improved performance over the REINFORCE algorithm but shows instability in learning. While it combines the low variance of REINFORCE and low bias of the DQN algorithm, it still suffers from occasional sharp drops in performance, posing a risk of training failure.

Next, we will explore the PPO algorithm, which was developed to address these instabilities with a simple yet effective solution.

Chapter 9

Policy-Based Reinforcement Learning: PPO Algorithm

9. Policy-Based PPO Algorithm

The PPO (Proximal Policy Optimization) algorithm is a reinforcement learning algorithm that improves upon the A2C algorithm (or more precisely, the TRPO algorithm) by using importance sampling and clipping techniques. Typically, the TRPO (Trust Region Policy Optimization) algorithm is introduced before PPO, but TRPO is a complex algorithm that employs various theories, making it difficult to understand. Since PPO generally outperforms TRPO in terms of performance, this book will directly introduce PPO without covering TRPO.

9.1 Importance Sampling

Before diving into the PPO algorithm, let's revisit importance sampling, which was discussed earlier. Importance sampling is used to estimate the expected value of a function f(x) under a probability distribution p(x), especially when it's challenging to generate samples from p(x). In this case, samples are instead drawn from an easier-to-sample probability distribution q(x), and these samples are used to estimate the expected value of f(x) under p(x).

$$E_{X \sim P}[f(X)] = \sum P(X)\, f(X)$$
$$= \sum Q(X)\, \left[\, \frac{P(X)}{Q(X)}\, f(X)\, \right]$$
$$= E_{X \sim Q}\left[\, \frac{P(X)}{Q(X)}\, f(X)\, \right]$$

P(X)	Probability distribution P of variable x in a certain environment
Q(X)	Probability distribution Q of variable x in another environment
f(X)	Function of x; any function is possible (e.g., sin, cos, $2x+3$, etc.)
$E_{X \sim P}[f(X)]$	Expected value when applying function f to variable X following probability distribution P
$\sum P(X)f(X)$	Expected value of function $f(X)$ of variable X under probability distribution P

Importance Sampling

In importance sampling, P and Q represent probability distributions from different environments. Since a policy can also be viewed as a probability distribution (easily understood by looking at the softmax function), it's helpful to think of P and Q as different policies used by the agent. To calculate the expected value in an environment with probability distribution Q using samples X collected from an environment with probability distribution P, we simply multiply by the ratio of the two probability distributions.

$$E_{X \sim \pi_\theta}[f(X)] = \sum \pi_\theta\, f(X)$$

$$= \sum \pi_{\theta old}\left[\, \frac{\pi_\theta}{\pi_{\theta old}}\, f(X)\, \right]$$

$$= E_{X \sim \pi_{\theta old}}\left[\, \frac{\pi_\theta}{\pi_{\theta old}}\, f(X)\, \right]$$

Application of Importance Sampling

In reinforcement learning, to calculate the expected value in an environment with policy $\pi\theta$ using data X collected under a different policy $\pi\theta$ old, we simply multiply by the ratio of the two policies within the formula for the expected value under $\pi\theta$.

Now, let's look at why the concept of importance sampling is necessary in PPO. In the A2C algorithm, the same policy is used both for gathering experiences and for updating the policy, which is generally known as on-policy learning. Normally, it seems intuitive to gather experiences with one policy and then improve upon that same policy. However, this approach has a downside: experiences gathered under the previous version of the policy must be discarded once the policy is updated, as the old experiences become less relevant to the new policy. This on-policy approach is inherently less efficient for learning.

A more efficient learning method is to reuse experiences and allow a single policy to gather a larger amount of experiences, which are then used to update the neural network. In this case, the gathering policy and the training policy differ, making standard learning problematic. Since the policy changes with each mini-batch update of the neural network, the new policy quickly diverges from the policy used to gather experiences.

This is where importance sampling becomes crucial. Through importance sampling, we can bridge the gap between the policy used to gather experiences and the updated policy, allowing us to reuse experiences effectively. Since importance sampling is a mathematically proven concept, it's more practical to focus on applying it rather than diving deeply into its underlying theory.

9.2 Off-Policy Policy Gradient

| Policy Gradient | $\nabla_\theta J(\theta) = E_{\pi\theta}[\nabla_\theta log\pi_\theta(a|s)\, R_s^a]$ | ① |

$$\doteq E_{\pi\theta}[\nabla_\theta log\pi_\theta(a|s)\, A_s^a] \qquad ②$$

| Chain rule | $= E_{\pi\theta}[\dfrac{\nabla_\theta\pi_\theta(a|s)}{\pi_\theta(a|s)}\, A_s^a]$ | ③ |

$y = \log f(x)$

$y' = \dfrac{f(x)'}{f(x)}$

$$= E_{\pi\theta old}[\dfrac{\pi_\theta(a|s)}{\pi_{\theta old}(a|s)}\, \dfrac{\nabla_\theta\pi_\theta(a|s)}{\pi_\theta(a|s)}\, A_s^a] \qquad ④$$

$$= E_{\pi\theta old}[\dfrac{\nabla_\theta\pi_\theta(a|s)}{\pi_{\theta old}(a|s)}\, A_s^a] \qquad ⑤$$

$$= E_{\pi\theta old}[\nabla_\theta(\dfrac{\pi_\theta(a|s)}{\pi_{\theta old}(a|s)}\, A_s^a)] \qquad ⑥$$

| Cost Function | $= -\dfrac{\pi_\theta(a|s)}{\pi_{\theta old}(a|s)}\, A_s^a$ | ⑦ |

Transitioning to Off-Policy

Equation ① represents the policy gradient we've explored so far.

Let's examine how to modify it for off-policy learning. Equation ②

introduces advantage to control data variance. Equation ③
reformulates the gradient using the chain rule to simplify
calculation. Since the chain rule is a well-established mathematical
theory, we'll apply it directly without further explanation.

In Equation ④, we introduce importance sampling to combine two
unrelated probability distributions. Here, $\pi\theta$ is the target policy we
want to improve, while $\pi\theta$ old is the behavior policy used to gather
experiences. Using importance sampling, we multiply by the ratio of
the two policies. The numerator $\pi\theta$ cancels out with the
denominator $\pi\theta$ old in the policy gradient, leaving only one instance

of each policy. This leads us to Equation ⑤. In Equation ⑥, we
bring the gradient symbol to the front, grouping the policy ratio and
advantage within parentheses.

Finally, we obtain a cost function in Equation ⑦ that enables us to update the policy network using gradient descent.

9.3 Clipping Technique

Now, let's explore clipping, a core concept in the PPO algorithm. The term "clipping" might initially sound complex, but it's actually quite simple. Rather than a complex mathematical theory, clipping is more of a straightforward idea.

http://www.iautocar.co.kr
Problems with High Learning Speed

Imagine a car navigating a curve. If the car is moving at high speed, as in scenario ①, even if the driver turns the wheel to change direction, the car might go off the edge due to its momentum.

However, if the car slows down slightly, as in scenario ②, it can safely navigate the curve with minimal risk. In reinforcement learning, if learning occurs too quickly, similar to scenario ①, it can result in reduced learning efficiency and may even cause the episode to end before reaching its goal. Controlling the rate of change, as in scenario ②, allows for improved learning efficiency.

In PPO, the clipping technique is used to control the learning speed effectively.

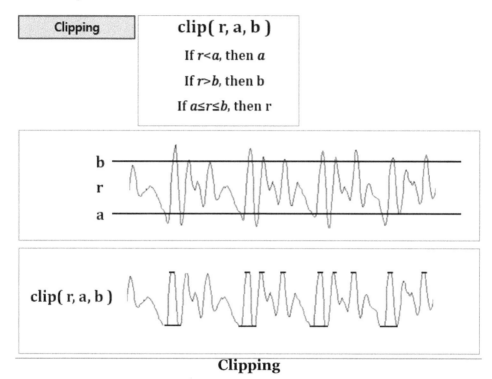

Clipping

Clipping is a technique that sets lower (a) and upper (b) bounds on data, ensuring input values remain within a specific range. In the formula clip(r, a, b),

r

r is the input value,

a

a is the lower bound, and

b

b is the upper bound. If

r

r is less than

a

a, the output is

a

a; if

r

r is greater than

b

b, the output is

b

b.

When input data with a consistent waveform is provided, values exceeding the upper bound

b

b and lower bound

a

a are replaced by

b

b and

a

a, respectively. Only the data within the bounds is output as is.

$$r(\theta) = \frac{\pi_\theta(a|s)}{\pi_{\theta old}(a|s)} \qquad ①$$

Cost Function $\quad \min(\ r_t(\theta)\ A_t,\ clip(r_t(\theta), 1 - \varepsilon, 1 + \varepsilon)\ A_t\ ) \qquad ②$

②-1   ②-2

Original Loss   **Clipped Loss**

Cost Function Using Clipping

First, we replace the ratio of the policy used for data collection to the updated policy with the variable r(θ) in Equation ①. Now, the cost function we used previously can be modified to Equation ②-1. In the new cost function, the smaller value between ②-1 and ②-2 is selected for updating the neural network. Equation ②-2 is a clipping function where ☐ defines the upper and lower bounds of the clipping. Choosing an appropriate ☐ value is crucial for efficient learning in reinforcement learning.

9.4 Generalized Advantage Estimation (GAE)

GAE, or Generalized Advantage Estimation, is an advanced concept derived from the advantage discussed in Chapter 8. In A2C, the agent is executed for a single timestep to gather experiences and train the neural network. However, in PPO, the agent runs for multiple timesteps, and the accumulated experiences are learned in batches. During this process, the advantage is also used, with each timestep's data discounted by a depreciation rate to compute a discounted advantage.

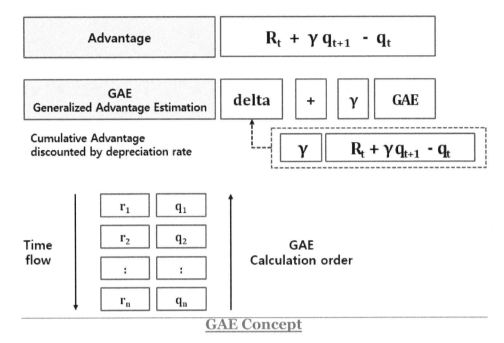

GAE Concept

In short, GAE (Generalized Advantage Estimation) is the cumulative advantage discounted by a discount rate. When an agent gains experience, it logs the rewards (r) and Q values (q) sequentially over time, which are later used to calculate the advantage. The reward obtained at the initial execution (t=1) and the reward just before the end of the episode (t=n) are valued differently due to the application of a discount factor (γ). For example, if an episode runs for five time steps, the reward gained at the end will be discounted four times by the factor.

Since advantage calculations also rely on rewards and Q values, both need to be discounted at each time step. Consequently, the final reward and Q value, which should carry the most significant discount factor, are calculated first in the GAE calculation process.

9.5 Basic Structure of the PPO Algorithm

The basic structure of the PPO (Proximal Policy Optimization) algorithm is very similar to that of the A2C (Advantage Actor-Critic) algorithm. The main differences are in the cost function composition of the policy neural network and the use of GAE to enable batch training of the neural network.

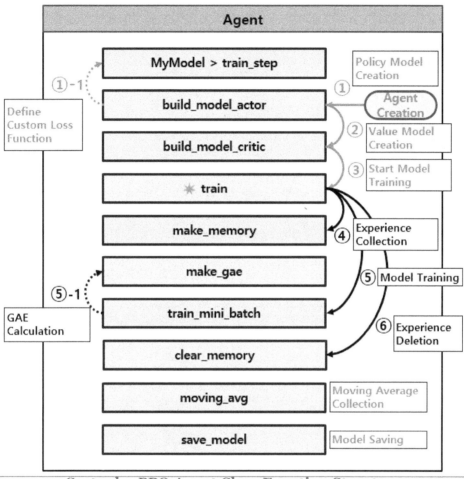

Cartpole_PPO Agent Class Function Structure

The Agent class in the PPO algorithm consists of 10 functions. Most of these functions have similar roles and functionalities as in the A2C algorithm, with only slight differences in how experiences are collected and how the model is trained.

(4) Unlike the REINFORCE algorithm, which continuously collects experience throughout an episode, the PPO algorithm collects experience over a fixed number of time steps. The number of time steps for collecting experience is chosen by the user, and finding an optimal value is crucial as it impacts algorithm performance.

(5) Once experience has been collected, model training begins. Before starting training, it is essential to calculate the GAE (Generalized Advantage Estimation). Using the make_gae function (5-1), the agent calculates and uses the Advantage and Target values.

(6) After training completes, the stored experiences are deleted, preparing the agent to collect new experiences.

Now that we've reviewed the basic structure of the algorithm, let's delve into the code to better understand the PPO algorithm, focusing particularly on the K.clip function in MyModel and the make_gae function within the Agent class.

9.6 PPO Algorithm Full Code Review

In this section, we'll go through the code for the PPO algorithm, focusing on the K.clip function used within the MyModel class and the make_gae function within the Agent class.

```python
import tensorflow as tf
import tensorflow.keras.backend as K
from tensorflow.keras.layers import Input, Dense, Flatten
from tensorflow.keras.optimizers import Adam
import gym
import numpy as np
import random as rand
LOSS_CLIPPING = 0.1
class Agent(object):
    def __init__(self):

        self.env = gym.make('CartPole-v1')
        self.state_size = self.env.observation_space.shape[0]
        self.action_size = self.env.action_space.n
        self.value_size = 1

        self.node_num = 24
        self.learning_rate_actor = 0.0005
        self.learning_rate_critic = 0.0005
        self.epochs_cnt = 5
        self.model_actor = self.build_model_actor()
```

```python
        self.model_critic = self.build_model_critic()

        self.discount_rate = 0.98
        self.smooth_rate = 0.95
        self.penalty = -400

        self.episode_num = 500
        self.mini_batch_step_size = 32

        self.moving_avg_size = 20
        self.reward_list= []
        self.count_list = []
        self.moving_avg_list = []

        self.states, self.states_next, self.action_matrixs = [],[],[]
        self.dones, self.action_probs, self.rewards = [],[],[]
        self.DUMMY_ACTION_MATRIX = np.zeros((1,1,self.action_size))
        self.DUMMY_ADVANTAGE = np.zeros((1,1,self.value_size))

    class MyModel(tf.keras.Model):
        def train_step(self, data):
            in_datas, out_action_probs = data
            states, action_matrixs, advantages = in_datas[0], in_datas[1],
                                        in_datas[2]
            with tf.GradientTape() as tape:
                y_pred = self(states, training=True)
                new_policy = K.max(action_matrixs*y_pred, axis=-1)
                old_policy = K.max(action_matrixs*out_action_probs, axis=-1)
                r = new_policy/(old_policy)
                clipped = K.clip(r, 1-LOSS_CLIPPING, 1+LOSS_CLIPPING)
                loss = -K.minimum(r*advantages, clipped*advantages)

            trainable_vars = self.trainable_variables
            gradients = tape.gradient(loss, trainable_vars)
            self.optimizer.apply_gradients(zip(gradients, trainable_vars))

    def build_model_actor(self):
        input_states = Input(shape=(1,self.state_size), name='input_states')
        input_action_matrixs = Input(shape=(1,self.action_size),
                                name='input_action_matrixs')
        input_advantages = Input(shape=(1,self.value_size),
```

```python
                              name='input_advantages')
        x = (input_states)
        x = Dense(self.node_num, activation='relu')(x)
        out_actions = Dense(self.action_size, activation='softmax',
                              name='output')(x)

        model = self.MyModel(inputs=[input_states, input_action_matrixs,
                                input_advantages], outputs=out_actions)
        model.compile(optimizer=Adam(lr=self.learning_rate_actor))

        model.summary()
        return model

    def build_model_critic(self):
        input_states = Input(shape=(1,self.state_size), name='input_states')
        x = (input_states)
        x = Dense(self.node_num, activation='relu')(x)
        out_values = Dense(self.value_size, activation='linear', name='output')(x)

        model = tf.keras.models.Model(inputs=[input_states],
                                outputs=[out_values])
        model.compile(optimizer=Adam(lr=self.learning_rate_critic),
                        loss='mean_squared_error'
                        )
        model.summary()
        return model

    def train(self):
        for episode in range(self.episode_num):
            state = self.env.reset()
            self.env.max_episode_steps = 500
            count, reward_tot = self.make_memory(episode, state)
            self.train_mini_batch()
            self.clear_memory()

            if count < 500:
                reward_tot = reward_tot-self.penalty

            self.reward_list.append(reward_tot)
            self.count_list.append(count)
```

```python
        self.moving_avg_list.append(self.moving_avg(self.count_list,self.moving_av
        g_size))

        if(episode % 10 == 0):
            print("episode:{}, moving_avg:{}, rewards_avg:{}"
                        .format(episode, self.moving_avg_list[-1],
                            np.mean(self.reward_list)))
        self.save_model()

    def make_memory(self, episode, state):
        reward_tot = 0
        count = 0
        reward = np.zeros(self.value_size)
        advantage = np.zeros(self.value_size)
        target = np.zeros(self.value_size)
        action_matrix = np.zeros(self.action_size)
        done = False

        while not done:
            count+ =1
            state_t = np.reshape(state,[1, 1, self.state_size])
            action_matrix_t = np.reshape(action_matrix,[1, 1, self.action_size])

            action_prob = self.model_actor.predict([state_t,
                            self.DUMMY_ACTION_MATRIX,
                            self.DUMMY_ADVANTAGE])
            action = np.random.choice(self.action_size, 1, p=action_prob[0][0])[0]
            action_matrix = np.zeros(self.action_size) #초기화
            action_matrix[action] = 1
            state_next, reward, done, none = self.env.step(action)

            state_next_t = np.reshape(state_next,[1, 1, self.state_size])

            if count < 500 and done:
                reward = self.penalty

            self.states.append(np.reshape(state_t, [1,self.state_size]))
            self.states_next.append(np.reshape(state_next_t, [1,self.state_size]))
            self.action_matrixs.append(np.reshape(action_matrix,
                                [1,self.action_size]))
            self.dones.append(np.reshape(0 if done else 1, [1,self.value_size]))
```

195

```python
            self.action_probs.append(np.reshape(action_prob, [1,self.action_size]))
            self.rewards.append(np.reshape(reward, [1,self.value_size]))

            if(count % self.mini_batch_step_size == 0):
                self.train_mini_batch()
                self.clear_memory()
            reward_tot += reward
            state = state_next

        return count, reward_tot

    def make_gae(self, values, values_next, rewards, dones):
        delta_adv, delta_tar, adv, target = 0, 0, 0, 0
        advantages = np.zeros(np.array(values).shape)
        targets = np.zeros(np.array(values).shape)
        for t in reversed(range(0, len(rewards))):
            delta_adv = rewards[t] + self.discount_rate * values_next[t] * dones[t]
                            - values[t]
            delta_tar = rewards[t] + self.discount_rate * values_next[t] * dones[t]
            adv = delta_adv + self.smooth_rate*self.discount_rate * dones[t] * adv
            target = delta_tar + self.smooth_rate*self.discount_rate * dones[t] *
                    target
            advantages[t] = adv
            targets[t] = target
        return advantages, targets

    def train_mini_batch(self):

        if len(self.states) == 0:
            return

        states_t = np.array(self.states)
        states_next_t = np.array(self.states_next)
        action_matrixs_t = np.array(self.action_matrixs)
        action_probs_t = np.array(self.action_probs)
        rewards_t = np.array(self.rewards)
        values = self.model_critic.predict(states_t)
        values_next = self.model_critic.predict(states_next_t)

        advantages, targets = self.make_gae(values, values_next, self.rewards,
                        self.dones)
```

```
        advantages_t = np.array(advantages)
        targets_t = np.array(targets)

        self.model_actor.fit([states_t, action_matrixs_t, advantages_t],
                        [action_probs_t], epochs=self.epochs_cnt,
                        verbose=0)
        self.model_critic.fit(states_t, targets_t, epochs=self.epochs_cnt, verbose=0)

    def clear_memory(self):
        self.states, self.states_next, self.action_matrixs = [],[],[]
        self.dones, self.action_probs, self.rewards = [],[],[]

    def moving_avg(self, data, size=10):
        if len(data) > size:
            c = np.array(data[len(data)-size:len(data)])
        else:
            c = np.array(data)
        return np.mean(c)

    def save_model(self):
        self.model_actor.save("./model/ppo")
        print("*****end learing")

if __name__ == "__main__":
    agent = Agent()
    agent.train()
```

CartPole_PPO.py

When comparing the code for the A2C and PPO algorithms, the improvements may not seem extensive at first glance. However, running both algorithms and examining the results clearly shows a significant performance boost with PPO. Currently, PPO is a prominent algorithm widely applied across various fields. It's no exaggeration to say that the various algorithms studied up to this point serve as foundational steps toward understanding PPO.

9.7 Examining the Detailed Structure of the PPO Algorithm

```
   self.env = gym.make('CartPole-v1')
   self.state_size = self.env.observation_space.shape[0]
   self.action_size = self.env.action_space.n
   self.value_size = 1

   self.node_num = 24
   self.learning_rate_actor = 0.0005
   self.learning_rate_critic = 0.0005
(1) self.epochs_cnt = 5
   self.model_actor = self.build_model_ac
   self.model_critic = self.build_model_c

   self.discount_rate = 0.98
(2) self.smooth_rate = 0.95
   self.penalty = -400

   self.episode_num = 500
   self.mini_batch_step_size = 32

   self.moving_avg_size = 20
   self.reward_list= []
   self.count_list = []
   self.moving_avg_list = []

   self.states, self.states_next, self.action_matrixs = [],[],[]
   self.dones, self.action_probs, self.rewards = [],[],[]
   self.DUMMY_ACTION_MATRIX = np.zeros((1,1,self.action_size))
   self.DUMMY_ADVANTAGE = np.zeros((1,1,self.value_size))
```

Attributes of the Cartpole_PPO Agent Class

In the PPO algorithm, the attributes of the Agent class are largely similar to those in the A2C algorithm.

(1) Learning Rate (learning_rate_actor and learning_rate_critic):

Unlike A2C, PPO separates the learning rates for the policy network and the value network, using learning_rate_actor and learning_rate_critic respectively. This distinction is necessary because each network has a unique role and handles different data, requiring a learning rate tailored to its specific function. In this example, both rates are set to the same value of 0.0005, but model tuning will involve finding the optimal values for each.

(2) Smooth Rate (smooth_rate): The PPO algorithm introduces a smooth_rate attribute in the training settings. This attribute, typically set to a value less than 1, helps reduce the variance that may occur when discounting future rewards. By smoothing out the reward signal, it aids in stabilizing the training process.

These adjustments to the attributes enable the PPO algorithm to refine its learning dynamics, making it more adaptive and stable in various environments.

```
LOSS_CLIPPING = 0.1     (1)
class MyModel(tf.keras.Model):
    def train_step(self, data):

      in_datas, out_action_probs = data
      states, action_matrixs, advantages = in_datas[0], in_datas[1], in_datas[2]

      with tf.GradientTape() as tape:
        y_pred = self(states, training=True)
 (2)    new_policy = K.max(action_matrixs*y_pred, axis=-1)
        old_policy = K.max(action_matrixs*out_action_probs, axis=-1)
 (3)    r = new_policy/(old_policy)
 (4)    clipped = K.clip(r, 1-LOSS_CLIPPING, 1+LOSS_CLIPPING)
 (5)    loss = -K.minimum(r*advantages, clipped*advantages)

      trainable_vars = self.trainable_variables
      gradients = tape.gradient(loss, trainable_vars)
      self.optimizer.apply_gradients(zip(gradients, trainable_vars))
```

Cartpole_PPO: MyModel Class

The user-defined MyModel class inherits from Keras's Model class. Thus, all variables within MyModel operate as tensors, making it challenging to apply regular variables within the class.

(1) LOSS_CLIPPING Variable: The LOSS_CLIPPING variable, which specifies the clipping range, is defined as a global variable outside the Agent class. This allows it to be accessed from any part of the program, ensuring consistent use of the clipping range.

(2) Calculating New Policy Probabilities: The model needs to calculate the probabilities for the new policy. The selected action is provided through the action_matrix input. If the first action is chosen, [1, 0] is inputted; if the second action is chosen, [0, 1] is used. Multiplying this input by the model-predicted probabilities for each action (e.g., [0.7, 0.3]) isolates the probability for the chosen action. For example, selecting the first action ([1, 0]) with action probabilities [0.7, 0.3] results in [0.7, 0], and taking the max value yields 0.7.

(3) Calculating Importance Sampling Ratio: After calculating the probabilities for the past policy, the ratio between the new and old probabilities is computed for importance sampling. This ratio helps ensure that updates respect the likelihood of actions under both the new and old policies.

(4) Using the CLIPPING_LOSS Variable: The CLIPPING_LOSS variable is used to compute the value of the clipping function, which constrains the updates within a specified range to stabilize training.

(5) Cost Function: Finally, the cost function is determined by taking the smaller value between (a) the product of the policy ratio and the advantage and (b) the product of the clipped result and the advantage. This approach helps prevent overly large updates to the policy, enhancing stability.

This series of steps in MyModel ensures efficient policy updates while maintaining stability, making it well-suited for reinforcement learning tasks.

```
def train(self):
  for episode in range(self.episode_num):
    state = self.env.reset()
    self.env.max_episode_steps = 500
    count, reward_tot = self.make_memory(episode, state)
    self.train_mini_batch()
    self.clear_memory()

    if count < 500:
        reward_tot = reward_tot-self.penalty

    self.reward_list.append(reward_tot)
    self.count_list.append(count)
    self.moving_avg_list.append(self.moving_avg(self.count_list,self.moving_avg_size))

    if(episode % 10 == 0):
        print("episode:{}, moving_avg:{}, rewards_avg:{}"
        .format(episode, self.moving_avg_list[-1], np.mean(self.reward_list)))
  self.save_model()
```

(1) Setting Maximum Execution Steps
(2) Experience Collection
(3) Model Training

Cartpole_PPO: train Function

In the Cartpole_PPO algorithm, the build_model_actor and build_model_critic functions are identical in structure and functionality to those in the A2C algorithm. The train function is responsible for collecting experiences and training the model.

(1) Setting the Maximum Execution Steps: First, the maximum number of steps for the Cartpole environment is specified. By setting a specific value in the max_episode_steps attribute, the cartpole simulation will terminate after reaching that limit, even if the pole hasn't fallen. The program will then return True for game termination.

(2) Experience Collection with make_memory: The make_memory function collects experiences until the game ends, storing them in the class variables states, states_next, action_matrixs, dones, action_probs, and rewards. Once the collected experiences reach the size specified in the mini_batch_step_size variable, the train_mini_batch function is called to train the model. After training, all collected experiences are cleared.

(3) Final Training with train_mini_batch: After make_memory completes, train_mini_batch is called one final time to process any remaining data that didn't fill a complete mini-batch. This ensures that all collected experiences are used for training, with the remaining data trained as a final batch.

The train function thus handles the full experience collection and model training cycle, optimizing the PPO algorithm by training at specified intervals and utilizing all gathered data effectively.

```
def make_memory(self, episode, state):
  reward_tot = 0
  count = 0
  reward = np.zeros(self.value_size)
  advantage = np.zeros(self.value_size)
  target = np.zeros(self.value_size)
  action_matrix = np.zeros(self.action_size)
  done = False

  while not done:
    count+=1
    state_t = np.reshape(state,[1, 1, self.state_size])
    action_matrix_t = np.reshape(action_matrix,[1, 1, self.action_size])

    action_prob = self.model_actor.predict([state_t, self.DUMMY_ACTION_MATRIX,
                                            self.DUMMY_ADVANTAGE])
    action = np.random.choice(self.action_size, 1, p=action_prob[0][0])[0]
    action_matrix = np.zeros(self.action_size) #초기화
    action_matrix[action] = 1
    state_next, reward, done, none = self.env.step(action)

    state_next_t = np.reshape(state_next,[1, 1, self.state_size])

    if count < 500 and done:
      reward = self.penalty

    self.states.append(np.reshape(state_t, [1,self.state_size]))
    self.states_next.append(np.reshape(state_next_t, [1,self.state_size]))
    self.action_matrixs.append(np.reshape(action_matrix, [1,self.action_size]))
(1) self.dones.append(np.reshape(0 if done else 1, [1,self.value_size]))
    self.action_probs.append(np.reshape(action_prob, [1,self.action_size]))
    self.rewards.append(np.reshape(reward, [1,self.value_size]))

    if(count % self.mini_batch_step_size == 0):
      self.train_mini_batch()
(2)   self.clear_memory()
    reward_tot += reward
    state = state_next

  return count, reward_tot
```

Cartpole_PPO: make_memory Function

The make_memory function in the PPO algorithm is responsible for gathering experiences and periodically training the model. It performs actions like predicting behavior, selecting actions, generating matrices, and storing experiences, similar to the REINFORCE algorithm. Here, we'll focus on the features unique to

PPO.

(1) Setting the dones Variable: The dones variable is set to either 0 or 1 to indicate whether the game has ended. Although the original done variable holds True/False values, it must be processed as 0/1 to be used in the make_gae function. If the game has ended, it is set to 0; otherwise, it is set to 1.

(2) Calling train_mini_batch Periodically: Based on the frequency set in the mini_batch_step_size attribute of the Agent class, the train_mini_batch function is called to train the model, after which the data is cleared.

The make_memory function thus manages the collection and processing of experiences in batches, ensuring that the PPO algorithm can train periodically without overloading the memory with unnecessary data.

```
def make_gae(self, values, values_next, rewards, dones):
    delta_adv, delta_tar, adv, target = 0, 0, 0, 0
    advantages = np.zeros(np.array(values).shape)
    targets = np.zeros(np.array(values).shape)

(1) for t in reversed(range(0, len(rewards))):
(2)     delta_adv = rewards[t] + self.discount_rate * values_next[t] * dones[t] - values[t]
(3)     delta_tar = rewards[t] + self.discount_rate * values_next[t] * dones[t]
(4)     adv = delta_adv + self.smooth_rate*self.discount_rate * dones[t] * adv
(5)     target = delta_tar + self.smooth_rate*self.discount_rate * dones[t] * target

        advantages[t] = adv
        targets[t] = target

    return advantages, targets
```

Cartpole_PPO: make_gae Function

The make_gae function calculates the discounted advantages and targets, using a method similar to that for computing discounted returns in the REINFORCE algorithm.

(1) Reversing through Rewards: The function first iterates backward through the array of stored rewards, taking the last index (the reward from the final time step) and moving backward. From the

agent's perspective, the last reward should be the most heavily discounted. The calculation involves repeatedly applying the discount factor, making the first calculated value carry the most discount.

(2) Calculating Advantage for Each Time Step: The advantage for each time step is calculated by taking the current reward, adding the discounted predicted value of the next time step, and then subtracting the predicted value of the current time step.

(3) Calculating Target for Each Time Step: The target is calculated by taking the current reward and adding the discounted predicted value of the next time step.

(4) Applying Additional Discounts to the Advantage: When calculating the discounted advantage, the previous time step's advantage is multiplied by the discount_rate and the smooth_rate to reduce variance. If the game has ended (indicated by done set to 0), the calculation excludes any future values, as there's no next step. In this case, the advantage is simply the reward minus the predicted value.

(5) Calculating Discounted Target: The discounted target is computed similarly to the discounted advantage, applying both the discount factor and smooth rate where relevant.

The make_gae function thus refines the advantage and target calculations with careful discounting, leveraging both the discount_rate and smooth_rate to stabilize training and improve learning efficiency.

```
def train_mini_batch(self):

    if len(self.states) == 0:
      return

    states_t = np.array(self.states)
    states_next_t = np.array(self.states_next)
    action_matrixs_t = np.array(self.action_matrixs)
    action_probs_t = np.array(self.action_probs)
    rewards_t = np.array(self.rewards)

    values = self.model_critic.predict(states_t)
(1)
    values_next = self.model_critic.predict(states_next_t)

(2) advantages, targets = self.make_gae(values, values_next, self.rewards, self.dones)
    advantages_t = np.array(advantages)
    targets_t = np.array(targets)
    self.model_actor.fit([states_t, action_matrixs_t, advantages_t],
                  [action_probs_t], epochs=self.epochs_cnt, verbose=0)
    self.model_critic.fit(states_t, targets_t, epochs=self.epochs_cnt, verbose=0)
```

Cartpole_PPO: train_mini_batch Function

The train_mini_batch function trains the model based on the experiences collected by the make_memory function.

(1) Predicting Values for GAE Calculation: To compute Generalized Advantage Estimation (GAE), the function first predicts the value of the current state. Then, it predicts the value for the next state, providing both values required for calculating the advantage and target.

(2) Calculating Advantage and Target with make_gae: Using the make_gae function, the function computes the advantage and target values. These values are then converted into NumPy arrays for use in model predictions and updates.

9.8 Analyzing PPO Algorithm Training Results

After training with the PPO algorithm, the results show significant performance improvements compared to REINFORCE and A2C.

When applied to more complex environments beyond the simple Cartpole scenario, the performance difference of the PPO algorithm becomes even more pronounced, demonstrating its robustness and adaptability to challenging tasks.

Model: "my_model_39"

Layer (type)	Output Shape	Param #	Connected to
input_states (InputLayer)	[(None, 1, 4)]	0	
dense_78 (Dense)	(None, 1, 24)	120	input_states[0][0]
input_action_matrixs (InputLaye	[(None, 1, 2)]	0	
input_advantages (InputLayer)	[(None, 1, 1)]	0	
output (Dense)	(None, 1, 2)	50	dense_78[0][0]

Total params: 170
Trainable params: 170
Non-trainable params: 0

Model: "model_39"

Layer (type)	Output Shape	Param #
input_states (InputLayer)	[(None, 1, 4)]	0
dense_79 (Dense)	(None, 1, 24)	120
output (Dense)	(None, 1, 1)	25

Total params: 145
Trainable params: 145
Non-trainable params: 0

episode:0, moving_avg:24.0, rewards_avg:23.0
episode:10, moving_avg:20.545454545454547,
rewards_avg:19.545454545454547
episode:20, moving_avg:20.05, rewards_avg:19.238095238095237
episode:30, moving_avg:22.25, rewards_avg:20.64516129032258
episode:40, moving_avg:23.3, rewards_avg:20.73170731707317
episode:50, moving_avg:21.5, rewards_avg:20.588235294411765
episode:60, moving_avg:25.05, rewards_avg:21.81967213114754
episode:70, moving_avg:24.05, rewards_avg:21.281690140845072
episode:80, moving_avg:27.4, rewards_avg:22.950617283950617

```
episode:90, moving_avg:32.1, rewards_avg:23.439560439560438
episode:100, moving_avg:28.2, rewards_avg:23.792079207920793
episode:110, moving_avg:33.45, rewards_avg:25.063063063063062
episode:120, moving_avg:38.45, rewards_avg:26.049586776859503
episode:130, moving_avg:36.5, rewards_avg:26.65648854961832
episode:140, moving_avg:34.1, rewards_avg:27.04964539007092
episode:150, moving_avg:35.9, rewards_avg:27.748344370860927
episode:160, moving_avg:40.25, rewards_avg:28.565217391304348
episode:170, moving_avg:40.35, rewards_avg:29.105263157894736
episode:180, moving_avg:42.75, rewards_avg:30.022099447513813
episode:190, moving_avg:43.95, rewards_avg:30.554973821989527
episode:200, moving_avg:43.95, rewards_avg:31.308457711442784
episode:210, moving_avg:48.45, rewards_avg:32.156398104265406
episode:220, moving_avg:58.55, rewards_avg:33.68325791855204
episode:230, moving_avg:59.05, rewards_avg:34.3982683982684
episode:240, moving_avg:54.0, rewards_avg:35.28630705394191
episode:250, moving_avg:66.9, rewards_avg:36.908366533864545
episode:260, moving_avg:72.4, rewards_avg:38.053639846743295
episode:270, moving_avg:92.5, rewards_avg:40.93726937269373
episode:280, moving_avg:100.45, rewards_avg:42.42348754448398
episode:290, moving_avg:90.05, rewards_avg:44.243986254295535
episode:300, moving_avg:108.65, rewards_avg:46.75747508305648
episode:310, moving_avg:137.4, rewards_avg:50.17041800643087
episode:320, moving_avg:151.15, rewards_avg:53.1993769470405
episode:330, moving_avg:150.4, rewards_avg:56.166163141993955
episode:340, moving_avg:163.4, rewards_avg:59.60703812316716
episode:350, moving_avg:206.5, rewards_avg:64.67806267806267
episode:360, moving_avg:252.4, rewards_avg:70.2354570637119
episode:370, moving_avg:254.45, rewards_avg:74.85983827493261
episode:380, moving_avg:270.6, rewards_avg:80.70866141732283
episode:390, moving_avg:263.3, rewards_avg:84.45780051150895
episode:400, moving_avg:209.0, rewards_avg:87.06234413965088
episode:410, moving_avg:223.85, rewards_avg:91.19464720194647
episode:420, moving_avg:274.15, rewards_avg:95.91211401425178
episode:430, moving_avg:207.95, rewards_avg:96.57308584686776
episode:440, moving_avg:107.65, rewards_avg:96.39909297052154
episode:450, moving_avg:83.9, rewards_avg:95.96674057649668
episode:460, moving_avg:86.8, rewards_avg:95.93926247288503
episode:470, moving_avg:82.75, rewards_avg:95.36305732484077
episode:480, moving_avg:79.95, rewards_avg:95.23284823284823
episode:490, moving_avg:116.7, rewards_avg:96.19144602851324
INFO:tensorflow:Assets written to: ./model/ppoWassets
*****end learing
```

Execution Results of cartpole_PPO

In the execution results of the PPO model, after around 350

episodes, the moving average begins to exceed 200. At about 420 episodes, the moving average peaks before gradually decreasing. However, by around episode 490, both the moving average and overall average start to increase again. This suggests that extending the training episodes could lead to improved performance, allowing the model to learn more effectively.

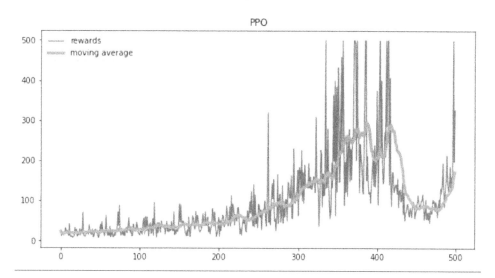

visualization of the PPO training performance

Here's an in-depth analysis of PPO training performance with a graph to provide a clearer picture of the trends and challenges discussed. From the previous log analysis, we know that:

Peak Performance Around Episode 400: Training performance peaked near episode 400, indicating that the model had effectively learned the environment and achieved a high level of stability and control.

Reaching the Maximum Execution Steps: The model frequently reached the 500-step maximum per episode, demonstrating strong performance at this stage.

Performance Decline Followed by Improvement: After peaking, performance gradually declined but then began improving again in the later 400s. This could suggest an overfitting or instability issue, underscoring the importance of tuning to achieve consistent performance improvements.

Reinforcement Learning Algorithm Tuning

While understanding reinforcement learning algorithms is essential, tuning is also critical. Tuning can focus on:

Neural Network Parameters: Adjusting learning rate, network architecture, and other neural network parameters.

Reinforcement Learning Algorithm Parameters: Adjusting discount factors, exploration-exploitation balance, and algorithm-specific parameters like the clipping rate in PPO.

Though ideally, gaining insights from a deep understanding of both neural networks and reinforcement learning concepts (and the underlying mathematical foundations) is invaluable, this can take years to master. Efficient tuning techniques can, however, help achieve significant performance improvements with minimal effort.

Chapter 10

Neural Network Tuning

10. Neural Network Tuning

To effectively tune a neural network, you need a solid understanding of how it functions. In previous chapters, we examined step-by-step how a linear function develops into a neural network. Through this, we studied the roles of the cost function, activation function, and gradient descent. The knowledge required for neural network tuning doesn't come from any special papers or theories; it starts right here. For instance, by exploring the limitations of early activation functions and how they evolved, you can gain ideas for tuning activation functions.

Now, let's deepen our understanding of how neural networks operate and explore their concepts more thoroughly, then apply tuning techniques to the neural network used in the PPO algorithm.

10.1 Overview of Neural Network Tuning

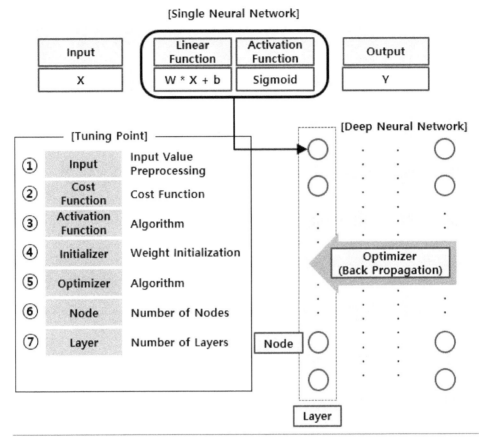

[Single Neural Network]

[Tuning Point]

[Deep Neural Network]

Neural Network Tuning Points

There are various tuning points when designing a neural network. Here, we'll focus on the elements necessary for tuning the PPO algorithm.

When explaining neural networks, a single neural network— commonly used to illustrate the concept—is composed of input, linear functions, activation functions, and output. Additionally, an optimization function is required to update the weights. In this single neural network, the linear and activation functions are combined into nodes, and stacking these nodes row-wise forms a layer. Multiple layers can then be stacked in columns to form a deep network.

(1) Preprocessing Input Values: One of the first tuning points is preprocessing input values. Preprocessing involves transforming the values so that the varied forms of input data don't negatively impact learning.

(2) Cost Function: The cost function measures the difference between predicted and actual values. Previously, we mainly used Mean Squared Error (MSE), but nowadays, Cross Entropy is widely used. Entropy is the number of bits required to represent information, and cross-entropy is the information needed to represent the entirety of two probability distributions. The closer these distributions are, the fewer bits are needed; if they differ significantly, more information is required.

(3) Activation Function: The activation function transforms the output of the linear model into a non-linear value. For instance, the sigmoid function compresses values between 0 and 1. However, using sigmoid as an activation function can cause various issues when networks grow or the training data increases. By examining the pros and cons of different activation functions, we can find one that enhances the performance of the PPO algorithm.

(4) Weight Initialization: The model's weights need to be initialized. In linear models, weights W and b are initialized randomly. However, if entirely random values are used, finding suitable weights may take a long time, or, in unfavorable cases, the model may not converge at all. Choosing appropriate initial weights is a crucial issue in neural network tuning.

(5) Optimization Algorithm: The optimization algorithm adjusts weights in the direction of minimizing error, with the learning rate as a key tuning point. Through partial derivatives, the optimization algorithm adjusts weights based on the learning rate. However, gradient descent has several drawbacks, and we'll explore various algorithms developed to address these issues.

(6)(7) Number of Nodes and Layers: Determining how many nodes to use in each hidden layer and how many hidden layers to build is always a challenging problem. Rather than detailing how to tune nodes and layers, we'll conclude this section by covering commonly discussed points on neural network tuning.

10.2 Input Data Preprocessing

Neural networks, which first apply a linear model y=wx+b and then extract non-linear output through an activation function (e.g., sigmoid), are sensitive to the scale of data. In a linear model, larger inputs yield larger outputs.

Consider input data with two variables: height and eyesight. The average male height is around 175 cm, while average eyesight is about 1.0. If we train the model with these raw data values, height data would be weighted more heavily, influencing the model's learning outcome more than eyesight data.

Input preprocessing helps reduce inefficiencies by addressing the substantial differences in scale across variables. Key preprocessing techniques include standardization and normalization.

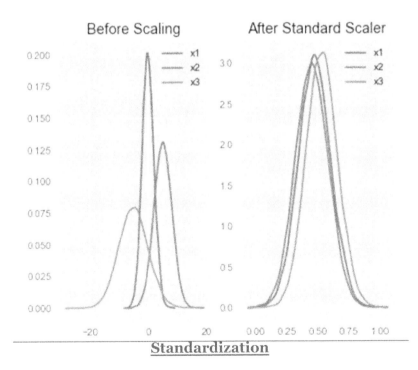

Standardization

Standardization is a technique for transforming data by converting it to a standard normal distribution. This method is commonly

214

applied to data with a Gaussian distribution. A Gaussian distribution refers to data that forms a bell shape, while a standard normal distribution is a symmetrical bell shape centered around the mean. Standardization involves processing data that may be skewed to the left or right, or that has an uneven bell shape, and transforming it into a symmetrical bell shape centered around the mean.

Norm	• Methods for Measuring the Magnitude of a Vector
	$$\|\mathbf{x}\|_p := \left(\sum_{i=1}^{n} \|x_i\|^p \right)^{1/p}$$ · n : Number of Elements · x : Distance Between Two Vectors · L1 Norm : p가 1 · L2 Norm : p가 2 (default)

Vector Norm

Before exploring normalization, let's first understand the concept of the norm of a vector. The norm of a vector can be calculated using a complex formula, where setting the value of p to 1 yields the L1 norm, and setting p to 2 yields the L2 norm. Most functions that calculate the norm default to the L2 norm if no specific value is given. In simple terms, the norm can be thought of as a measurement of the vector's magnitude, making it easier to understand.

Normalization	• Dividing the vector by its norm to normalize its magnitude to 1
	Normalization(x) = x / ‖x‖

Normalization

Now that we understand norms, let's look at the concept of normalization. Normalization is the process of dividing each element of a vector by its norm. This calculation changes the absolute values of all elements to be less than 1. The term "vector" may seem unexpected here, but it becomes easier to understand if you think of the set of input variables x for the model as a vector.

For example, if there are four input variables, x={x1, x2, x3, x4}, each variable is an element of the vector.

Rather than focusing too much on the formula itself, it is better to normalize test data and visualize the results to observe the effects of normalization.

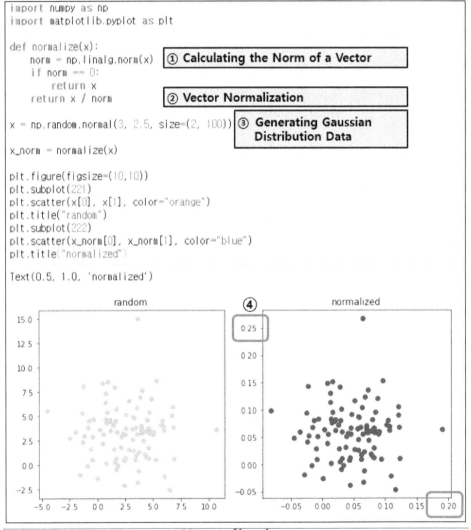

```
import numpy as np
import matplotlib.pyplot as plt

def normalize(x):
    norm = np.linalg.norm(x)      ① Calculating the Norm of a Vector
    if norm == 0:
        return x
    return x / norm               ② Vector Normalization

x = np.random.normal(3, 2.5, size=(2, 100))   ③ Generating Gaussian
                                                  Distribution Data
x_norm = normalize(x)

plt.figure(figsize=(10,10))
plt.subplot(221)
plt.scatter(x[0], x[1], color="orange")
plt.title("random")
plt.subplot(222)
plt.scatter(x_norm[0], x_norm[1], color="blue")
plt.title("normalized")

Text(0.5, 1.0, 'normalized')
```

Normalization

Numpy provides various linear algebra functions through the linalg package.

By using the norm function in the linalg package, you can calculate the norm of a vector. The default is the L2 norm, but if you specify 1 for the ord argument, it will calculate the L1 norm instead.

Dividing each element by the vector's norm gives normalized data.

Before normalizing data, you can create test data using the random.normal function. This function generates 100 two-dimensional data points with a mean of 3 and a standard deviation of 2.5.

Now, visualize and compare the generated test data with the normalized data. You'll see that the distribution remains the same, but the overall magnitude of the data has decreased.

10.3 Choosing a Cost Function

To understand the commonly used concept of cross-entropy, let's first discuss entropy. Entropy represents the number of bits required to optimally encode information. For example, to represent all possible outcomes of a dice game, you'd need 3 bits to cover numbers 1 through 6 in binary. However, a coin toss game only needs 1 bit, as it involves only 0 and 1. Therefore, a coin toss has lower entropy than a dice game. Lower entropy implies greater efficiency in handling information.

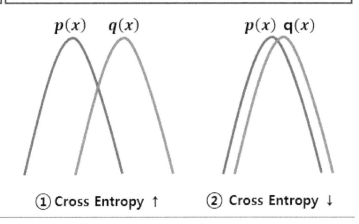

Cross Entropy	• Discrete Probability Distribution
	• H(p, q) = - $\sum_{x \in X} p(x) log\ q(x)$
	• Continuous Probability Distribution
	• H(p, q) = - $\int_x p(x) log\ q(x)$

$p(x)$ $q(x)$ $p(x)$ $q(x)$

① Cross Entropy ↑   ② Cross Entropy ↓

Cross Entropy

Cross-entropy refers to the multiplication (crossing) of two probability distributions. It represents the amount of information required to optimally express the difference between two probability distributions. Thus, when the difference between two distributions is large, the cross-entropy value also increases. While the formulas differ slightly for discrete probability distributions (where values can be clearly distinguished like integers) versus continuous probability distributions (where values cannot be distinctly separated like real numbers), the concept remains intuitively similar. It's best to focus on understanding this conceptually rather than in terms of exact formulas.

When we denote the true probability as P(x) and the predicted probability as Q(x), calculating cross-entropy reveals the degree of difference between the two probabilities. Adjusting the weights to reduce the cross-entropy value brings the two probabilities closer. In case (1), the distributions differ significantly, resulting in a high cross-entropy value, whereas in case (2), the distributions are more similar, yielding a lower cross-entropy value. Our goal is to find neural network weights that produce a distribution resembling (2).

If we define the target policy as P(x) and the learned policy as Q(x), using cross-entropy as a cost function can sufficiently train the policy neural network. Recently, cross-entropy has become more widely used than Mean Squared Error (MSE) as a cost function. When the neural network's output is binary, Binary Cross-Entropy is used as the cost function, and when there are more than two classes, Sparse Cross-Entropy is applied.

10.4 Activation Algorithms

In the early explanations of neural networks, we discussed the sigmoid function, a non-linear function with a step-like output (though it is slightly curved rather than strictly linear to allow differentiation). Although the sigmoid function was widely used in early neural networks, its inherent drawbacks have led to a decline in its usage today. Here, we'll examine issues that can arise in the learning process depending on the activation function, as well as explore the characteristics and evolution of various activation functions.

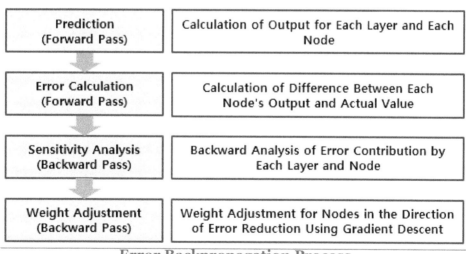

Prediction (Forward Pass)	Calculation of Output for Each Layer and Each Node
Error Calculation (Forward Pass)	Calculation of Difference Between Each Node's Output and Actual Value
Sensitivity Analysis (Backward Pass)	Backward Analysis of Error Contribution by Each Layer and Node
Weight Adjustment (Backward Pass)	Weight Adjustment for Nodes in the Direction of Error Reduction Using Gradient Descent

Error Backpropagation Process

Error backpropagation is the process of calculating the error and adjusting weights by moving backward through the network to minimize the error. The first step in training a neural network is the forward pass, where outputs are calculated for each layer and each node in sequence. Next, the error—the difference between the predicted output and the actual value—is calculated.

After determining the error, the network performs a backward pass through each layer and node, calculating each one's contribution to the total error. Finally, gradient descent is used to adjust the weights of each node in the direction that reduces the error (error backpropagation). This process is repeated over multiple epochs using the training data.

Vanishing Gradient	The phenomenon of rapidly diminishing gradients toward the input layer
Exploding Gradient	The phenomenon of rapidly exploding gradients toward the input layer

Gradient Vanishing and Exploding

One of the reasons neural network training can fail is due to the issues of gradient vanishing and gradient exploding. In backpropagation, weights should be adjusted in the direction that reduces error through gradient descent. However, if the initial weights are set too small or if the activation function's output range is much smaller than the input values, gradient vanishing can occur, causing the weights in the input layer to barely change.

Conversely, if the initial weights are set too large or the activation function's output range is too large, gradient exploding may occur, leading to excessively large changes in the weights of the input layer.

These problems of gradient vanishing and exploding can be mitigated to some extent by using appropriate weight initialization techniques and selecting effective activation functions.

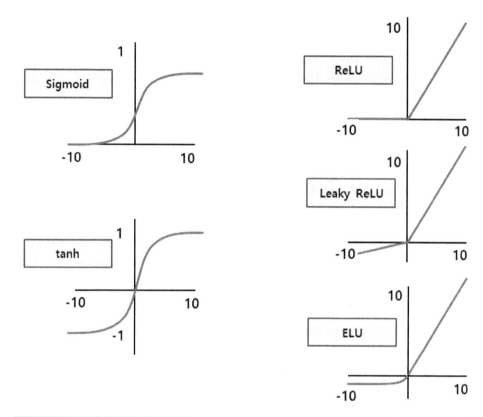

Various Activation Functions

The initially developed sigmoid function has an output range between 0 and 1 ($0 \leq y \leq 1$). Since it compresses any large input to a value within this range, repeated use of this function can significantly reduce the magnitude of values, leading to gradient vanishing issues.

To address the drawbacks of the sigmoid function, the tanh (hyperbolic tangent) function was introduced, with an output range between -1 and 1. While this range is twice as large as that of the sigmoid, the values are still relatively small, and thus gradient vanishing remains a concern.

Next came the ReLU (Rectified Linear Unit) function, which has become widely used today. In ReLU, values less than zero are output as 0, while positive values are output as themselves. This function finally resolved the gradient vanishing issue often

221

encountered with activation functions. However, a drawback of ReLU is the Dying ReLU problem, where nodes receive only values less than zero, resulting in constant outputs of 0, effectively rendering the nodes inactive.

To address this, the Leaky ReLU function was developed. It operates the same as ReLU for positive inputs, but for negative inputs, it outputs a small value proportional to the input. While the output for negative values is not large, it is greater than zero, thus avoiding the Dying ReLU problem and keeping neural network nodes functional.

The ELU (Exponential Linear Units) function was also designed to solve the Dying ReLU problem. For positive values, ELU behaves like ReLU, but for negative values, it has a steep gradient near zero and a flatter gradient further away from zero. ELU provides a smaller variance in output than Leaky ReLU, but its use of an exponential function increases computational cost, potentially slowing down processing.

Recently, Leaky ReLU and ELU have become more popular as neural network activation functions than the standard ReLU.

10.5 Weight Initialization

For efficient training, the initial values assigned to weights are crucial. Failure to initialize weights properly can lead to vanishing or exploding gradient issues. Various initialization methods have been developed to suit different activation functions, but here we'll focus on two widely discussed methods: Glorot Initialization and He Initialization.

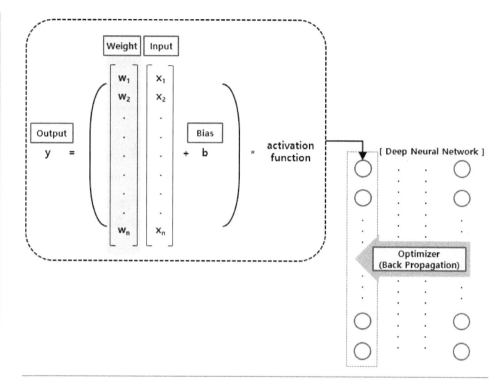

Neural Network Weights

A neural network is composed of multiple layers and nodes, with each node consisting of a linear function and an activation function. A one-dimensional array is used as input, with each element in the array assigned a weight. The number of weights matches the number of input data points, and as the network learns more complex data structures, the number of weights increases exponentially.

Alongside weights, a bias term is also used. For each node, only one bias value is applied regardless of the number of inputs, so when tuning a neural network, the focus of initialization tends to be on weights rather than biases.

For example, if there are 10 input data points and 20 nodes, each node has 10 weights, resulting in a total of 200 weights across all 20 nodes. Neural network training is the process of determining the appropriate values for these weights. As the number of layers and nodes increases, so does the total number of weights. While a complex neural network can represent more intricate data, it also requires a larger number of weights to be learned. Consequently, as networks become more complex, they require more data and longer training times to achieve effective learning.

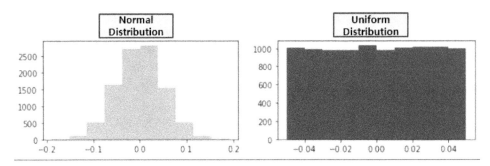

Normal Distribution and Uniform Distribution

Initialized data typically follows either a normal distribution or a uniform distribution. A normal distribution is bell-shaped and symmetric around a central value, while a uniform distribution spreads data evenly across a specified range. The choice of distribution for initializing weights depends on various factors, such as the characteristics of the input data, network size, activation function, and type of output data. Thus, weight initialization should be adjusted according to the specific context.

One fundamental method to reduce the likelihood of gradient vanishing or exploding during initialization is to set weights so that the variance of input and output values is equal across each layer. Variance refers to how much values deviate from the mean. When the variances of input and output data are equal, the sum of input values and output values can be balanced. This balance helps prevent data from diminishing or exploding as it flows through the network during training.

Uniform Distribution	Normal Distribution	

Glorot	$r = \sqrt{\dfrac{6}{n_{in}+nout}}$	$\sigma = \sqrt{\dfrac{6}{n_{in}+nout}}$
He	$r = \sqrt{2}\sqrt{\dfrac{6}{n_{in}+nout}}$	$\sigma = \sqrt{2}\sqrt{\dfrac{6}{n_{in}+nout}}$

- R : Range of Values
- σ : Variance
- n_{in} : Number of Input Nodes
- n_{out} : Number of Output Nodes

Glorot Initialization and He Initialization

Both Glorot and He initialization methods provide ways to initialize data based on either a normal or uniform distribution. While conceptually similar, Glorot initialization was developed before the ReLU algorithm and is more suited to functions like sigmoid and tanh, whereas He initialization is tailored for the ReLU algorithm.

The formulas for Glorot and He initialization are similar, with the main difference being that He initialization multiplies the formula used in Glorot initialization by a factor of 2. In the previous figure's formulas, uniform distribution specifies the range over which data is generated, while normal distribution specifies the variance of the data. Rather than focusing on the specific formulas, it's best to remember the general concepts and application areas of Glorot and He initialization.

10.6 Optimization Algorithms

When explaining artificial intelligence, gradient descent is used to adjust weights to minimize the cost function. Although gradient descent is the simplest neural network optimization algorithm, it has several mathematical drawbacks. Let's explore these limitations in the learning process and examine various algorithms developed to overcome them.

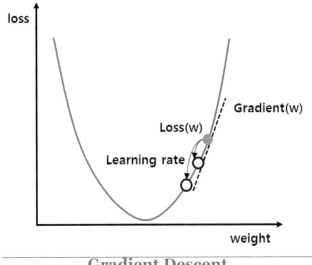

Gradient Descent

Let's take another look at Gradient Descent (GD). Gradient descent is an algorithm that finds the minimum of a function (cost function) by moving in the direction of the gradient, calculated through partial derivatives. The first step is to find the gradient with respect to the weight w, which indicates the direction to move w to reduce the cost function. In this figure, the positive gradient suggests that moving w in the decreasing direction will lower the cost function.

This leads to the question of how much to decrease w. If we decrease it too much, we might overshoot the minimum; if we decrease it too little, the learning process may be too slow. This adjustment amount is determined by the learning rate.

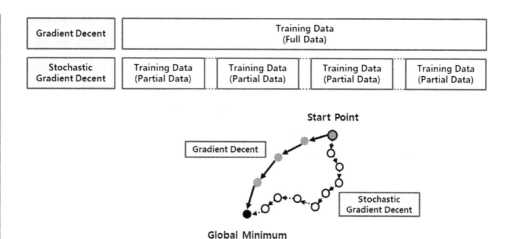

Gradient Descent and Stochastic Gradient Descent

A major drawback of Gradient Descent (GD) is that it requires the entire dataset for each weight update, which can make training slow when dealing with large datasets.

To address this, Stochastic Gradient Descent (SGD) was developed. SGD incorporates the concept of probability by sampling small batches of data for training, rather than using the full dataset each time. By repeating this process multiple times, SGD achieves an effect similar to training on the entire dataset.

In practice, SGD often results in faster training times and higher accuracy than standard gradient descent.

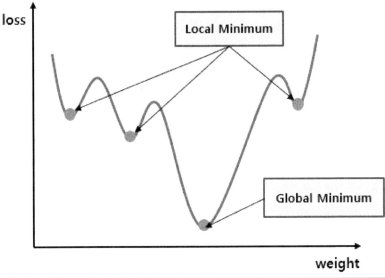

Local Minima and Global Minimum

The cost function curve we previously examined was smooth, making it relatively straightforward for an algorithm to find the minimum. However, in most neural networks, the cost function curve is irregular, as shown in the previous figure, where the cost fluctuates up and down during training.

The dips along the cost function curve represent local minima—points where the function has the lowest value in a small neighborhood but not necessarily across the entire curve. The deepest dip, where the function has its absolute lowest value, is the global minimum. This global minimum is the target that optimization functions aim to find.

A limitation of gradient descent and stochastic gradient descent is that they can get "stuck" in a local minimum, unable to reach the global minimum. At a local minimum, the gradient can be zero, leading the algorithm to interpret it as the smallest possible value.

Momentum	• Adding momentum to weight updates • Enables weight updates even in flat regions where the gradient is zero, due to inertia
AdaGrad	• Adaptive Gradient • Adjusting the learning rate alongside weight changes • Designed to decrease the learning rate as weights are updated
RMSProp	• Improves on the AdaGrad algorithm's drawback of diminishing learning rates over time • Designed so that recent data has a greater influence on learning rate adjustments
Adam	• Combination of the Momentum and RMSProp algorithms • Enables stable learning of the loss function minimum by adjusting both weights and learning rate

Various Optimization Algorithms

To avoid getting stuck in local minima and to effectively find the global minimum, several optimization algorithms have been developed. The first of these was the momentum algorithm, which improves algorithm performance by adjusting weights with added momentum. By adding inertia (momentum) to weight changes, the algorithm can move past local minima. An additional advantage of the momentum algorithm is faster optimization, as it modifies weights with an added push. However, a downside is that the momentum can sometimes cause overshooting, continuing past the point where movement should ideally stop.

Next came the AdaGrad algorithm, which adjusts the learning rate instead of weight changes. If the learning rate is too low, training takes too long; if too high, it can diverge, disrupting the learning process. AdaGrad addresses this by implementing learning rate decay, automatically adjusting the learning rate as weights are updated.

The RMSProp algorithm builds on AdaGrad by modifying the learning rate so that recent data has more influence on weight adjustments. RMSProp works well in more complex environments, offering improvements over AdaGrad.

The Adam algorithm combines the features of both the momentum and RMSProp algorithms. It uses a momentum variable for weight adjustments and a learning rate adjustment variable, helping it reliably find the minimum of the cost function. Adam is one of the most widely used optimization algorithms today.

10.7 Discussion on the Number of Nodes and Hidden Layers

Choosing the number of hidden layers and setting the number of nodes in each layer is a constant challenge for those working with neural networks. Although various approaches continue to be discussed, a general solution has not yet emerged. Here, we will introduce a few notable approaches to structuring hidden layers and nodes, based on extensive discussions in the field.

General Discussion	All data can be represented with a single hidden layer
	More hidden layers and nodes enable representation of more complex data
	Using too few nodes in hidden layers can lead to underfitting
	Using too many neurons in hidden layers can lead to overfitting
Empirical Discussion	The number of hidden layer nodes should be between the size of the input layer and the output layer
	The number of hidden layer nodes should be two-thirds of the input layer size plus the output layer size
	The number of hidden layer nodes should be less than twice the size of the input layer

Discussion on the Number of Nodes and Hidden Layers

Discussions on the number of nodes and hidden layers can be

divided into general and empirical discussions. General discussions are based on theories and experiments that have been shown to hold true broadly, while empirical discussions may vary depending on the specific learning environment of the neural network.

In general, it is suggested that most data can be represented with a single hidden layer. This implies that in many learning environments, additional hidden layers may not be necessary, and learning can be achieved with only a few layers.

More hidden layers and nodes allow for the representation of more complex data. For instance, in the case of GPT-3, which is widely discussed in the field of natural language processing, millions of nodes are used, indicating that representing complex data may require a large number of hidden layers and nodes.

If too few nodes are used in hidden layers, underfitting can occur; with too many nodes, overfitting can arise. Underfitting happens when the neural network is too simplistic and cannot capture the characteristics of the training data, resulting in poor predictive performance. Overfitting, on the other hand, means the neural network is over-optimized for the training data, leading to a significant drop in prediction accuracy when tested on new data.

Moving on to empirical discussions, these are more situational and can be used selectively depending on the training context. One approach is to estimate the number of hidden layer nodes based on the relationship between the input layer and output layer sizes. This is particularly useful when the dimensionality of the input data (number of variables) is large.

10.8 Tuning the Neural Network in the PPO Algorithm

Let's dive into tuning the neural network used in the PPO algorithm. Although many tuning techniques have been introduced, the latest techniques are not always the best. Even if a technique has theoretical limitations, it may perform well depending on the characteristics of the training data. Judging which technique is most suitable for the data is not straightforward. Therefore, understanding the theory and refining optimal techniques through diverse experiences and experiments is essential.

[Tunning Neural Network]	
Input	Normalize
Activation Function	Relu
Initializer	glorot_normal
Optimizer	Adam
Node	24
Layer	1

PPO Neural Network Tuning

Let's start by tuning the input values for the Cartpole PPO neural network. Four input values are used, and normalization is applied to ensure uniform data scales across variables.

Next, we'll tune the activation function. While the current activation function is ReLU, theoretically, newer functions like Leaky ReLU and ELU might be more suitable for tuning. However, in the Cartpole PPO, ReLU actually delivers better performance than these newer algorithms.

Now we need to select a weight initialization algorithm. Previously, we discussed two initialization algorithms, with Glorot initialization being more suitable for tanh activation functions compared to the He algorithm. For the data distribution, both normal and uniform distributions are options, but the normal distribution performs better for Cartpole PPO. Therefore, glorot_ normal was chosen for weight initialization.

As for the optimization algorithm, we retained Adam, as it's currently one of the most widely used algorithms, known for strong performance. Let's modify the program to apply these tuning adjustments and observe the results.

10.9 Applying Tuning Code to PPO Algorithm

Most of the code remains the same as in previous chapters, with additional functions for activation functions, weight initialization, and input tuning.

```python
import tensorflow as tf
import tensorflow.keras.backend as K
from tensorflow.keras.layers import Input, Dense, Flatten
from tensorflow.keras.optimizers import Adam
import gym
import numpy as np
import random as rand
LOSS_CLIPPING = 0.2
class Agent(object):
    def __init__(self):
        self.env = gym.make('CartPole-v1')
        self.state_size = self.env.observation_space.shape[0]
        self.action_size = self.env.action_space.n
        self.value_size = 1
        self.node_num = 24
        self.learning_rate_actor = 0.0005
        self.learning_rate_critic = 0.0005
        self.epochs_cnt = 5
        self.model_actor = self.build_model_actor()
        self.model_critic = self.build_model_critic()

        self.discount_rate = 0.98
        self.smooth_rate = 0.95
        self.penalty = -400

        self.episode_num = 500
        self.mini_batch_step_size = 32

        self.moving_avg_size = 20
        self.reward_list= []
        self.count_list = []
        self.moving_avg_list = []

        self.states, self.states_next, self.action_matrixs = [],[],[]
        self.dones, self.action_probs, self.rewards = [],[],[]
```

```python
        self.DUMMY_ACTION_MATRIX = np.zeros((1,1,self.action_size))
        self.DUMMY_ADVANTAGE = np.zeros((1,1,self.value_size))

    class MyModel(tf.keras.Model):
        def train_step(self, data):
            in_datas, out_action_probs = data
            states, action_matrixs, advantages = in_datas[0], in_datas[1],
                                        in_datas[2]
            with tf.GradientTape() as tape:
                y_pred = self(states, training=True)
                new_policy = K.max(action_matrixs*y_pred, axis=-1)
                old_policy = K.max(action_matrixs*out_action_probs, axis=-1)
                r = new_policy/(old_policy)
                clipped = K.clip(r, 1-LOSS_CLIPPING, 1+LOSS_CLIPPING)
                loss = -K.minimum(r*advantages, clipped*advantages)
            # Compute gradients
            trainable_vars = self.trainable_variables
            gradients = tape.gradient(loss, trainable_vars)
            # Update weights
            self.optimizer.apply_gradients(zip(gradients, trainable_vars))

    def build_model_actor(self):
        input_states = Input(shape=(1,self.state_size), name='input_states')
        input_action_matrixs = Input(shape=(1,self.action_size),
                                name='input_action_matrixs')
        input_advantages = Input(shape=(1,self.value_size),
                                name='input_advantages')
        x = (input_states)
        x = Dense(self.node_num, activation="relu",
                kernel_initializer='glorot_normal')(x)
        out_actions = Dense(self.action_size, activation='softmax',
                        name='output')(x)

        model = self.MyModel(inputs=[input_states, input_action_matrixs,
                                input_advantages], outputs=out_actions)
        model.compile(optimizer=Adam(lr=self.learning_rate_actor))

        model.summary()
        return model

    def build_model_critic(self):
```

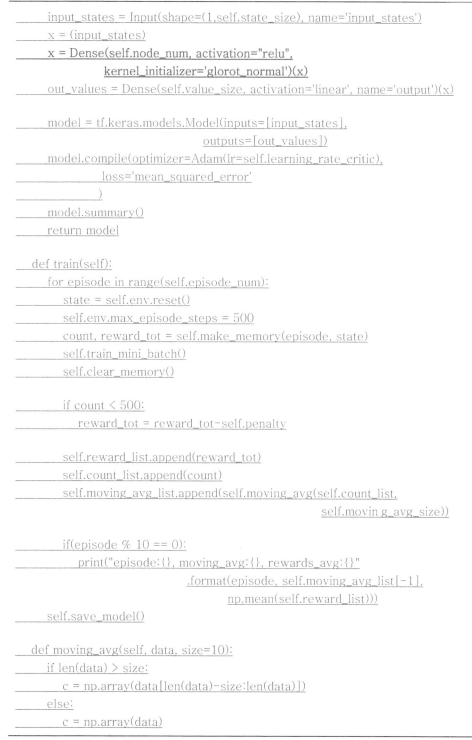

```
        input_states = Input(shape=(1,self.state_size), name='input_states')
        x = (input_states)
        x = Dense(self.node_num, activation="relu",
                    kernel_initializer='glorot_normal')(x)
        out_values = Dense(self.value_size, activation='linear', name='output')(x)

        model = tf.keras.models.Model(inputs=[input_states],
                                outputs=[out_values])
        model.compile(optimizer=Adam(lr=self.learning_rate_critic),
                    loss='mean_squared_error'
                    )
        model.summary()
        return model

    def train(self):
        for episode in range(self.episode_num):
            state = self.env.reset()
            self.env.max_episode_steps = 500
            count, reward_tot = self.make_memory(episode, state)
            self.train_mini_batch()
            self.clear_memory()

            if count < 500:
                reward_tot = reward_tot-self.penalty

            self.reward_list.append(reward_tot)
            self.count_list.append(count)
            self.moving_avg_list.append(self.moving_avg(self.count_list,
                                            self.movin g_avg_size))

            if(episode % 10 == 0):
                print("episode:{}, moving_avg:{}, rewards_avg:{}"
                            .format(episode, self.moving_avg_list[-1],
                                np.mean(self.reward_list)))
        self.save_model()

    def moving_avg(self, data, size=10):
        if len(data) > size:
            c = np.array(data[len(data)-size:len(data)])
        else:
            c = np.array(data)
```

```python
        return np.mean(c)

    def clear_memory(self):
        self.states, self.states_next, self.action_matrixs = [],[],[]
        self.dones, self.action_probs, self.rewards = [],[],[]

    def make_memory(self, episode, state):
        reward_tot = 0
        count = 0
        reward = np.zeros(self.value_size)
        advantage = np.zeros(self.value_size)
        target = np.zeros(self.value_size)
        action_matrix = np.zeros(self.action_size)
        done = False

        while not done:
            count+ =1
            state_t = np.reshape(self.normalize(state),[1, 1, self.state_size])
            action_matrix_t = np.reshape(action_matrix,[1, 1, self.action_size])

            action_prob = self.model_actor.predict([state_t,
                                self.DUMMY_ACTION_MATRIX,
                                self.DUMMY_ADVANTAGE])
            action = np.random.choice(self.action_size, 1, p=action_prob[0][0])[0]
            action_matrix = np.zeros(self.action_size) #초기화
            action_matrix[action] = 1
            state_next, reward, done, none = self.env.step(action)

            state_next_t = np.reshape(self.normalize(state_next),[1, 1,
                                        self.state_size])

            if count < 500 and done:
                reward = self.penalty

            self.states.append(np.reshape(state_t, [1,self.state_size]))
            self.states_next.append(np.reshape(state_next_t, [1,self.state_size]))
            self.action_matrixs.append(np.reshape(action_matrix,
                                [1,self.action_size]))
            self.dones.append(np.reshape(0 if done else 1, [1,self.value_size]))
            self.action_probs.append(np.reshape(action_prob, [1,self.action_size]))
            self.rewards.append(np.reshape(reward, [1,self.value_size]))
```

```python
            if(count % self.mini_batch_step_size == 0):
                self.train_mini_batch()
                self.clear_memory()
            reward_tot += reward
            state = state_next

        return count, reward_tot

    def make_gae(self, values, values_next, rewards, dones):
        delta_adv, delta_tar, adv, target = 0, 0, 0, 0
        advantages = np.zeros(np.array(values).shape)
        targets = np.zeros(np.array(values).shape)
        for t in reversed(range(0, len(rewards))):
            delta_adv = rewards[t] + self.discount_rate * values_next[t] * dones[t]
                            - values[t]
            delta_tar = rewards[t] + self.discount_rate * values_next[t] * dones[t]
            adv = delta_adv + self.smooth_rate*self.discount_rate * dones[t] * adv
            target = delta_tar + self.smooth_rate*self.discount_rate * dones[t] *
                            target
            advantages[t] = adv
            targets[t] = target
        return advantages, targets


    def normalize(self, x):
        norm = np.linalg.norm(x)
        if norm == 0:
            return x
        return x / norm

    def train_mini_batch(self):

        if len(self.states) == 0:
            return

        states_t = np.array(self.states)
        states_next_t = np.array(self.states_next)
        action_matrixs_t = np.array(self.action_matrixs)
        action_probs_t = np.array(self.action_probs)
        rewards_t = np.array(self.rewards)
```

```
        values = self.model_critic.predict(states_t)
        values_next = self.model_critic.predict(states_next_t)

        advantages, targets = self.make_gae(values, values_next, self.rewards,
                                self.dones)
        advantages_t = np.array(advantages)
        targets_t = np.array(targets)
        self.model_actor.fit([states_t, action_matrixs_t, advantages_t],
                                [action_probs_t], epochs=5, verbose=0)
        self.model_critic.fit(states_t, targets_t, epochs=5, verbose=0)

    def save_model(self):
        self.model_actor.save("./model/ppo_tuned")
        print("*****end learing")

if __name__ == "__main__":
    agent = Agent()
    agent.train()
```

cartpole_PPO_tuned.py

The normalize function, responsible for variable initialization, utilizes the norm function from Numpy's linalg package. Before inputting the state values into the neural network, the normalize function is called to normalize these values.

10.10 Analysis of PPO Algorithm Tuning Results

After applying several neural network tuning techniques and running the PPO algorithm, you can observe a noticeable performance improvement. In reinforcement learning, not only is the choice of algorithm crucial, but how the neural network is designed also plays a significant role.

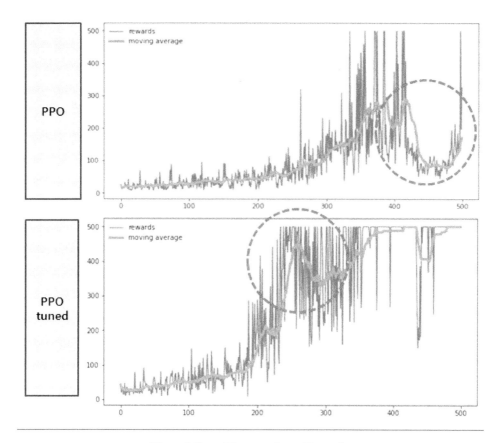

Algorithm Execution Results

Let's compare the results of the standard PPO algorithm with the tuned PPO algorithm. The original PPO algorithm demonstrated remarkable performance between episodes 350 and 400, often reaching the maximum execution limit of 500 steps. However, after episode 400, the execution count gradually declined, dropping to around 100 steps near episode 450. While performance improved slightly toward the end, the results were somewhat inconsistent.

In contrast, the tuned PPO algorithm showed a steady increase in execution steps starting near episode 100, with the upward trend continuing throughout. Around episode 220, the tuned algorithm reached the maximum execution limit of 500 steps, demonstrating peak performance.

This completes our exploration of neural network tuning. Now, we are left with the task of tuning the various parameters used in the PPO algorithm. This book presents two approaches for solving this: one is grid search, which involves specifying a range and randomly sampling parameters to evaluate performance, and the other is a tuning method that applies Bayesian statistical theory. Each method has its advantages and disadvantages, which we'll explore in detail in the following chapters.

Chapter 11

Grid Search-Based
Optimization Technique

11. Grid Search-Based Optimization Technique

One advantage of computers is their ability to automate simple,
repetitive tasks. Grid search leverages this advantage, using a
predefined range of values and randomly selecting and testing them
to find the best-performing configuration. Grid search is
conceptually simple and structurally straightforward, making it
quick and easy for anyone to apply.

11.1 Concept of Grid Search

Until now, we've been manually tuning parameters by observing
training results and adjusting values individually. The strength of
computer operations lies in automating repetitive tasks, and
random search fully utilizes this strength by selecting and testing
values at random. With a computer, once rules are defined, it can
repeat tasks endlessly, making random search potentially very
efficient.

However, a drawback of random search is the possibility of
selecting values that are unhelpful. For example, a typical learning
rate is around 0.01, but random search might select values like 0.9
or 0.0000001, which would be ineffective for training.

One advantage of computers is their ability to automate simple,
repetitive tasks. Grid search leverages this advantage, using a
predefined range of values and randomly selecting and testing them
to find the best-performing configuration. Grid search is

conceptually simple and structurally straightforward, making it quick and easy for anyone to apply.

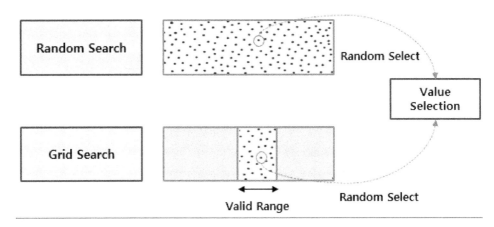

Random Search and Grid Search

To address the drawbacks of random search, the grid search technique was developed. As the name suggests, grid search involves defining a baseline or range and selecting values within that specified range. For grid search to be effective, it's helpful to have a rough idea of the valid value range for each parameter.

There are two notable special cases of this formula, obtained by setting $\lambda = 0$ and $\lambda = 1$.

$$\text{GAE}(\gamma, 0): \quad \hat{A}_t := \delta_t \qquad = r_t + \gamma V(s_{t+1}) - V(s_t) \qquad (17)$$

$$\text{GAE}(\gamma, 1): \quad \hat{A}_t := \sum_{l=0}^{\infty} \gamma^l \delta_{t+l} = \sum_{l=0}^{\infty} \gamma^l r_{t+l} - V(s_t) \qquad (18)$$

Excerpt from GAE paper

Discount Factor Gamma Range: 0.99 (most common), 0.8 to 0.9997

Discount Factor Gamma also known as: Discount (gamma) (PPO Paper), gamma (RLlib), gamma (ppo2 baselines), gamma (ppo baselines), gamma (Unity ML), discount (TensorForce)

GAE Parameter Lambda Range: 0.9 to 1

GAE Parameter Lambda also known as: GAE Parameter (lambda) (PPO Paper), lambda (RLlib), lambda (ppo2 baselines), lambda (ppo baselines), lambda (Unity ML), gae_lambda (TensorForce)

https://www.codecademy.com/articles/normalization

Internet Search Methods

There are several ways to determine valid parameter ranges, with internet searches being the most common. You can find resources from experts who have tuned the algorithm you're working on and use this data as a reference.

Another approach is to manually adjust parameters to find the optimal range. While basic ideas can be obtained from internet research, testing parameters directly provides a more precise range by allowing you to see results firsthand. This approach accounts for differences that may arise due to computer specifications or program versions.

Finally, setting valid ranges by thoroughly understanding how the algorithm works is a robust approach. Neural networks and the PPO algorithm involve various mathematical concepts. By fully understanding these, you can gauge the range in which parameters are likely to perform well.

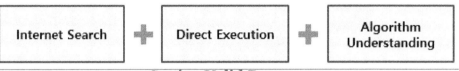

Setting Valid Ranges

Once you've established valid parameter ranges using the three methods mentioned earlier, you're ready to create a program to perform grid search on these parameters.

11.2 Coding Grid Search

```
def random_select()  Dictionary
    config_data = {   Creation
        'layer_num_actor'      :rand.randint(1,2),
        'node_num_actor'       :rand.randint(12,128),
        'epochs_actor'         :rand.randint(3,6),  Generate an Integer
        'layer_num_critic'     :rand.randint(1,2),  between 12 and 128
        'node_num_critic'      :rand.randint(12,128),
        'epochs_critic'        :rand.randint(3,6),

        'learning_rate_actor'  :rand.uniform(0.0001,0.001),
        'learning_rate_critic' :rand.uniform(0.0001,0.001),
        'discount_rate'        :rand.uniform(0.9,0.99),
        'smooth_rate'          :rand.uniform(0.9,0.99),
        'penalty'              :rand.randint(-500,-10),
        'mini_batch_step_size' :rand.randint(4,80),
        'loss_clipping'        :rand.uniform(0.1,0.3)
    }
    return config_data
                                         Generate a Float between
                                         0.1 and 0.3
```

Creating the random_select Function

Once the valid range is set, you need to determine whether the generated numbers should be integers or floats. If integers are required, use the randint function to generate numbers within the specified range. For floats, use the uniform function to create numbers within the range.

The generated data is stored in a dictionary structure as key-value pairs for easy access. This allows you to retrieve values conveniently, such as with config_data['layer_num_actor'].

```
def __init__(self, config_data):        Modify Constructor Function
    self.env = gym.make('CartPole-v1')
    self.state_size = self.env.observation_space.shape[0]
    self.action_size = self.env.action_space.n
    self.value_size = 1

    self.layer_num_actor = config_data['layer_num_actor']
    self.node_num_actor = config_data['node_num_actor']
    self.epochs_actor = config_data['epochs_actor']           Extract Values
    self.layer_num_critic = config_data['layer_num_critic']        from
    self.node_num_critic = config_data['node_num_critic']     config_data
    self.epochs_critic = config_data['epochs_critic']          Dictionary

    self.learning_rate_actor = config_data['learning_rate_actor']
    self.learning_rate_critic = config_data['learning_rate_critic']
    self.discount_rate = config_data['discount_rate']
    self.smooth_rate = config_data['smooth_rate']
    self.penalty = config_data['penalty']
    self.mini_batch_step_size = config_data['mini_batch_step_size']
    self.loss_clipping = config_data['loss_clipping']
```

Modifying the Agent Class

In the previous Agent class, the constructor did not take any specific arguments. For grid search, however, the constructor will receive a dictionary as an argument containing values selected from within the valid range. Each Agent class variable is then initialized one by one using the values from the config_data dictionary.

```
class MyModel(tf.keras.Model):   Custom Loss Function
    def train_step(self, data):
        .....
        states, action_matrixs, advantages = in_datas[0], in_datas[1], in_datas[2]
        loss_clipping = in_datas[3]

        with tf.GradientTape() as tape:
            .....
            LOSS_CLIPPING = K.mean(loss_clipping)
            loss = -K.minimum(r*advantages, K.clip(r, 1-LOSS_CLIPPING, 1+LOSS_CLIPPING)*advantages)
            .....


    def build_model_actor(self):    Model Creation
        .....
        input_loss_clipping = Input(shape=(1,self.value_size), name='input_loss_clipping')
        .....
        model = self.MyModel(inputs=[input_states, input_action_matrixs, input_advantages, input_loss_clipping],
                        outputs=out_actions)
        .....


    def train_mini_batch(self):    Model Training
        .....
        loss_clipping = [self.loss_clipping for j in range(len(self.states))]
        loss_clipping_t = np.reshape(loss_clipping, [len(self.states),1,1])
        .....
        self.model_actor.fit([states_t, action_matrixs_t, advantages_t, loss_clipping_t], [action_probs_t],
```

Passing the LOSS_CLIPPING Variable

Previously, the LOSS_CLIPPING variable was declared outside the Agent class, making it accessible across different parts of the code. However, in a grid search environment, the value of LOSS_CLIPPING should be controlled by the programmer, requiring it to be passed from outside the class to within the class repeatedly.

Another challenge is that the LOSS_CLIPPING variable is used within the MyModel class, which operates on tensorized data. To handle this, some adjustments are necessary to ensure that the LOSS_CLIPPING variable is passed like other neural network training variables across key points: the MyModel class, which defines the custom loss function; the build_model_actor function, which creates the model; and the train_mini_batch function, which handles model training. These modifications will allow LOSS_CLIPPING to be integrated smoothly within the neural network training process.

```
results = []
print("***** start r|Specify Execution Count
for i in range(100):  |for Grid Search          Convert Grid Setting Variables Using
    config_data = random_select()            random_select Function
    agent = Agent(config_data)
    print("*config:", config_data)     Create Agent Class
    agent.train()
    result = []              Train Model
    result.append(config_data)
    result.append(agent.moving_avg_list[len(agent.moving_avg_list)-1])
    result.append(np.mean(agent.reward_list))
    results.append(result)                Save Model Training Results
    print("*result:", i, agent.moving_avg_list[len(agent.moving_avg_list)-1]
                    , np.mean(agent.reward_list))
    print("-"*100)
print("***** end random search *****")
```

Executing Grid Search

Grid search is a technique that iteratively substitutes values within a programmer-specified range to evaluate model performance. To run grid search, a loop is used to define the number of iterations. Next, the random_select function randomly selects values within the valid range and passes them as inputs to the constructor of the Agent class.

The Agent class, receiving these tuning parameters, initializes the algorithm and neural network and then begins training. Once training is complete, the moving_avg_list (20-episode moving average rewards) and reward_list (overall average rewards) are saved as internal variables in the Agent class.

After each training session, the values stored in the Agent's internal variables, along with the selected parameters, are saved to the results variable. When all grid search iterations are complete, the parameters that yielded the highest overall average rewards can be identified.

11.3 Full Grid Search Code

Now, let's apply all the previously coded components to the PPO algorithm and finalize the grid search code.

```python
import tensorflow as tf
import tensorflow.keras.backend as K
from tensorflow.keras.layers import Input, Dense, Flatten
from tensorflow.keras.optimizers import Adam
import gym
import numpy as np
import random as rand
class Agent(object):
    def __init__(self, config_data):
        self.env = gym.make('CartPole-v1')
        self.state_size = self.env.observation_space.shape[0]
        self.action_size = self.env.action_space.n
        self.value_size = 1

        self.layer_num_actor = config_data['layer_num_actor']
        self.node_num_actor = config_data['node_num_actor']
        self.epochs_actor = config_data['epochs_actor']
        self.layer_num_critic = config_data['layer_num_critic']
        self.node_num_critic = config_data['node_num_critic']
        self.epochs_critic = config_data['epochs_critic']

        self.learning_rate_actor = config_data['learning_rate_actor']
        self.learning_rate_critic = config_data['learning_rate_critic']
        self.discount_rate = config_data['discount_rate']
        self.smooth_rate = config_data['smooth_rate']
        self.penalty = config_data['penalty']
        self.mini_batch_step_size = config_data['mini_batch_step_size']
        self.loss_clipping = config_data['loss_clipping']
        self.episode_num = 200
        self.moving_avg_size = 20

        self.model_actor = self.build_model_actor()
        self.model_critic = self.build_model_critic()

        self.states, self.states_next, self.action_matrixs, self.dones = [],[],[],[]
        self.action_probs, self.rewards = [],[]
        self.DUMMY_ACTION_MATRIX = np.zeros((1,1,self.action_size))
        self.DUMMY_ADVANTAGE = np.zeros((1,1,self.value_size))

        self.reward_list= []
        self.count_list = []
        self.moving_avg_list = []

class MyModel(tf.keras.Model):
    def train_step(self, data):
        in_datas, out_action_probs = data
```

```python
        states, action_matrixs = in_datas[0], in_datas[1]
        advantages, loss_clipping = in_datas[2], in_datas[3]
        with tf.GradientTape() as tape:
            y_pred = self(states, training=True)
            new_policy = K.max(action_matrixs*y_pred, axis=-1)
            old_policy = K.max(action_matrixs*out_action_probs, axis=-1)
            r = new_policy/(old_policy)

            LOSS_CLIPPING = K.mean(loss_clipping)

            loss = -K.minimum(r*advantages,
                        K.clip(r, 1-LOSS_CLIPPING,
                        1+LOSS_CLIPPING)*advantages)
        trainable_vars = self.trainable_variables
        gradients = tape.gradient(loss, trainable_vars)
        self.optimizer.apply_gradients(zip(gradients, trainable_vars))

    def build_model_actor(self):
        input_states = Input(shape=(1,self.state_size), name='input_states')
        input_action_matrixs = Input(shape=(1,self.action_size),
                                            name='input_action_matrixs')
        input_advantages = Input(shape=(1,self.value_size),
                                    name='input_advantages')
        input_loss_clipping = Input(shape=(1,self.value_size),
                                    name='input_loss_clipping')

        x = (input_states)
        for i in range(1,self.layer_num_actor+1):
            x = Dense(self.node_num_actor, activation="relu",
                            kernel_initializer='glorot_normal')(x)
        out_actions = Dense(self.action_size, activation='softmax',
                            name='output')(x)

        model = self.MyModel(inputs=[input_states, input_action_matrixs,
                                        input_advantages,
                                        input_loss_clipping],
                                    outputs=out_actions)
        model.compile(optimizer=Adam(lr=self.learning_rate_actor))

        return model

    def build_model_critic(self):
        input_states = Input(shape=(1,self.state_size), name='input_states')

        x = (input_states)
        for i in range(1,self.layer_num_critic+1):
```

```python
        x = Dense(self.node_num_actor, activation="relu",
                        kernel_initializer='glorot_normal')(x)
    out_values = Dense(self.value_size, activation='linear', name='output')(x)

    model = tf.keras.models.Model(inputs=[input_states],
                            outputs=[out_values])
    model.compile(optimizer=Adam(lr=self.learning_rate_critic),
                        loss = "binary_crossentropy"
            )
    return model

def train(self):
    for episode in range(self.episode_num):
        state = self.env.reset()
        count, reward_tot = self.make_memory(episode, state)
        self.train_mini_batch()
        self.clear_memory()

        if count < 500:
            reward_tot = reward_tot-self.penalty

        self.reward_list.append(reward_tot)
        self.count_list.append(count)
        self.moving_avg_list.append(self.moving_avg(self.count_list,
                                            self.moving_avg_size))

def moving_avg(self, data, size=10):
    if len(data) > size:
        c = np.array(data[len(data)-size:len(data)])
    else:
        c = np.array(data)
    return np.mean(c)

def clear_memory(self):
    self.states, self.states_next, self.action_matrixs, self.done = [],[],[],[]
    self.action_probs, self.rewards = [],[]

def make_memory(self, episode, state):
    reward_tot = 0
    count = 0
    reward = np.zeros(self.value_size)
    advantage = np.zeros(self.value_size)
    target = np.zeros(self.value_size)
    action_matrix = np.zeros(self.action_size)
    done = False
```

```python
while not done:
    count += 1
    state_t = np.reshape(self.normalize(state),[1, 1, self.state_size])
    action_matrix_t = np.reshape(action_matrix,[1, 1, self.action_size])

    action_prob = self.model_actor.predict([state_t,
                                self.DUMMY_ACTION_MATRIX,
                                self.DUMMY_ADVANTAGE])
    action = np.random.choice(self.action_size, 1, p=action_prob[0][0])[0]
    action_matrix = np.zeros(self.action_size) # 초기 기억
    action_matrix[action] = 1
    state_next, reward, done, none = self.env.step(action)

    state_next_t = np.reshape(self.normalize(state_next),
                            [1, 1, self.state_size])

    if count < 500 and done:
        reward = self.penalty

    self.states.append(np.reshape(state_t, [1,self.state_size]))
    self.states_next.append(np.reshape(state_next_t, [1,self.state_size]))
    self.action_matrixs.append(np.reshape(action_matrix,
                                        [1,self.action_size]))
    self.dones.append(np.reshape(0 if done else 1, [1,self.value_size]))
    self.action_probs.append(np.reshape(action_prob, [1,self.action_size]))
    self.rewards.append(np.reshape(reward, [1,self.value_size]))

    if(count % self.mini_batch_step_size == 0):
        self.train_mini_batch()
        self.clear_memory()
    reward_tot += reward
    state = state_next

    return count, reward_tot

def make_gae(self, values, values_next, rewards, dones):
    delta_adv, delta_tar, adv, target = 0, 0, 0, 0
    advantages = np.zeros(np.array(values).shape)
    targets = np.zeros(np.array(values).shape)
    for t in reversed(range(0, len(rewards))):
        delta_adv = rewards[t] + self.discount_rate * values_next[t] * dones[t]
                        - values[t]
        delta_tar = rewards[t] + self.discount_rate * values_next[t] * dones[t]
        adv = delta_adv + self.smooth_rate * self.discount_rate * dones[t] * adv
        target = delta_tar + self.smooth_rate * self.discount_rate * dones[t] *
                    target
```

```python
            advantages[t] = adv
            targets[t] = target
        return advantages, targets

    def normalize(self, x):
            norm = np.linalg.norm(x)
        if norm == 0:
            return x
        return x / norm

        def train_mini_batch(self):

        if len(self.states) == 0:
            return

        states_t = np.array(self.states)
        states_next_t = np.array(self.states_next)
        action_matrixs_t = np.array(self.action_matrixs)
        action_probs_t = np.array(self.action_probs)
        loss_clipping = [self.loss_clipping for j in range(len(self.states))]
        loss_clipping_t = np.reshape(loss_clipping, [len(self.states),1,1])

        values = self.model_critic.predict(states_t)
        values_next = self.model_critic.predict(states_next_t)

        advantages, targets = self.make_gae(values, values_next,
                                            self.rewards, self.dones)
        advantages_t = np.array(advantages)
        targets_t = np.array(targets)

        self.model_actor.fit([states_t, action_matrixs_t, advantages_t,
                            loss_clipping_t],
                            [action_probs_t],
                            epochs=self.epochs_actor, verbose=0)
        self.model_critic.fit(states_t, targets_t,
                            epochs=self.epochs_critic, verbose=0)

if __name__ == "__main__":
    def random_select():
        config_data = {
            'layer_num_actor':rand.randint(1,2),
            'node_num_actor':rand.randint(12,128),
            'epochs_actor':rand.randint(3,6),
            'layer_num_critic':rand.randint(1,2),
            'node_num_critic':rand.randint(12,128),
            'epochs_critic':rand.randint(3,6),
```

```
            'learning_rate_actor' :rand.uniform(0.0001,0.001),
            'learning_rate_critic':rand.uniform(0.0001,0.001),
            'discount_rate'     :rand.uniform(0.9,0.99),
            'smooth_rate'       :rand.uniform(0.9,0.99),
            'penalty'           :rand.randint(-500,-10),
            'mini_batch_step_size':rand.randint(4,80),
            'loss_clipping'     :rand.uniform(0.1,0.3)
        }
        return config_data
results = []
print("***** start random search *****")
for i in range(100):
    config_data = random_select()
    agent = Agent(config_data)
    print("*config:", config_data)
    agent.train()
    result = []
    result.append(config_data)
    result.append(agent.moving_avg_list[len(agent.moving_avg_list)-1])
    result.append(np.mean(agent.reward_list))
    results.append(result)
    print("*result:", i, agent.moving_avg_list[len(agent.moving_avg_list)-1],
                            np.mean(agent.reward_list))
    print("-"*100)
print("***** end random search *****")
```

cartpole_PPO_gridsearch.py

The complete code for grid search appears as follows. With minor
modifications to the PPO algorithm, it can be implemented easily.
Grid search is popular for algorithm tuning because it is simple to
understand and straightforward to code. However, it is time-
consuming, with the primary factor affecting duration being the
number of grid search iterations. Greater computing power reduces
the required time, making high-performance CPUs and ample
memory crucial.

253

11.4 Grid Search Execution Results

Now, let's run the grid search program and analyze the results based on the logs.

```
***** start random search *****
*config: {'layer_num_actor': 2, 'node_num_actor': 95, 'epochs_actor': 6, 'layer_num_c
ritic': 2, 'node_num_critic': 124, 'epochs_critic': 5, 'learning_rate_actor': 0.0001821320
3036520845, 'learning_rate_critic': 0.0005814962731170509, 'discount_rate': 0.96203
4926159223, 'smooth_rate': 0.9155998432226305, 'penalty': -101, 'mini_batch_step_si
ze': 48, 'loss_clipping': 0.10779084820831981}
*result: 0 321.8 155.71
-----------------------------------------------------------------------------------
*config: {'layer_num_actor': 2, 'node_num_actor': 36, 'epochs_actor': 4, 'layer_num_c
ritic': 1, 'node_num_critic': 92, 'epochs_critic': 6, 'learning_rate_actor': 0.0001482984
3010839537, 'learning_rate_critic': 0.0009351140107065621, 'discount_rate': 0.95580
29876140309, 'smooth_rate': 0.9556677031316966, 'penalty': -146, 'mini_batch_step_
size': 64, 'loss_clipping': 0.2653178577438546}
*result: 1 19.6 18.11
-----------------------------------------------------------------------------------
*config: {'layer_num_actor': 2, 'node_num_actor': 79, 'epochs_actor': 4, 'layer_num_cr
itic': 2, 'node_num_critic': 117, 'epochs_critic': 3, 'learning_rate_actor': 0.00053319984
49545821, 'learning_rate_critic': 0.00015263631697136885, 'discount_rate': 0.988269
5356654484, 'smooth_rate': 0.9117588412415741, 'penalty': -389, 'mini_batch_step_siz
e': 29, 'loss_clipping': 0.28416359005681013}
*result: 2 388.0 280.42
-----------------------------------------------------------------------------------
......
......
......
-----------------------------------------------------------------------------------
*config: {'layer_num_actor': 2, 'node_num_actor': 90, 'epochs_actor': 3,
'layer_num_critic': 1, 'node_num_critic': 25, 'epochs_critic': 4, 'learning_rate_actor':
0.00042486048723834645, 'learning_rate_critic': 0.00020446135647386553,
'discount_rate': 0.9676650193263128, 'smooth_rate': 0.95982013706074, 'penalty': -
437, 'mini_batch_step_size': 48, 'loss_clipping': 0.2000142797197637}

*result: 99 139.75 94.68


-----------------------------------------------------------------------------------

***** end random search *****
```

Execution Results of cartpole_ PPO_**gridsearch.py**

When you run the grid search program, you can observe results like the following:

In the Config section, the parameter values chosen for that specific routine are displayed.

In the Result section, you can see the execution count, the 20-episode moving average, and the overall average reward.

If the total execution count is low, you may be able to visually identify the best-performing parameters. However, when grid search has been executed many times, resulting in a large dataset, it can be challenging to manually identify the optimal parameters.

Since all data is stored in the results list variable, sorting this data within the variable provides a more efficient way to review the results and find the best parameters.

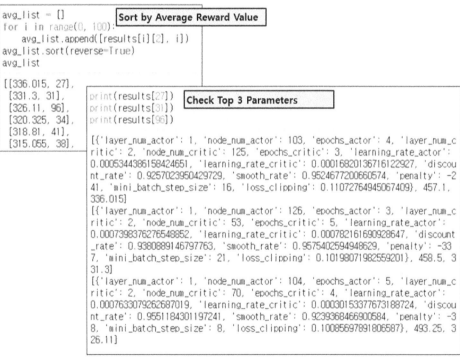

Grid Search Result Analysis

The grid search results are stored in the results variable, with the average reward value located in the third position. Since the average reward is a key metric for evaluating overall algorithm performance, the results are sorted in descending order based on this value. After identifying the indices of the top 3 values, you can check the corresponding parameters in the results variable.

11.5 Applying Grid Search Parameter Tuning

Now, let's apply the optimal parameters identified through grid search to the PPO algorithm and observe the best possible results.

```
. . . . .
LOSS_CLIPPING = 0.11072764945067409
class Agent(object):
    def __init__(self):
        self.env = gym.make('CartPole-v1')
        self.state_size = self.env.observation_space.shape[0]
        self.action_size = self.env.action_space.n
        self.value_size = 1

        self.layer_num_actor = 1
        self.node_num_actor = 103
        self.epochs_actor = 4
        self.layer_num_critic = 2
        self.node_num_critic = 125
        self.epochs_critic = 3

        self.learning_rate_actor = 0.0005344386158424651
        self.learning_rate_critic = 0.00016820136716122927
        self.discount_rate = 0.9257023950429729
        self.smooth_rate = 0.9524677200660574
        self.penalty = -241
        self.mini_batch_step_size = 16

        self.episode_num = 300

        self.moving_avg_size = 20

        self.model_actor = self.build_model_actor()
        self.model_critic = self.build_model_critic()
. . . . .
```

Setting Parameters in cartpole_PPO_gridsearch_test.py

Once you've identified the parameter values with the highest average reward, set these values in the PPO algorithm and observe

256

the results. While manually tuning parameters earlier, you might have used easy-to-remember values. However, in grid search, values are randomly selected within the valid range, so float values with more than 15 decimal places may appear. This poses no issue for execution, so simply set the parameters as they are found from grid search and run the program to evaluate performance.

```
import matplotlib.pyplot as plt
plt.figure(figsize=(10,5))
plt.plot(agent.reward_list, label='rewards')
plt.plot(agent.moving_avg_list, linewidth=4, label='moving average')
plt.legend(loc='upper left')
plt.title('PPO')
plt.show()
```

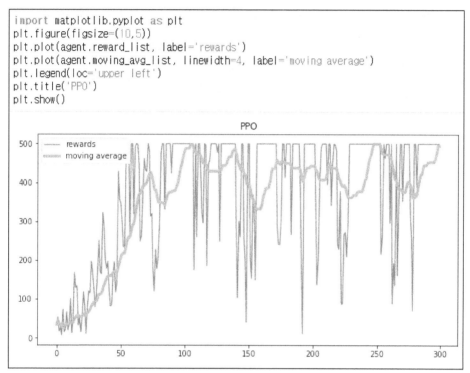

Analyzing Execution Results

Let's visualize the algorithm's execution results with a graph. Compared to the manually tuned PPO algorithm, the grid search-tuned version reaches the maximum execution count significantly faster. Here, we ran 100 iterations, but by extending the valid range and increasing the iteration count, we may find parameter values that reach the maximum execution faster.

As mentioned earlier, grid search is highly intuitive; as long as you understand the PPO algorithm, anyone can use this method. However, a drawback is that the algorithm relies on random functions, so previous runs can't be reused. Grid search generates entirely new parameter values for each test, leading to completely

257

different experiments each time.

In the next chapter, we'll explore Bayesian tuning, a method that can reuse past experience. Although Bayesian tuning is theoretically designed to improve performance by reusing prior results, in practice, it sometimes performs worse than grid search. This discrepancy may be due to limited understanding of the Bayesian approach or insufficient training time, among other reasons.

Rather than viewing Bayesian tuning as superior to grid search, it's better to see it as an alternative approach. Adopting the mindset of using tuning methods suited to the specific context will lead to more effective tuning.

Chapter 12

Bayesian Optimization Technique

12. Bayesian Optimization Technique

In this chapter, we will discuss the Bayesian optimization technique. Unlike grid search, which selects values at random, Bayesian optimization uses an algorithm to select parameters more efficiently. Although Bayesian optimization is theoretically superior, it doesn't always yield the best performance. However, due to its frequent use in algorithm tuning, it's worth studying in depth.

In this book, we'll use a specialized Python package developed for Bayesian optimization. However, Keras, a popular neural network package, also provides a Keras Tuner class that includes a Bayesian optimization algorithm.

Let's explore the basic concepts and methods of Bayesian optimization and consider what further studies may be beneficial for effective algorithm tuning.

12.1 Frequentist Probability and Bayesian Probability

Before diving into Bayesian optimization, let's revisit the concept of probability. The typical concept of probability we're familiar with is frequentist probability. Frequentist probability is intuitive and can be easily calculated. For instance, we know the probability of rolling a 3 on a die is 1/6, which is easy to calculate mentally. However, if we roll a die 12 times, it doesn't necessarily mean that a 3 will appear exactly twice. It's only when we roll the die thousands or even hundreds of thousands of times that the proportion of 3s approaches 1/6, which is the essence of frequentist probability. In short, frequentist probability represents the long-term ratio of a specific event occurring when an event is repeated multiple times.

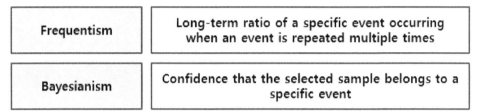

Frequentism	Long-term ratio of a specific event occurring when an event is repeated multiple times
Bayesianism	Confidence that the selected sample belongs to a specific event

Frequentist Probability and Bayesian Probability

Another concept of probability is Bayesian probability. Bayesian probability involves forming a hypothesis (or claim), testing it through actual execution, and refining it based on the results. For instance, let's say we hypothesize that the probability of rolling a 3 on a die is 1/4 because we believe the side opposite 3 has a slightly larger area. Now, we roll the die 60 times and count how often we get a 3. If it appears 10 times, the ratio is 1/6, so we might want to adjust our initial hypothesis. Now, let's update our hypothesis to 1/5 and roll the die another 60 times, collecting results to further refine our probability. This ongoing process of adjusting the hypothesis with new data to find an optimal probability is Bayesian probability. In essence, Bayesian probability can be defined as the confidence level in a hypothesis that a selected sample belongs to a specific event.

12.2 Calculating Bayesian Probability

Bayesian probability is considered one of the more complex areas of probability theory to grasp. While the basic theory isn't overly challenging, understanding the mathematical formulation and working through examples often requires significant background knowledge. Here, we'll cover the foundational concepts of Bayesian probability relevant to reinforcement learning tuning, omitting detailed theory and proofs to stay focused on the main topic.

As mentioned, Bayesian probability involves forming a hypothesis, testing it through execution, and refining it based on results. This concept is built directly into the formula for calculating Bayesian probability. Key components are prior probability and posterior probability: prior probability is the hypothesis formed before testing, while posterior probability is the improved hypothesis after reviewing and refining based on the results.

In other words, Bayesian probability can be described as the process of using execution results to refine prior probability into a more accurate posterior probability. The goal of Bayesian probability, therefore, is to calculate an accurate posterior probability.

$$P(D|H) = \frac{P(H|D)\ P(H)}{P(D)}$$

H	**Hypothesis** Expected information predicting "this is how it will be observed"
P(H)	**Prior** Confidence regarding the claim that a specific event occurred
D	**Data** Directly observed information from execution
P(D)	**Boundary Probability** Newly calculated probability based on the gathered information
P(D|H)	**Posterior** Updated prior probability after receiving new information
P(H|D)	**Likelihood** Probability that the observed D originated from distribution H

Relationship Between Prior and Posterior Probabilities

The goal of Bayesian probability is to calculate a more accurate posterior probability, represented by the target variable $P(H|D)$. Here: D (Data) is the information collected through execution, H (Hypothesis) is the assumption that the data will be observed in a certain way, and $P(H)$ is the prior probability.

The purpose of this formula is to update the prior probability into a posterior probability using the collected data. $P(D)$ is called the marginal probability (or boundary probability), representing a new probability calculated based on the gathered information. For example, if we assume the probability of rolling a 3 on a die is 1/4 (prior probability), then roll the die 60 times and get a 3 ten times, the newly calculated probability of 1/6 is the marginal probability.

P(D|H) is known as likelihood and represents the probability that the observed D originated from distribution H. Since understanding likelihood in depth can be challenging, for now, it's helpful to think of it as the relationship between the prior probability and the observed data.

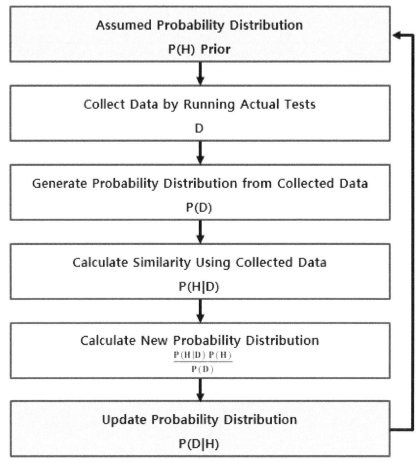

Bayesian Probability Calculation Process

The posterior probability can be calculated by dividing the prior probability by the marginal probability and then multiplying by the likelihood. This formula allows a hypothesis to be refined into a more reliable one through direct experimentation.

Applying Bayesian probability to reinforcement learning model tuning means that, starting from a hypothesis about an optimal parameter setting, the model can be run to gather results and update the parameters to improve them based on the observed data.

To make Bayesian probability easier to understand, let's consider an example involving the height data of 10th-grade male students. This isn't real data but will help illustrate the concept.

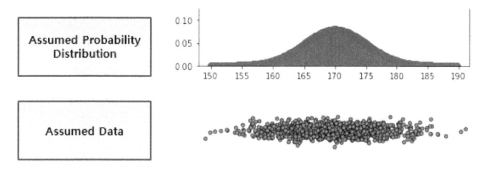

Prior Probability Distribution

Let's start by looking at the prior probability distribution. Suppose we assume that the heights of students range from 150 to 190 cm and follow a normal distribution with a mean of 170 cm. This is our prior probability. In this distribution, most data points cluster around the mean of 170, with fewer data points appearing closer to the extremes of 150 and 190.

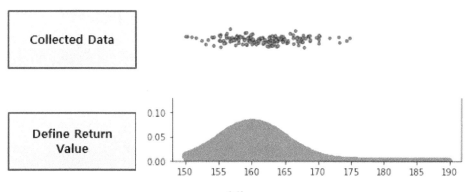

Marginal Probability Distribution

Now, let's look at the data collected by randomly selecting and measuring the heights of 3,000 students. This measured data has a mean of 160 and shows a distribution that tapers off toward both ends. Additionally, the data is skewed to the left, rather than being centered.

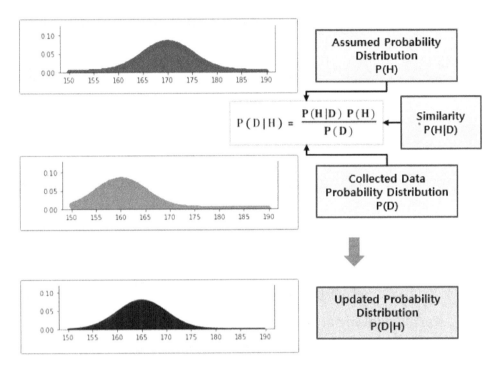

Calculating the Posterior Probability Distribution

Now, let's calculate the posterior probability distribution using the assumed probability distribution (prior probability distribution) and the collected data distribution (marginal probability distribution). Visually examining the resulting posterior probability distribution reveals that the mean falls somewhere between the prior and marginal distributions. The exact posterior distribution can be easily calculated by taking the ratio of the two distributions and multiplying it by the likelihood. Although understanding and calculating likelihood can be challenging, using the package introduced later simplifies this process significantly.

12.3 Introduction to Bayesian Optimization Packages

Bayesian optimization incorporates various theories beyond Bayesian probability, making it time-consuming to master fully. Therefore, this book focuses on applying a Bayesian optimization package to reinforcement learning algorithm tuning with an understanding of Bayesian probability concepts. As you'll experience during practice, a basic understanding of Bayesian probability is sufficient to work with the package.

The Bayesian Optimization package, developed by Fernando Nogueira in 2014, is a Python package for implementing Bayesian optimization. Although similar functionality is available in Keras Tuner, this book introduces the Bayesian Optimization package, which is designed to be easy to use even without an in-depth understanding of Bayesian probability. For more details, visit https://github.com/fmfn/BayesianOptimization.

Program Installation

The Bayesian Optimization package includes various algorithms, such as GP (Gaussian Process), UCB (Upper Confidence Bound), and EI (Expected Improvement). However, this book will not delve into each of these algorithms in detail. Just keep in mind that Bayesian optimization is not a simple method; rather, it's a complex algorithm that combines multiple optimization techniques.

```
'''
@Misc{,
    author = {Fernando Nogueira},
    title = {{Bayesian Optimization}: Open source constrained
                            global optimization tool for {Python}},
    year = {2014--},
    url = " https://github.com/fmfn/BayesianOptimization"
}
'''

from bayes_opt import BayesianOptimization

def black_box_function(x, y):
    return -x ** 2 - (y - 1) ** 2 + 1

pbounds = {'x': (2, 4), 'y': (-3, 3)}

optimizer = BayesianOptimization(
    f=black_box_function,
    pbounds=pbounds,
    random_state=1,
)

optimizer.maximize(
    init_points=2,
    n_iter=3,
)
```

iter	target	x	y
1	-7.135	2.834	1.322
2	-7.78	2.0	-1.186
3	-7.11	2.218	-0.7867
4	-12.4	3.66	0.9608
5	-6.999	2.23	-0.7392

Basic Structure of the Program: bayesian.ipynb

The first step when using the Bayesian Optimization package is to define the objective function you want to optimize. This objective function can take various forms, and the optimization algorithm will automatically find the parameters that maximize the function's return value.

For testing, create a function called black_box_function, which takes x and y as inputs and returns the result of the formula $-x^2-(y-1)^2+1$. Here, the parameters to be optimized are x and y, and the objective function to be optimized is black_box_function.

Next, define the range within which the parameters can vary, known as Parameter Bounds (pbounds). Set the range of x and y as a dictionary structure.

Now, combine all of these to create an instance of the BayesianOptimization class, which will perform the optimization. Pass the objective function and parameters as arguments, and set the seed value for the random function used within the class.

Calling the maximize function provided by the BayesianOptimization class starts the optimization process. The maximize function takes two arguments:

init_points: Specifies the number of times to run the objective function with randomly selected parameters. While random runs do not apply optimization, they help gather diverse information.

n_iter: Specifies the number of times to perform optimization. Using the information collected from the random runs, the algorithm will carry out optimization for the specified number of iterations.

```
'''
@Misc{,
    author = {Fernando Nogueira},
    title = {{Bayesian Optimization}: Open source constrained
                              global optimization tool for {Python}},
    year = {2014--},
    url = " https://github.com/fmfn/BayesianOptimization"
}
'''
print(optimizer.max)

{'target': -6.999472814518675, 'params': {'x': 2.2303920156083024, 'y': -0.7392021938893159}}
```

Max Attribute: bayesian.ipynb

If you perform optimization only a few times, you can visually inspect the results to identify the optimal parameters. However, as the number of optimization runs increases, manually checking each result becomes impractical. The BayesianOptimization class includes an internal variable called max, which stores the highest-performing return value of the objective function along with its associated parameters. This makes it easy to access the best results without needing to inspect each outcome visually.

```
'''
@Misc{,
    author = {Fernando Nogueira},
    title = {{Bayesian Optimization}: Open source constrained
                        global optimization tool for {Python}},
    year = {2014--},
    url = " https://github.com/fmfn/BayesianOptimization"
}
'''
for i, res in enumerate(optimizer.res):
    print("Iteration {}: \n\t{}".format(i, res))
Iteration 0:
        {'target': -7.135455292718879, 'params': {'x': 2.8340440094051482, 'y': 1.3219469606529488}}
Iteration 1:
        {'target': -7.779531005607566, 'params': {'x': 2.0002287496346898, 'y': -1.1860045642089614}}
Iteration 2:
        {'target': -7.109925819441113, 'params': {'x': 2.2175526295255183, 'y': -0.7867249801593896}}
Iteration 3:
        {'target': -12.397162416009818, 'params': {'x': 3.660003815774634, 'y': 0.9608275029525108}}
Iteration 4:
        {'target': -6.999472814518675, 'params': {'x': 2.2303920156083024, 'y': -0.7392021938893159}}
```

Res Attribute: bayesian.ipynb

The BayesianOptimization class also contains an internal variable called res, which stores the optimization results step-by-step in a list format. While the optimization process outputs intermediate results to the screen as it runs, you may want to analyze these results step-by-step after the process is complete. In such cases, the res class variable is a useful resource for reviewing each stage of the optimization.

```
'''
@Misc{,
    author = {Fernando Nogueira},
    title = {{Bayesian Optimization}: Open source constrained
                                global optimization tool for {Python}},
    year = {2014--},
    url = " https://github.com/fmfn/BayesianOptimization"
}
'''
optimizer.set_bounds(new_bounds={"x": (-2, 3)})

optimizer.maximize(
    init_points=0,
    n_iter=5,
)

|   iter  |  target  |    x    |    y    |
-------------------------------------------------
|   6     | -2.942   |  1.98   |  0.8567 |
|   7     | -0.4597  |  1.096  |  1.508  |
|   8     |  0.5304  | -0.6807 |  1.079  |
|   9     | -5.33    | -1.526  |  3.0    |
|   10    | -5.419   | -2.0    | -0.5552 |
=================================================
```

Set_bounds Function: bayesian.ipynb

The BayesianOptimization class provides a set_bounds function
that allows you to change the parameter ranges during the
optimization process. This means you can initially set parameter
ranges when creating an instance of the BayesianOptimization class,
perform optimization, analyze the results, and then adjust the
parameters to continue training with new ranges.

Using the set_bounds function offers the advantage of reusing the
previous optimization process, leveraging the data gathered with
the initial parameters.

```
' ' '
@Misc{,
    author = {Fernando Nogueira},
    title = {{Bayesian Optimization}: Open source constrained
                          global optimization tool for {Python}},
    year = {2014--},
    url = " https://github.com/fmfn/BayesianOptimization"
}
' ' '
optimizer.probe(
    params={"x": 0.5, "y": 0.7},
    lazy=True,
)

optimizer.probe(
    params=[-0.3, 0.1],
    lazy=True,
)

optimizer.maximize(init_points=0, n_iter=0)

|   iter    |  target   |    x     |    y     |
-------------------------------------------------
|   11      |  0.66     |   0.5    |   0.7    |
|   12      |  0.1      |  -0.3    |   0.1    |
=================================================
```

Probe Function: bayesian.ipynb

If you have doubts about the set parameter ranges, the probe function allows you to perform optimization with specific parameters independently of the predefined ranges. By using the probe function, you can specify parameter values for targeted optimization.

The argument lazy=True ensures that the probe function only executes after the maximize function is called, allowing for a controlled and sequential optimization process.

```
'''
@Misc{,
    author = {Fernando Nogueira},
    title = {{Bayesian Optimization}: Open source constrained
                              global optimization tool for {Python}},
    year = {2014--},
    url = " https://github.com/fmfn/BayesianOptimization"
}
'''
from bayes_opt.logger import JSONLogger
from bayes_opt.event import Events

logger = JSONLogger(path="./bayesian/logs.json")
optimizer.subscribe(Events.OPTIMIZATION_STEP, logger)

optimizer.maximize(
    init_points=2,
    n_iter=3,
)
```

iter	target	x	y
13	-12.48	-1.266	-2.446
14	-3.854	-1.069	-0.9266
15	-3.594	0.7709	3.0
16	0.8237	0.03431	1.419
17	0.9721	-0.1051	0.8701

Saving to JSON File: bayesian.ipynb

The JSONLogger class allows you to save various events occurring during the training process to a file in JSON format. After creating a JSONLogger instance, you can call the subscribe function of the BayesianOptimization class and pass the JSONLogger object. Then, when the maximize function is called, events will be recorded in the JSON file.

```
'''
@Misc{,
    author = {Fernando Nogueira},
    title = {{Bayesian Optimization}: Open source constrained
                              global optimization tool for {Python}},
    year = {2014--},
    url = " https://github.com/fmfn/BayesianOptimization"
}
'''
from bayes_opt.util import load_logs

new_optimizer = BayesianOptimization(
    f=black_box_function,
    pbounds={"x": (-2, 2), "y": (-2, 2)},
    verbose=2,
    random_state=7,
)

load_logs(new_optimizer, logs=["./bayesian/logs.json"])

new_optimizer.maximize(
    init_points=2,
    n_iter=3,
)

|   iter    |  target   |     x     |     y     |
-------------------------------------------------
|    1      |  -1.887   |  -1.695   |   1.12    |
|    2      |   0.928   |  -0.2464  |   0.8939  |
|    3      |  -4.825   |   2.0     |  -0.351   |
|    4      |  -3.456   |   2.0     |   1.675   |
|    5      |  -0.5305  |  -0.7284  |   2.0     |
=================================================
```

Reusing JSON File: bayesian.ipynb

Events recorded in a JSON file can be reloaded and reused. By creating a new BayesianOptimization instance and calling the load_logs function with the instance and the path to the saved JSON file, you can leverage previous training data for more efficient learning.

Now that we've covered the basic functions of the Bayesian optimization package, let's explore how to use this package to enhance the performance of reinforcement learning algorithms.

12.4 Using the Bayesian Optimization Package

```
def black_box_function(layer_num_actor, node_num_actor, epochs_actor,
                       layer_num_critic, node_num_critic, epochs_critic,
                       learning_rate_actor, learning_rate_critic,
                       discount_rate, smooth_rate,
                       penalty, mini_batch_step_size, loss_clipping
                       ):
    config_data = {
        'layer_num_actor':layer_num_actor,
        'node_num_actor':node_num_actor,
        'epochs_actor':epochs_actor,
        'layer_num_critic':layer_num_critic,
        'node_num_critic':node_num_critic,            Tuning Parameter
        'epochs_critic':epochs_critic,

        'learning_rate_actor' :learning_rate_actor,
        'learning_rate_critic':learning_rate_critic,
        'discount_rate'       :discount_rate,
        'smooth_rate'         :smooth_rate,
        'penalty'             :penalty,
        'mini_batch_step_size':mini_batch_step_size,
        'loss_clipping'       :loss_clipping
    }
    agent = Agent(config_data)
    agent.train()
    return np.mean(agent.reward_list)       Define Return Value
```

Defining the Objective Function: cartpole_PPO_bayesian.ipynb

The objective function is named black_box_function, as in the previous example. This function determines the parameters to tune, runs the program based on these parameters, and returns the results. Here, the program being executed is the Agent class, which performs reinforcement learning. The function calls the train function to train the Agent class, accumulates the rewards from the entire training process, and calculates the average reward to return.

The goal of the optimization is to find the parameter values that maximize the average return value.

```
pbounds = {
            'layer_num_actor':(1,2),
            'node_num_actor':(12,128),
            'epochs_actor':(3,6),
            'layer_num_critic':(1,2),
            'node_num_critic':(12,128),
            'epochs_critic':(3,6),

            'learning_rate_actor' :(0.0001,0.001),
            'learning_rate_critic':(0.0001,0.001),
            'discount_rate'        :(0.9,0.99),
            'smooth_rate'          :(0.9,0.99),
            'penalty'              :(-500,-10),
            'mini_batch_step_size':(4,80),
            'loss_clipping'        :(0.1,0.3)
        }
```

Specifying Parameter Ranges: cartpole_PPO_bayesian.ipynb

The range for the parameters to be tuned can be set in a dictionary format using the pbounds variable. All parameters with defined ranges are selected as floating-point values during the optimization process. Therefore, any parameters requiring integer inputs for the reinforcement learning process must be explicitly converted to integers.

```
def __init__(self, config_data):
    self.env = gym.make('CartPole-v1')
    self.state_size = self.env.observation_space.shape[0]
    self.action_size = self.env.action_space.n
    self.value_size = 1
                                                          Convert to
                                                           Integer
    self.layer_num_actor = int(round(config_data['layer_num_actor'],0))
    self.node_num_actor = int(round(config_data['node_num_actor'],0))
    self.epochs_actor = int(round(config_data['epochs_actor'],0))
    self.layer_num_critic = int(round(config_data['layer_num_critic'],0))
    self.node_num_critic = int(round(config_data['node_num_critic'],0))
    self.epochs_critic = int(round(config_data['epochs_critic'],0))

    self.learning_rate_actor = config_data['learning_rate_actor']
    self.learning_rate_critic = config_data['learning_rate_critic']
    self.discount_rate = config_data['discount_rate']
    self.smooth_rate = config_data['smooth_rate']
    self.penalty = int(round(config_data['penalty'],0))
    self.mini_batch_step_size = int(round(config_data['mini_batch_step_size'],0))
    self.loss_clipping = config_data['loss_clipping']
```

Setting Agent Class Variables: cartpole_PPO_bayesian.ipynb

As previously mentioned, all parameters passed to the Agent class during training are in float format. Therefore, it is essential to forcibly convert parameters like layer_num_actor and node_num_actor to integers to ensure proper configuration.

```
optimizer = BayesianOptimization(
    f=black_box_function,
    pbounds=pbounds,
    random_state=1,
)

optimizer.maximize(
    init_points=5,          5 Random Runs,
    n_iter=20               20 Optimizations,
)                           50 Total Runs
```

Performing Optimization: cartpole_PPO_bayesian.ipynb

Now, create an instance of the BayesianOptimization class using the predefined objective function and tuning dictionary. Run the maximize function to begin training. Set the init_points argument to 5 to randomly execute the reinforcement learning agent five times for diverse data collection. Then, set the n_iter argument to 20 to perform the optimization process 20 times.

12.5 Complete Bayesian Optimization Code

Now, let's integrate the code we created earlier with the PPO algorithm to finalize the Bayesian optimization code. This will allow us to leverage Bayesian optimization fully for tuning the PPO algorithm.

```
import tensorflow as tf
import tensorflow.keras.backend as K
from tensorflow.keras.layers import Input, Dense, Flatten
from tensorflow.keras.optimizers import Adam
import gym
import numpy as np
import random as rand
from bayes_opt import BayesianOptimization
```

```python
class Agent(object):

    def __init__(self, config_data):
        self.env = gym.make('CartPole-v1')
        self.state_size = self.env.observation_space.shape[0]
        self.action_size = self.env.action_space.n
        self.value_size = 1

        self.layer_num_actor = int(round(config_data['layer_num_actor'],0))
        self.node_num_actor = int(round(config_data['node_num_actor'],0))
        self.epochs_actor = int(round(config_data['epochs_actor'],0))
        self.layer_num_critic = int(round(config_data['layer_num_critic'],0))
        self.node_num_critic = int(round(config_data['node_num_critic'],0))
        self.epochs_critic = int(round(config_data['epochs_critic'],0))

        self.learning_rate_actor = config_data['learning_rate_actor']
        self.learning_rate_critic = config_data['learning_rate_critic']
        self.discount_rate = config_data['discount_rate']
        self.smooth_rate = config_data['smooth_rate']
        self.penalty = int(round(config_data['penalty'],0))
        self.mini_batch_step_size = \
                    int(round(config_data['mini_batch_step_size'],0))
        self.loss_clipping = config_data['loss_clipping']
        self.episode_num = 100
        self.moving_avg_size = 20

        self.model_actor = self.build_model_actor()
        self.model_critic = self.build_model_critic()

        self.states, self.states_next, self.action_matrixs, self.dones = [],[],[],[]
        self.action_probs, self.rewards = [],[]

        self.DUMMY_ACTION_MATRIX = np.zeros((1,1,self.action_size))
        self.DUMMY_ADVANTAGE = np.zeros((1,1,self.value_size))

        self.reward_list= []
        self.count_list = []
        self.moving_avg_list = []

    class MyModel(tf.keras.Model):
        def train_step(self, data):
            in_datas, out_action_probs = data
                    states, action_matrixs = in_datas[0], in_datas[1]
            advantages, loss_clipping = in_datas[2], in_datas[3]
            with tf.GradientTape() as tape:
                y_pred = self(states, training=True)
```

```python
            new_policy = K.max(action_matrixs*y_pred, axis=-1)
            old_policy = K.max(action_matrixs*out_action_probs, axis=-1)
            r = new_policy/(old_policy)

            LOSS_CLIPPING = K.mean(loss_clipping)
            loss = -K.minimum(r*advantages,
                    K.clip(r, 1-LOSS_CLIPPING,
                        1+LOSS_CLIPPING)*advantages)
        trainable_vars = self.trainable_variables
        gradients = tape.gradient(loss, trainable_vars)
        self.optimizer.apply_gradients(zip(gradients, trainable_vars))

    def build_model_actor(self):
        input_states = Input(shape=(1,self.state_size), name='input_states')
        input_action_matrixs = Input(shape=(1,self.action_size),
                                            name='input_action_matrixs')
        input_advantages = Input(shape=(1,self.value_size), name='input_advantages')
        input_loss_clipping = Input(shape=(1,self.value_size),
                                        name='input_loss_clipping')


        x = (input_states)
        for i in range(1,self.layer_num_actor+1):
            x = Dense(self.node_num_actor, activation="relu",
                            kernel_initializer='glorot_normal')(x)
        out_actions = Dense(self.action_size, activation='softmax',
                            name='output')(x)

        model = self.MyModel(inputs=[input_states, input_action_matrixs,
                                        input_advantages,
                                        input_loss_clipping],
                                outputs=out_actions)
        model.compile(optimizer=Adam(lr=self.learning_rate_actor))

        return model

    def build_model_critic(self):
        input_states = Input(shape=(1,self.state_size), name='input_states')

        x = (input_states)
        for i in range(1,self.layer_num_critic+1):
            x = Dense(self.node_num_actor, activation="relu",
                            kernel_initializer='glorot_normal')(x)
        out_values = Dense(self.value_size, activation='linear', name='output')(x)

        model = tf.keras.models.Model(inputs=[input_states],
```

```python
                                    outputs=[out_values])
        model.compile(optimizer=Adam(lr=self.learning_rate_critic),
                        loss = "binary_crossentropy"
            )
        return model

    def train(self):
        for episode in range(self.episode_num):
            state = self.env.reset()
            count, reward_tot = self.make_memory(episode, state)
            self.train_mini_batch()
            self.clear_memory()

            if count < 500:
                reward_tot = reward_tot-self.penalty

            self.reward_list.append(reward_tot)
            self.count_list.append(count)
            self.moving_avg_list.append(self.moving_avg(self.count_list,
                                                self.moving_avg_size))

    def moving_avg(self, data, size=10):
        if len(data) > size:
            c = np.array(data[len(data)-size:len(data)])
        else:
            c = np.array(data)
        return np.mean(c)

    def clear_memory(self):
        self.states, self.states_next, self.action_matrixs, self.done = [],[],[],[]
        self.action_probs, self.rewards = [],[]

    def make_memory(self, episode, state):
        reward_tot = 0
        count = 0
        reward = np.zeros(self.value_size)
        advantage = np.zeros(self.value_size)
        target = np.zeros(self.value_size)
        action_matrix = np.zeros(self.action_size)
        done = False

        while not done:
            count+=1
            state_t = np.reshape(self.normalize(state),[1, 1, self.state_size])
            action_matrix_t = np.reshape(action_matrix,[1, 1, self.action_size])
```

```python
            action_prob = self.model_actor.predict([state_t,
                                    self.DUMMY_ACTION_MATRIX,
                                    self.DUMMY_ADVANTAGE])
            action = np.random.choice(self.action_size, 1, p=action_prob[0][0])[0]
            action_matrix = np.zeros(self.action_size) # 초기화
            action_matrix[action] = 1
            state_next, reward, done, none = self.env.step(action)

            state_next_t = np.reshape(self.normalize(state_next),
                                    [1, 1, self.state_size])

            if count < 500 and done:
                reward = self.penalty

            self.states.append(np.reshape(state_t, [1,self.state_size]))
            self.states_next.append(np.reshape(state_next_t, [1,self.state_size]))
            self.action_matrixs.append(np.reshape(action_matrix,
                                    [1,self.action_size]))
            self.dones.append(np.reshape(0 if done else 1, [1,self.value_size]))
            self.action_probs.append(np.reshape(action_prob, [1,self.action_size]))
            self.rewards.append(np.reshape(reward, [1,self.value_size]))

            if(count % self.mini_batch_step_size == 0):
                self.train_mini_batch()
                self.clear_memory()
            reward_tot += reward
            state = state_next

        return count, reward_tot

    def make_gae(self, values, values_next, rewards, dones):
        delta_adv, delta_tar, adv, target = 0, 0, 0, 0
        advantages = np.zeros(np.array(values).shape)
        targets = np.zeros(np.array(values).shape)
        for t in reversed(range(0, len(rewards))):
            delta_adv = rewards[t] + self.discount_rate * values_next[t] * dones[t]
                                    - values[t]
            delta_tar = rewards[t] + self.discount_rate * values_next[t] * dones[t]
            adv = delta_adv + self.smooth_rate * self.discount_rate * dones[t] * adv
            target = delta_tar + self.smooth_rate * self.discount_rate * dones[t] *
                                                            target

            advantages[t] = adv
            targets[t] = target
        return advantages, targets
```

```python
    def normalize(self, x):
        norm = np.linalg.norm(x)
        if norm == 0:
            return x
        return x / norm

    def train_mini_batch(self):

        if len(self.states) == 0:
            return

        states_t = np.array(self.states)
        states_next_t = np.array(self.states_next)
        action_matrixs_t = np.array(self.action_matrixs)
        action_probs_t = np.array(self.action_probs)
        loss_clipping = [self.loss_clipping for j in range(len(self.states))]
        loss_clipping_t = np.reshape(loss_clipping, [len(self.states),1,1])

        values = self.model_critic.predict(states_t)
        values_next = self.model_critic.predict(states_next_t)

        advantages, targets = self.make_gae(values, values_next, self.rewards,
                                                              self.dones)
        advantages_t = np.array(advantages)
        targets_t = np.array(targets)

        self.model_actor.fit([states_t, action_matrixs_t, advantages_t,
                            loss_clipping_t], [action_probs_t],
                            epochs=self.epochs_actor, verbose=0)
        self.model_critic.fit(states_t, targets_t,
                            epochs=self.epochs_critic, verbose=0)

if __name__ == "__main__":
    def black_box_function(layer_num_actor, node_num_actor, epochs_actor,
                layer_num_critic, node_num_critic, epochs_critic,
                learning_rate_actor, learning_rate_critic,
                discount_rate, smooth_rate,
                penalty, mini_batch_step_size, loss_clipping
                ):
        config_data = {
            'layer_num_actor':layer_num_actor,
            'node_num_actor':node_num_actor,
            'epochs_actor':epochs_actor,
            'layer_num_critic':layer_num_critic,
            'node_num_critic':node_num_critic,
            'epochs_critic':epochs_critic,
```

```python
        'learning_rate_actor' :learning_rate_actor,
        'learning_rate_critic':learning_rate_critic,
        'discount_rate'       :discount_rate,
        'smooth_rate'         :smooth_rate,
        'penalty'             :penalty,
        'mini_batch_step_size':mini_batch_step_size,
        'loss_clipping'       :loss_clipping
    }
    agent = Agent(config_data)
    agent.train()
    return np.mean(agent.reward_list)

pbounds = {
        'layer_num_actor':(1,2),
        'node_num_actor':(12,128),
        'epochs_actor':(3,6),
        'layer_num_critic':(1,2),
        'node_num_critic':(12,128),
        'epochs_critic':(3,6),
        'learning_rate_actor' :(0.0001,0.001),
        'learning_rate_critic':(0.0001,0.001),
        'discount_rate'       :(0.9,0.99),
        'smooth_rate'         :(0.9,0.99),
        'penalty'             :(-500,-10),
        'mini_batch_step_size':(4,80),
        'loss_clipping'       :(0.1,0.3)
    }

optimizer = BayesianOptimization(
    f=black_box_function,
    pbounds=pbounds,
    random_state=1,
)
optimizer.maximize(
    init_points=5,
    n_iter=20
)
```

Now, let's combine all the necessary functions for Bayesian optimization to complete the program for tuning the PPO algorithm. Bayesian optimization requires running the Cartpole simulation for a certain number of episodes, followed by an additional optimization phase, making it more time-consuming than grid search. However, Bayesian optimization theoretically offers the advantage of achieving good performance with fewer runs.

12.6 Analyzing Bayesian Optimization Results

Run the PPO algorithm with the Bayesian optimization code applied and analyze the results based on the logs.

iter	target	discou...	epochs...	epochs...	layer_...	layer_...	learni...	learni...	loss_c...	mini_b...	node_n...	node_n...	penalty	smooth...
1	37.65	0.9375	5.161	3.0	1.302	1.147	0.000183	0.000267	0.1691	34.15	74.5	60.63	-164.2	0.9184
2	23.1	0.979	3.082	5.011	1.417	1.559	0.000226	0.000278	0.2601	77.59	48.36	92.31	-70.57	0.9805
3	32.31	0.9077	3.117	3.509	1.878	1.098	0.000479	0.000962	0.2066	56.58	48.6	91.63	-91.03	0.9016
4	25.11	0.9675	5.967	5.244	1.28	1.789	0.000192	0.000503	0.2817	26.31	45.38	27.08	-490.5	0.9611
5	34.92	0.919	3.797	4.475	1.053	1.574	0.000232	0.000630	0.24	11.78	60.03	92.55	-297.1	0.9045
6	143.0	0.9626	3.623	3.248	1.306	1.548	0.000779	0.000576	0.1574	51.44	42.72	87.71	-87.47	0.9575
7	33.65	0.9424	3.826	5.102	1.779	1.849	0.000585	0.000741	0.2949	34.85	61.93	28.71	-420.1	0.9347
8	261.0	0.9561	5.377	4.037	1.091	1.536	0.000949	0.000489	0.1358	17.45	90.82	122.4	-133.1	0.9446

| 9 | 29.04 | 0.9352 | 3.343 | 5.206 | 1.199 | 1.062 | 0.000959 |
0.000135 | 0.2367 | 44.62 | 119.1 | 51.09 | -47.23 | 0.9792 |

| 10 | 23.04 | 0.9682 | 5.624 | 4.292 | 1.77 | 1.288 | 0.000258 |
0.000582 | 0.2948 | 36.58 | 83.53 | 23.39 | -362.3 | 0.9589 |

| 11 | 42.52 | 0.9226 | 3.466 | 5.953 | 1.183 | 1.364 | 0.000418 |
0.000281 | 0.2086 | 10.69 | 119.6 | 18.01 | -368.9 | 0.9539 |

| 12 | 50.81 | 0.9216 | 5.941 | 4.988 | 1.431 | 1.603 | 0.000164 |
0.000936 | 0.2232 | 17.56 | 75.3 | 126.5 | -123.4 | 0.9677 |

| 13 | 28.11 | 0.9274 | 3.438 | 5.431 | 1.271 | 1.792 | 0.000169 |
0.000275 | 0.2057 | 17.54 | 85.69 | 24.01 | -315.8 | 0.9555 |

| 14 | 15.64 | 0.9223 | 4.879 | 4.707 | 1.951 | 1.056 | 0.000329 |
0.000266 | 0.2299 | 61.55 | 55.41 | 118.3 | -390.9 | 0.928 |

| 15 | 17.65 | 0.9873 | 4.764 | 4.072 | 1.858 | 1.077 | 0.000435 |
0.000464 | 0.2783 | 39.85 | 55.34 | 21.24 | -484.9 | 0.9184 |

| 16 | 20.63 | 0.9692 | 3.7 | 5.935 | 1.737 | 1.245 | 0.000185 |
0.000744 | 0.1418 | 72.77 | 38.84 | 66.25 | -443.6 | 0.954 |

| 17 | 28.45 | 0.9384 | 4.063 | 5.433 | 1.973 | 1.702 | 0.000253 |
0.000483 | 0.2822 | 20.95 | 14.45 | 56.22 | -360.9 | 0.9325 |

| 18 | 31.68 | 0.9874 | 4.124 | 5.531 | 1.317 | 1.099 | 0.000648 |
0.000143 | 0.1877 | 64.63 | 66.42 | 46.25 | -324.1 | 0.9804 |

| 19 | 112.5 | 0.9468 | 5.848 | 4.31 | 1.338 | 1.942 | 0.000230 |
0.000143 | 0.1504 | 17.42 | 119.2 | 72.16 | -343.8 | 0.9182 |

| 20 | 207.3 | 0.9015 | 4.888 | 4.1 | 1.926 | 1.801 | 0.000619 |
0.000111 | 0.1151 | 16.53 | 112.0 | 74.65 | -344.8 | 0.9123 |

| 21 | 334.6 | 0.9138 | 4.136 | 3.069 | 1.813 | 1.29 | 0.000704 |
0.000732 | 0.2671 | 18.73 | 119.2 | 74.68 | -347.1 | 0.9321 |

| 22 | 15.76 | 0.9723 | 5.409 | 3.821 | 1.124 | 1.855 | 0.000676 |
0.000359 | 0.189 | 50.06 | 46.28 | 89.35 | -84.37 | 0.9848 |

| 23 | 90.43 | 0.9503 | 4.78 | 4.383 | 1.522 | 1.837 | 0.000163 |
0.000425 | 0.1385 | 25.44 | 123.0 | 72.82 | -348.1 | 0.9822 |

| 24 | 33.81 | 0.9737 | 3.471 | 4.316 | 1.198 | 1.542 | 0.000170 |
0.000305 | 0.2157 | 17.06 | 121.6 | 77.53 | -353.6 | 0.9655 |

| 25 | 166.0 | 0.9869 | 4.916 | 5.744 | 1.673 | 1.487 | 0.000203 |
0.000690 | 0.2577 | 17.62 | 88.07 | 117.1 | -135.2 | 0.9771 |

===

Execution Results of cartpole_PPO_**bayesian.py**

When you run the Bayesian optimization program, the results will appear as follows. In line with the previously set parameter values, the program runs a total of 25 times. If a better-performing set of parameters is found during the execution, it is highlighted in purple. Here, the final purple-highlighted result represents the optimal parameters identified by the program.

```
target_list = []
i=0
for res in optimizer.res:
    target_list.append([res["target"], i])
    i=i+1
target_list.sort(reverse=True)
target_list
```

Sort by Execution Results

```
[[334.62, 20],
 [260.99, 7],
 [207.33, 19],
 [165.97, 24],
 [142.99, 5],
 [112.53, 18],
 [90.43, 22],
 [50.81, 11],
 [42.52, 10],
 [37.65, 0],
 [34.92, 4],
 [33.81, 23],
 [33.65, 6],
 [32.31, 2],
 [31.68, 17],
 [29.04, 8],
 [28.45, 16],
 [28.11, 12],
 [25.11, 3],
 [23.1, 1],
 [23.04, 9],
 [20.63, 15],
 [17.65, 14],
 [15.76, 21],
 [15.64, 13]]
```

Identify Optimal Parameters

```
print("*result:" , optimizer.res[20]['params'])

*result: {'discount_rate': 0.9138068228055699, 'epochs_actor': 4.13579
6340297432, 'epochs_critic': 3.068824820615902, 'layer_num_actor': 1.8
127168005702576, 'layer_num_critic': 1.2899196661865222, 'learning_rat
e_actor': 0.0007044665544668867, 'learning_rate_critic': 0.00073253232
36616151, 'loss_clipping': 0.2671282081035625, 'mini_batch_step_size':
18.73240705651665, 'node_num_actor': 119.19096504720964, 'node_num_cri
tic': 74.68079589490598, 'penalty': -347.12015260105, 'smooth_rate':
0.9321116290822046}
```

Analyzing Bayesian Optimization Results

Sort the Bayesian optimization results in order, and you'll see the highest value is 334.62. Although using the parameters corresponding to the highest value often yields the best performance for the reinforcement learning algorithm, sometimes the second or third highest values can perform even better. Therefore, it's beneficial to sort results by performance for additional testing.

Now, confirm the optimal parameters, apply them to the reinforcement learning model, and run the program to evaluate performance.

```
. . . . .
LOSS_CLIPPING = 0.2671282081035625
class Agent(object):
    def __init__(self):
        self.env = gym.make('CartPole-v1')
        self.state_size = self.env.observation_space.shape[0]
        self.action_size = self.env.action_space.n
        self.value_size = 1

        self.layer_num_actor = int(round(1.8127168005702576,0))
        self.node_num_actor = int(round(119.19096504720964,0))
        self.epochs_actor = int(round(4.135796340297432,0))

        self.layer_num_critic = int(round(1.2899196661865222,0))
        self.node_num_critic = int(round(74.68079589490598,0))
        self.epochs_critic = int(round(3.068824820615902,0))

        self.learning_rate_actor = 0.0007044665544668867
        self.learning_rate_critic = 0.0007325323236616151
        self.discount_rate = 0.9138068228055699
        self.smooth_rate = 0.9321116290822046
        self.penalty = int(round(-347.12015260105,0))
        self.mini_batch_step_size = int(round(18.73240705651665,0))

        self.episode_num = 300

        self.moving_avg_size = 20

        self.model_actor = self.build_model_actor()
        self.model_critic = self.build_model_critic()
. . . . .
```

Setting Parameters in cartpole_PPO_bayesian_test.py

In the Agent class, set the optimal parameters identified earlier. Since all parameters in Bayesian optimization are generated as floats, it is necessary to convert them to integers when assigning values to variables like layer_num_actor and node_num_actor.

```
import matplotlib.pyplot as plt
plt.figure(figsize=(10,5))
plt.plot(agent.reward_list, label='rewards')
plt.plot(agent.moving_avg_list, linewidth=4, label='moving average')
plt.legend(loc='upper left')
plt.title('PPO')
plt.show()
```

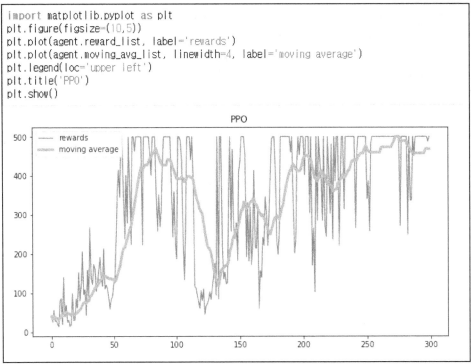

Execution Results of cartpole_PPO_bayesian_test.py

To make analysis easier, let's visualize the execution results. Although the parameters found through Bayesian optimization don't outperform those identified through grid search, the model reaches the maximum number of executions after around 60 runs, demonstrating better performance than the manually selected parameters.

Here, we simply called the maximize function to identify optimal parameters. By combining other functions like set_bound, probe, and load_logs, you can further improve tuning efficiency.

Comparing these results with those from grid search reveals that the performance is not necessarily better. Although Bayesian optimization theoretically requires less effort, the results in this case are somewhat opposite. This could be due to the specific characteristics of the Cartpole environment or the lack of utilization of Bayesian optimization's advanced features. Nonetheless,

Bayesian optimization is conceptually a superior technique, and it's recommended to apply it to other reinforcement learning problems you encounter in the future.

Chapter 13

In Conclusion

13. In Conclusion

If you've understood everything covered so far, you may feel inspired to improve a business environment or develop a new product. The reinforcement learning algorithms introduced in this book are foundational. Even now, new theories related to reinforcement learning are being published, and OpenAI is continually introducing new technologies. To advance as a skilled reinforcement learning expert, don't stop here—continue preparing in the following ways:

• Back to Basics

The foundational textbook for reinforcement learning is Reinforcement Learning: An Introduction by Richard S. Sutton. Much of the theory discussed here, as well as many resources available online, are based on this text.

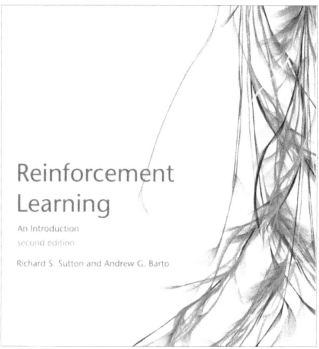

Reinforcement Learning: An Introduction

For those who find reading in English challenging, the translated version can be a good alternative. Reinforcement learning theory is fundamentally complex, so this book has introduced only the essential concepts, omitting many details from the textbook. If you build on what you've learned here to fully understand the textbook, you can progress to a much higher level.

Returning to the basics and reading the textbook is a valuable next step. If tackling it alone feels challenging, consider forming a study group for support.

• Studying Neural Network Techniques in Depth

The neural network techniques introduced here are very basic. Topics such as Convolutional Neural Networks (CNNs) for image processing and the increasingly popular Generative Adversarial Networks (GANs) were not covered. Neural networks have vast application potential, as demonstrated by CNNs and GANs. For example, transfer learning, a technique for reusing neural networks, finds remarkable application in GANs.

To enable autonomous driving, for instance, images captured by LIDAR need to be processed through a neural network, and the outcomes are then evaluated with reinforcement learning to make policy-based decisions. Although GANs are primarily used for generating new images, they fundamentally combine neural networks to create new outputs, making GAN-based reinforcement learning performance enhancement an active research area.

Consider studying a wider range of neural network techniques and exploring how they can improve reinforcement learning algorithms.

• Advancing Through OpenAI Spinning Up

OpenAI is a nonprofit organization dedicated to researching and sharing advances in artificial intelligence. OpenAI Spinning Up is a reinforcement learning educational platform provided by OpenAI.

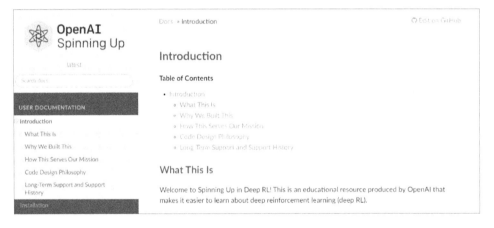

OpenAI Spinning Up

On this site, you'll find various resources, including specific methodologies for studying reinforcement learning. It introduces newer algorithms such as DDPG, which is more recent than PPO, and provides detailed explanations of the Mujoco game environment, where you can experiment with robot control.

OpenAI Spinning Up is a valuable resource for learning reinforcement learning theory in depth. While studying the latest reinforcement learning theories through research papers found online may be suitable for academics, OpenAI offers an excellent alternative for Developers.

• Mastering Neural Network Tools

Just as a chef with the best recipes but lacking knife skills might struggle in a high-end hotel kitchen, an AI practitioner must also master their tools.

Two leading packages for neural networks are TensorFlow and PyTorch. TensorFlow, developed and open-sourced by Google, is popular in industry for its scalability and feature variety. PyTorch, developed by Facebook, is widely used in academia due to its simplicity, and recently, many reinforcement learning algorithms developed with PyTorch have been made publicly available.

Both packages have unique advantages, so choose the one that best suits your needs and aim to master it for effective reinforcement learning development.

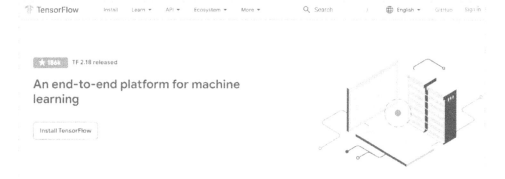

TensorFlow Website

There doesn't seem to be a widely available book that explains how to master TensorFlow. Since TensorFlow offers tutorials and guides directly on its official website, I recommend visiting the site to familiarize yourself with the package. Even studying just the tutorials can elevate your understanding to a solid theoretical level.

AI technology is being adopted across various industries, from AI speakers and drug discovery to defect inspection and photo enhancement solutions. However, reinforcement learning has yet to be fully utilized in industry. As readers may have noticed, reinforcement learning holds immense potential as an AI technology. Start mastering these skills now and apply them to your business; it will increase the value of your company and elevate your own expertise.